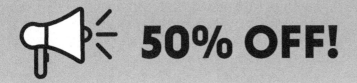 **50% OFF!**

MW00773928

AFOQT ONLINE TEST PREP COURSE

We consider it an honor and a privilege that you chose our AFOQT Study Guide. As a way of showing our appreciation and to help us better serve you, we have partnered with Mometrix Test Preparation to offer you 50% off their online AFOQT Prep Course.

Mometrix has structured their online course to perfectly complement your printed study guide. Many AFOQT courses are needlessly expensive and don't deliver enough value. With their course, you get access to the best AFOQT prep material, and you only pay half price.

WHAT'S IN THE AFOQT TEST PREP COURSE?

- ☑ **AFOQT Study Guide**: Get access to content that complements your study guide.

- ☑ **Progress Tracker**: Their customized course allows you to check off content you have studied or feel confident with.

- ☑ **1900+ Practice Questions**: With 1900+ practice questions and lesson reviews, you can test yourself again and again to build confidence.

- ☑ **AFOQT Flashcards**: Their course includes a flashcard mode consisting of over 325 content cards to help you study.

TO RECEIVE THIS DISCOUNT, VISIT THE WEBSITE AT

link.mometrix.com/afoqt

USE THE DISCOUNT CODE:
STARTSTUDYING

SCAN HERE

IF YOU HAVE ANY QUESTIONS OR CONCERNS, PLEASE
CONTACT MOMETRIX AT SUPPORT@MOMETRIX.COM

Mometrix
ONLINE COURSES

FREE VIDEO  FREE VIDEO

Essential Test Tips Video from Trivium Test Prep!

Dear Customer,

Thank you for purchasing from Trivium Test Prep! We're honored to help you prepare for your AFOQT exam.

To show our appreciation, we're offering a **FREE *AFOQT Essential Test Tips* Video by Trivium Test Prep**.* Our video includes 35 test preparation strategies that will make you successful on your big exam. All we ask is that you email us your feedback and describe your experience with our product. Amazing, awful, or just so-so: we want to hear what you have to say!

To receive your **FREE *AFOQT Essential Test Tips* Video**, please email us at 5star@ triviumtestprep.com. Include "Free 5 Star" in the subject line and the following information in your email:

1. The title of the product you purchased.
2. Your rating from 1 – 5 (with 5 being the best).
3. Your feedback about the product, including how our materials helped you meet your goals and ways in which we can improve our products.
4. Your full name and shipping address so we can send your **FREE *AFOQT Essential Test Tips* Video**.

If you have any questions or concerns please feel free to contact us directly at 5star@trivium-testprep.com.

Thank you!

- Trivium Test Prep Team

*To get access to the free video please email us at 5star@triviumtestprep.com, and please follow the instructions above.

AFOQT Study Guide 2025-2026:

1,100+ Practice Questions and Exam Prep Book for the Air Force Officer Qualifying Test

8th Edition

B. Hettinger

TABLE OF CONTENTS

ONLINE RESOURCES

To help you fully prepare for your AFOQT exam, Trivium includes online resources with the purchase of this study guide.

Practice Test

In addition to the practice test included in this book, we also offer an online exam. Since many exams today are computer based, getting to practice your test-taking skills on the computer is a great way to prepare.

Flash Cards

A convenient supplement to this study guide, Trivium flash cards enable you to review important terms easily on your computer or smartphone.

Cheat Sheets

Review the core skills you need to master the exam with easy-to-read Cheat Sheets.

From Stress to Success

Watch From Stress to Success, a brief but insightful YouTube video that offers the tips, tricks, and secrets experts use to score higher on the exam.

Reviews

Leave a review, send us helpful feedback, or sign up for Trivium promotions—including free books!

Access these materials at: **www.triviumtestprep.com/afoqt-online-resources**

INTRODUCTION

ongratulations on choosing to take the Air Force Officer Qualifying Test (AFOQT)! By purchasing this book, you've taken an important step on your path to joining the military.

This guide will provide you with a detailed overview of the AFOQT, so you know exactly what to expect on exam day. We'll take you through all the concepts covered on the exam and give you the opportunity to test your knowledge with practice questions. Even if it's been a while since you last took a major exam, don't worry; we'll make sure you're more than ready!

WHAT IS THE AFOQT?

Under the purview of the US Air Force, the AFOQT is a comprehensive exam used to measure aptitudes of candidates aspiring to enter the Air Force as an officer. This exam assesses candidates for acceptance into one of the Air Force commissioning programs. These programs include the Air Force Military Academy, Air Force Officer Training School (OTS), and the Air Force Reserve Officer Training Corps (Air Force ROTC). Results from this exam also determine a candidate's qualification for attendance to pilot and navigator training courses as well as nonaviation officer positions.

The AFOQT, written by several subject matter experts and revised in 2015, ensures the US Air Force recruits candidates that possess certain knowledge to meet the fundamental, rigid standards required of the modern and technical positions they will encounter as Air Force commissioned officers.

Only high school students applying for attendance in the US Air Force Military Academy, college students enrolled in their university ROTC program, and college graduates with bachelor's degrees are considered eligible to take the AFOQT.

WHAT'S ON THE AFOQT?

The AFOQT is broken down into twelve subtests. The entire exam is multiple choice, providing four or five possible answers with one being the correct or best answer. The exam is scored based on the total number of questions answered correctly. Therefore, test-takers are not penalized for guessing. Prior to starting some of the subtests, you may have the opportunity to answer some practice questions to ensure you understand what you are supposed to do. The exam itself requires three hours and thirty-six minutes; however, be prepared to allow at least five hours to account for administrative instruction, time between subtests, and two scheduled breaks.

Candidates must complete all subtests of the AFOQT, even if they are not applying to attend the pilot and navigator training courses. The subtests, approximate number of questions in each subtest, and the time allowed are shown in the following table.

What's on the AFOQT?

SUBTEST	APPROXIMATE NUMBER OF QUESTIONS	TIME LIMIT
1. Verbal Analogies	25	8 minutes
2. Arithmetic Reasoning	25	29 minutes
3. Word Knowledge	25	5 minutes
4. Math Knowledge	25	22 minutes
5. Reading Comprehension	25	38 minutes
6. Situational Judgment Test	50	35 minutes
7. Self-Description Inventory	220	40 minutes
8. Physical Science	20	10 minutes
9. Table Reading	40	7 minutes
10. Instrument Comprehension	25	5 minutes
11. Block Counting	30	4.5 minutes
12. Aviation Information	20	8 minutes
Total	530 multiple-choice questions	3 hours, 31 minutes

- **VERBAL ANALOGIES**: tests your knowledge of the relationship between words.
- **ARITHMETIC REASONING**: asks you to solve mathematical word problems using basic arithmetic equations, ratios, and statistics.
- **WORD KNOWLEDGE**: assesses your understanding of antonyms, synonyms, and the meaning of words (vocabulary).
- **MATH KNOWLEDGE**: asks you to calculate math equations using geometric and algebraic properties in addition to basic addition, subtraction, multiplication, and division.
- **READING COMPREHENSION**: gauges your comprehension of written passages.
- **SITUATIONAL JUDGMENT TEST**: examines your responses to decision-making situations junior officers typically encounter.
- **SELF-DESCRIPTION INVENTORY**: evaluates your individual character traits and attitudes using a personality test.
- **PHYSICAL SCIENCE**: explores the scope of your high school-level chemistry, physics, and Earth science knowledge.
- **TABLE READING**: asks you to identify values provided in a table or graph as rapidly as possible.
- **INSTRUMENT COMPREHENSION**: assesses your ability to recognize the response of an aircraft from graphics depicting instrument panel indicators.
- **BLOCK COUNTING**: provides a three-dimensional figure and asks you to count the number of blocks adjacent to or touching the block in question.
- **AVIATION INFORMATION**: tests your knowledge of aviation terminology and concepts, including the flight physics of fixed and rotary aircraft.

How is the AFOQT Scored?

Each subtest score is quantified in a percentile ranking between 0 and 99 percent. This ranking is relative to your score ranked against other candidates who took the same subtest. After each subtest is computed, certain subtest scores are combined to correlate into a composite score for one of six separate categories: Verbal, Quantitative (Math), Academic Aptitude, Pilot, Combat Systems Operator (CSO), and Air Battle Manager (ABM). The Situational Judgment test is its own composite score category. While all six composite scores are used to determine eligibility for pilot and other aviation training courses, only the Verbal, Academic Aptitude, Situational Judgment, and Quantitative (Math) categories are used for nonaviation candidates. Due to the concentrated skill required for pilot and CSO positions, candidates must score higher in all categories to be eligible for attendance in the aviation training courses. The following covers how to attain a composite score for each category.

Verbal

To become an Air Force officer in any nonaviation position, you must score at least 15 in this subtest. The composite score for this category is a combination of Verbal Analogies, Word Knowledge, and Reading Comprehension. This category identifies candidates with strong understanding of language, grammar, and literature.

Quantitative

To become an Air Force officer in any nonaviation position, you must score at least 10 in this subtest. The composite score for this category is a combination of Arithmetic Reasoning and Math Knowledge. This category identifies candidates with a strong mathematical background understanding formulas, proportions, and ratios.

Academic Aptitude

The composite score for this category is a combination of Verbal Analogies, Arithmetic Reasoning, Word Knowledge, and Math Knowledge. This category identifies candidates with a broad academic knowledge. There is no minimum score in this category to be eligible to become an Air Force officer.

Pilot

The composite score for this category is a combination of Math Knowledge, Table Reading, Instrument Comprehension, and Aviation Information. This category identifies those candidates with particular talent in understanding aviation concepts, analyzing aeronautical charts, and possessing a quick response to surroundings. Candidates applying to become a pilot must score a minimum of 25 in this category. Candidates applying to become a CSO must score a minimum of 10 in this category. This category is not considered if applying to a nonaviation training course.

CSO

The composite score for this category is a combination of Word Knowledge, Math Knowledge, Table Reading, and Block Counting. This category identifies those candidates with technical aptitude in spatial ability coupled with verbal skill. Candidates applying to become a pilot must score a minimum of 10 in this category. Candidates applying to become a CSO must score a minimum of 25 in this category. There is no minimum score in this category if applying to a nonaviation training course.

Although the minimum Pilot and CSO composite scores for pilot and other aviation training course candidates are 25 and 10, respectively, candidates must attain a combined total composite score of 50 from the Pilot and CSO categories.

ABM

The composite score for this category is a combination of Verbal Analogies, Math Knowledge, Table Reading, Instrument Comprehension, Block Counting, and Aviation Information. This category identifies those candidates with particular technical competence in spatial ability, analyzing aeronautical charts, ability to recognize aircraft attitude, and verbal aptitude. There is no minimum score in this category to be eligible to become an Air Force officer.

Situational Judgment

The score for this category is taken from the Situational Judgment test. There is no minimum score in this category to be eligible to become an Air Force officer.

Although there is no minimum score for certain composite categories, the Air Force balances recruitment quotas by selecting candidates who attain the highest scores on the AFOQT. It is in your best interest to prepare for this test by studying and completing practice sample exam questions, especially in subtests that are not your strongest areas.

RETAKING THE AFOQT

The AFOQT may be taken twice in your lifetime. The retake exam must be taken after 180 days from the date of the initial exam. The most recent AFOQT score is used, not the highest score between the two exams. The AFOQT score is valid for life; however, the Air Force has a maximum age requirement at time of commissioning.

HOW IS THE AFOQT ADMINISTERED?

If you are ready to take the AFOQT, contact your local recruiter. Your officer recruiter will determine your initial eligibility to apply for officer schooling or to join the Air Force as an officer and schedule you for the AFOQT.

On the day of the exam, you will need to bring valid photo identification. Testing materials are provided by the test proctor. Calculators are not allowed. Personal breaks are scheduled by the proctor. The proctor will provide all instructions for taking the exam, such as when to start and stop, and will allow practice questions as applicable. During the practice questions, the proctor cannot provide information on the question, possible answers, or test-taking strategies.

GETTING TO KNOW THE UNITED STATES AIR FORCE

The US Air Force is tasked with missions to provide the global air support through superior air power for intelligence gathering, surveillance, and reconnaissance. The Air Force allows the United States to swiftly respond to threats and protect our national interests worldwide. The Air Force also leads the space and missile program, requiring various positions from combat crew operators to astronauts.

The rank structure of the Air Force consists of enlisted and officers, and it is similar to that of the US Army. The AFOQT only applies to individuals pursuing a career as a US Air Force officer. The US Air Force offers officer careers in the following fields: aviation, computer science, space command, munitions, command and control, intelligence, health, operations support, logistics, and more. Once you are determined to be qualified for a career field, the Air Force provides you with the training necessary to carry out the duties and responsibilities.

THE MILITARY RECRUITMENT PROCESS

As stated before, passing the AFOQT is just one requirement to qualify for military service as an officer in the US Air Force. You may contact your local recruiter through your high school counselor or college adviser, or visit your local military recruitment center.

Once you contact your local recruiter, he or she will meet with you at the recruiting office, your school, or your home. During this meeting, the recruiter will conduct an interview to initiate the recruitment process. This process begins with the recruiter determining if you meet the basic qualification requirements. Expect a review of your education level, financial record, background investigation, interests, criminal record or drug history, height and weight, age, and citizenship. Once basic qualifications have been established, the recruiter refers you to an officer recruiter who will schedule you to take the AFOQT and a physical exam. After this, you will meet with your officer recruiter to discuss your AFOQT scores and any medical issue that may preclude your entrance to an officer commissioning school leading to an appointment as an officer. During this meeting, the officer recruiter will discuss which branch(es) of service you qualify for and possible career options for you to choose from. Your recruiter can respond to any concerns or questions you have along the way.

ABOUT THIS GUIDE

This guide will help you master the most important test topics and also develop critical test-taking skills. We have built features into our books to prepare you for your tests and increase your score. Along with a detailed summary of the test's format, content, and scoring, we offer an in-depth overview of the content knowledge required to pass the test. In the review you'll find sidebars that provide interesting information, highlight key concepts, and review content so that you can solidify your understanding of the exam's concepts. You can also test your knowledge with sample questions throughout the text and practice questions that reflect the content and format of the AFOQT. We're pleased you've chosen Trivium Test Prep to be a part of your military journey!

VERBAL ANALOGIES

An analogy compares two things, identifying an important way or ways the two are alike. The type of analogy in this test presents four items arranged in two pairs. For example:

HAND is to ARM as FOOT is to LEG

HAND and ARM is the first pair. FOOT and LEG is the second pair. The two items in Pair 1 have the same relationship that the two items in Pair 2 have. In this case, it is a part-to-whole relationship: a HAND is part of an ARM, just as a FOOT is part of a LEG.

There are twenty-five items on this analogy test. Each is multiple-choice and has five answer choices labeled (A), (B), (C), (D), and (E). The first section is structured so that only one word needs to be filled in:

1. NOMENCLATURE is to TERMINOLOGY as RACONTEUR is to
   (A) NARRATIVE
   (B) AUDIENCE
   (C) STORYTELLER
   (D) JARGON
   (E) COMMUNICATION

The last section is structured so that a pair of words is needed:

2. NOMENCLATURE is to TERMINOLOGY as
   (A) DEFERENCE is to DISRESPECT
   (B) DOUBTER is to BELIEVER
   (C) LASSITUDE is to LIVELINESS
   (D) GUILE is to FRANKNESS
   (E) RACONTEUR is to STORYTELLER

Answer: Each pair of words has the same meaning. NOMENCLATURE and TERMINOLOGY both describe a system for naming things; both a RACONTEUR and a STORYTELLER are persons who are skillful at telling stories.

TYPES OF ANALOGIES

Synonyms and Antonyms

SYNONYMS are words with identical or similar meanings. For example, *identical* and *alike* are synonyms. ANTONYMS are words with opposite meanings. For example, *opposite* and *matching* are antonyms.

In a SYNONYM ANALOGY, the two words in each pair are synonyms. For example:

CONFUSING is to PERPLEXING as
INTELLIGENT is to BRAINY

Confusing and *perplexing* are synonyms (have the same or similar meaning), and *intelligent* and *brainy* are synonyms, too.

In an ANTONYM ANALOGY, the two words in each pair are antonyms. For example:

COMPREHENSIBLE is to PERPLEXING as
SENSIBLE is to FOOLISH.

Comprehensible and *perplexing* are antonyms (words with opposite meanings), and *sensible* and *foolish* are antonyms, too.

Examples

1. DURABLE is to STURDY as ARID is to
    (A) PARCHED
    (B) THIRST
    (C) GLUTTONY
    (D) RESILIENT
    (E) FLIMSY

2. KEEN is to BLUNT as SACCHARINE is to
    (A) SALTY
    (B) SAVORY
    (C) DINGY
    (D) SOUR
    (E) SUGARY

Actions and Functions

In an ACTION ANALOGY, each pair contains a noun (person, animal, or thing) and a verb that describes an action that person, animal, or thing commonly performs. For example:

> HORSE is to GALLOPS as RUNNER is to SPRINTS.
>
> A HORSE GALLOPS, just as a RUNNER SPRINTS.

In a FUNCTION ANALOGY, each pair contains a noun and a verb that describes that person's, animal's, or thing's function (what it is supposed to do). For example:

> MICROPHONE is to AMPLIFY as
> WHEELBARROW is to TRANSPORT

A MICROPHONE's function is to AMPLIFY sound, just as a WHEELBARROW's function is to TRANSPORT things.

Examples

3. WORM is to SQUIGGLES as MOUSE is to
   (A) CLUMPS
   (B) FLUTTERS
   (C) SKITTERS
   (D) BOUNCES
   (E) CLANKS

4. SCISSORS are to CUT as TAPE is to
   (A) STICKY
   (B) TRANSPARENT
   (C) DEVICE
   (D) ATTACH
   (E) DISPENSER

Size, Degree, and Amount

The word pair in an analogy can also have a relationship of SIZE, DEGREE, or AMOUNT. Here is an example of a degree analogy that shows increasing intensity:

> SAD is to DESPONDENT as HAPPY is to ECSTATIC

Someone who is *extremely* SAD feels DESPONDENT; someone who is *extremely* HAPPY feels ECSTATIC.

The example below also shows a relationship of degree/amount:

> WHISPERS is to BELLOWS as DRIPS is to GUSHES

When a man WHISPERS he speaks very softly, and when he BELLOWS he shouts very loudly; when a tap DRIPS, a tiny amount of water comes out, and when a tap GUSHES, a large amount of water comes out.

HELPFUL HINT

You can use the tone of the words in an analogy to help fill in the missing parts. For example, SAD and DESPONDENT are both negative words. Because HAPPY is a positive word, the second word in the pair should also be positive.

5. FAMISHED is to HUNGRY as DRENCHED is to

    (A) SATURATED

    (B) DAMP

    (C) RAVENOUS

    (D) TIRED

    (E) FATIGUED

6. RARE is to ABUNDANT as MOMENTARY is to

    (A) SHORT

    (B) TRANSIENT

    (C) PUNY

    (D) PERPETUAL

    (E) FEEBLE

Part to Whole

In a **PART-TO-WHOLE ANALOGY**, the first word forms a part of the object described by the second word (or vice versa). For example:

> STEP is to STAIRCASE as KEY is to KEYBOARD

A STEP is one part of a STAIRCASE, just as a KEY is one part of a KEYBOARD.

Examples

7. WHEEL is to CAR as WING is to

    (A) AIRPLANE

    (B) RUNWAY

    (C) SOAR

    (D) TRANSPORTATION

    (E) ALOFT

8. WHISKER is to CAT as ANTENNA is to

    (A) THORAX

    (B) CLAW

    (C) TAIL

    (D) SNAKE

    (E) INSECT

Member to Group

In a **MEMBER-TO-GROUP ANALOGY**, the first word is a member of the group described by the second word (or vice versa). For example:

> KITTEN is to LITTER as
> KINDERGARTNER is to KINDERGARTEN

A KITTEN is one member of a LITTER, just as a KINDERGARTNER is one member of a KINDERGARTEN.

Examples

9. BIRD is to FLOCK as BUFFALO is to
   - (A) PACK
   - (B) CLUSTER
   - (C) HERD
   - (D) HERBIVORE
   - (E) PRAIRIE

10. VOTER is to ELECTORATE as CITIZEN is to
    - (A) CIVIL
    - (B) SOCIETY
    - (C) PASSPORT
    - (D) CITIZENSHIP
    - (E) IMMIGRANT

Units of Measurement

Analogies can also address the relationships between units of measurement. Here is an example of a UNIT-OF-MEASUREMENT ANALOGY:

OUNCE is to POUND as INCH is to FOOT

An OUNCE is a lighter unit for measuring weight than a POUND, just as an INCH is a shorter unit of measuring length than a FOOT.

Examples

11. KILOMETER is to DISTANCE as HOUR is to
    - (A) MINUTE
    - (B) SECOND
    - (C) CLOCK
    - (D) TIME
    - (E) SPACE

12. QUART is to GALLON as CUP is to
    - (A) QUART
    - (B) TEASPOON
    - (C) HALF GALLON
    - (D) TABLESPOON
    - (E) QUARTER CUP

Mathematical Analogies

A mathematical analogy describes the mathematical relationship between two values or words. These analogies will not require complex calculations.

Instead, they often focus on simple operations (such as multiplication) or general concepts (such as money). For example:

> 11 is to 13 as 15 is to 17
>
> 11 + 2 = 13, just as 15 + 2 = 17

Examples

13. 20 is to 5 as 100 is to
    (A) 10
    (B) 15
    (C) 20
    (D) 25
    (E) 30

14. DIME is to 0.1 as DOLLAR is to
    (A) 0.01
    (B) 0.05
    (C) 0.25
    (D) 0.75
    (E) 1.0

HOW TO ANSWER A MULTIPLE-CHOICE ANALOGY TEST ITEM

Step 1: Read the whole analogy and the answer choices.

1. NOMENCLATURE is to TERMINOLOGY as RACONTEUR is to
   (A)   NARRATIVE
   (B)   AUDIENCE
   (C)   STORYTELLER
   (D)   JARGON
   (E)   COMMUNICATION

Step 2: Zero in on the *completed* pair: NOMENCLATURE is to TERMINOLOGY

Figure out how the two words are related to each other. Ask: How is the word *nomenclature* related to the word *terminology*? Answer: These two words are synonyms—they mean approximately the same thing. If necessary, check the answer: An online thesaurus confirms that *terminology* and *nomenclature* are synonyms. They both mean "body or system of names or terms."

Step 3: Zero in on the incomplete pair: as RACONTEUR is to _____?

Ask: What relationship should *raconteur* and the missing word have? Answer: They should be synonyms. (Step 2 reveals this answer.)

Step 4: Create a statement that makes good sense of the analogy: *Nomenclature* is a synonym for *terminology*; *raconteur* is a synonym for _____.

Step 5: Find the answer that correctly completes the statement. If necessary, gather information that will help. In this case, find out what *raconteur* means. An online dictionary or thesaurus says that it means "storyteller or narrator." The correct answer is probably (C) STORYTELLER.

Step 6: Check the other answers to be sure they are incorrect. Might answer (A), (B), (D), or (E) be correct? (A) A *narrative* is a story, not a storyteller. (B) An *audience* is a group of listeners, not a storyteller. (D) *Jargon* is special language, not a storyteller. (E) *Communication* is the act of communicating—not a storyteller. Yes, (C) is the only correct answer. *Raconteur* and *storyteller* are synonyms.

ANSWER KEY

1. **(A)** DURABLE is a synonym for STURDY; ARID is a synonym for PARCHED.

2. **(D)** KEEN (*sharp*) means the opposite of BLUNT; SACCHARINE (*sugary*) means the opposite of SOUR.

3. **(C)** A WORM SQUIGGLES along the ground; a MOUSE SKITTERS across the floor.

4. **(D)** A person uses SCISSORS to CUT materials such as paper or cloth; a person uses TAPE to ATTACH one thing to another.

5. **(B)** Someone who is FAMISHED is extremely HUNGRY; something that is DRENCHED is extremely DAMP.

6. **(D)** There are only a few of something RARE, while there is a great number of something ABUNDANT; a MOMENTARY event lasts a very short time, while a PERPETUAL event or state goes on forever.

7. **(A)** A WHEEL is one part of a CAR; A WING is one part of an AIRPLANE.

8. **(E)** A WHISKER is one part of a CAT; an ANTENNA is one part of an INSECT.

9. **(C)** A BIRD is one member of a FLOCK; a BUFFALO is one member of a HERD.

10. **(B)** A VOTER is one member of the ELECTORATE; a CITIZEN is one member of SOCIETY.

11. **(D)** A KILOMETER is a unit of measurement that measures DISTANCE; an HOUR is a unit of measurement that measures TIME.

12. **(A)** There are four QUARTs in a GALLON; there are four CUPs in a QUART.

13. **(D)** 20 divided by 4 = 5; 100 divided by 4 = 25.

14. **(E)** A DIME is equal to 0.1 of a dollar; a DOLLAR is equal to 1.0 of a dollar.

2

ARITHMETIC REASONING

The Arithmetic Reasoning section includes 25 questions to be answered in 29 minutes. The questions test candidates' ability to solve word problems using basic mathematical principles such as ratios, percentages, and probability. These problems will not require the use of algebra or other advanced math topics. Instead, the focus will be on interpreting written scenarios and applying the correct mathematical operations.

TYPES OF NUMBERS

Numbers are placed in categories based on their properties.

- A **NATURAL NUMBER** is greater than 0 and has no decimal or fraction attached. These are also sometimes called counting numbers {1, 2, 3, 4, ...}.

- **WHOLE NUMBERS** are natural numbers and the number 0 {0, 1, 2, 3, 4, ...}.

- **INTEGERS** include positive and negative natural numbers and 0 {..., –4, –3, –2, –1, 0, 1, 2, 3, 4, ...}.

- A **RATIONAL NUMBER** can be represented as a fraction. Any decimal part must terminate or resolve into a repeating pattern. Examples include –12, $-\frac{4}{5}$, 0.36, 7.$\overline{7}$, 26$\frac{1}{2}$, etc.

- An **IRRATIONAL NUMBER** cannot be represented as a fraction. An irrational decimal number never ends and never resolves into a repeating pattern. Examples include $-\sqrt{7}$, π, and 0.34567989135...

- A **REAL NUMBER** is a number that can be represented by a point on a number line. Real numbers include all the rational and irrational numbers.

- An **IMAGINARY NUMBER** includes the imaginary unit i, where $i = \sqrt{-1}$ Because $i^2 = -1$, imaginary numbers produce a negative value when squared. Examples of imaginary numbers include $-4i$, $0.75i$, $i\sqrt{2}$ and $\frac{8}{3}i$.

- A **COMPLEX NUMBER** is in the form $a + bi$, where a and b are real numbers. Examples of complex numbers include $3 + 2i$, $-4 + i$, $\sqrt{3} - i\sqrt[3]{5}$ and $\frac{5}{8} - \frac{7i}{8}$. All imaginary numbers are also complex.

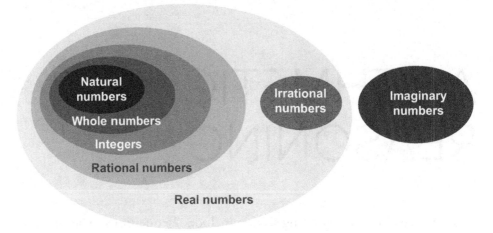

Figure 2.1. Types of Numbers

The **FACTORS** of a natural number are all the numbers that can multiply together to make the number. For example, the factors of 24 are 1, 2, 3, 4, 6, 8, 12, and 24. Every natural number is either prime or composite. A **PRIME NUMBER** is a number that is only divisible by itself and 1. (The number 1 is not considered prime.) Examples of prime numbers are 2, 3, 7, and 29. The number 2 is the only even prime number. A **COMPOSITE NUMBER** has more than two factors. For example, 6 is composite because its factors are 1, 6, 2, and 3. Every composite number can be written as a unique product of prime numbers, called the **PRIME FACTORIZATION** of the number. For example, the prime factorization of 90 is $90 = 2 \times 3^2 \times 5$. All integers are either even or odd. An even number is divisible by 2; an odd number is not.

HELPFUL HINT

If a real number is a natural number (e.g., 50), then it is also a whole number, an integer, and a rational number.

Properties of Number Systems

A system is **CLOSED** under an operation if performing that operation on two elements of the system results in another element of that system. For example, the integers are closed under the operations of addition, subtraction, and multiplication but not division. Adding, subtracting, or multiplying two integers results in another integer. However, dividing two integers could result in a rational number that is not an integer $(-2 \div 3 = \frac{-2}{3})$.

- The rational numbers are closed under all four operations (except for division by 0).
- The real numbers are closed under all four operations.
- The complex numbers are closed under all four operations.
- The irrational numbers are NOT closed under ANY of the four operations.

The **COMMUTATIVE PROPERTY** holds for an operation if order does not matter when performing the operation. For example, multiplication is commutative for integers: $(-2)(3) = (3)(-2)$.

The **ASSOCIATIVE PROPERTY** holds for an operation if elements can be regrouped without changing the result. For example, addition is associative for real numbers: $-3 + (-5 + 4) = (-3 + -5) + 4$.

The **DISTRIBUTIVE PROPERTY** of multiplication over addition allows a product of sums to be written as a sum of products: $a(b + c) = ab + ac$. The value a is distributed over the sum $(b + c)$. The acronym FOIL (First, Outer, Inner, Last) is a useful way to remember the distributive property.

When an operation is performed with an **IDENTITY ELEMENT** and another element a, the result is a. The identity element for multiplication on real numbers is 1 ($a \times 1 = a$), and for addition is 0 ($a + 0 = a$).

An operation of a system has an **INVERSE ELEMENT** if applying that operation with the inverse element results in the identity element. For example, the inverse element of a for addition is $-a$ because $a + (-a) = 0$. The inverse element of a for multiplication is $\frac{1}{a}$ because $a \times \frac{1}{a} = 1$.

Examples

1. Classify the following numbers as natural, whole, integer, rational, or irrational. (The numbers may have more than one classification.)

    (A) 72

    (B) $-\frac{2}{3}$

    (C) $\sqrt{5}$

2. Determine the real and imaginary parts of the following complex numbers.

    (A) 20

    (B) $10 - i$

    (C) $15i$

3. Answer True or False for each statement:

    (A) The natural numbers are closed under subtraction.

    (B) The sum of two irrational numbers is irrational.

    (C) The sum of a rational number and an irrational number is irrational.

4. Answer True or False for each statement:

    (A) The associative property applies for multiplication in the real numbers.

    (B) The commutative property applies to all real numbers and all operations.

POSITIVE AND NEGATIVE NUMBERS

POSITIVE NUMBERS are greater than 0, and **NEGATIVE NUMBERS** are less than 0. Both positive and negative numbers can be shown on a **NUMBER LINE**.

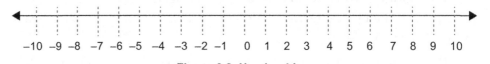

Figure 2.2. Number Line

The **ABSOLUTE VALUE** of a number is the distance the number is from 0. Since distance is always positive, the absolute value of a number is always positive. The absolute value of a is denoted $|a|$. For example, $|-2| = 2$ since -2 is two units away from 0.

Positive and negative numbers can be added, subtracted, multiplied, and divided. The sign of the resulting number is governed by a specific set of rules shown in the table below.

Table 2.1. Operations with Positive and Negative Numbers

ADDING REAL NUMBERS		SUBTRACTING REAL NUMBERS	
Positive + Positive = Positive	$7 + 8 = 15$	Negative – Positive = Negative	$-7 - 8 = -7 + (-8) = -15$
Negative + Negative = Negative	$-7 + (-8) = -15$	Positive – Negative = Positive	$7 - (-8) = 7 + 8 = 15$
Negative + Positive OR Positive + Negative = Keep the sign of the number with larger absolute value	$-7 + 8 = 1$ $7 + -8 = -1$	Negative – Negative = Change the subtraction to addition and change the sign of the second number; then use addition rules.	$-7 - (-8) = -7 + 8 = 1$ $-8 - (-7) = -8 + 7 = -1$

MULTIPLYING REAL NUMBERS		DIVIDING REAL NUMBERS	
Positive × Positive = Positive	$8 \times 4 = 32$	Positive ÷ Positive = Positive	$8 \div 4 = 2$
Negative × Negative = Positive	$-8 \times (-4) = 32$	Negative ÷ Negative = Positive	$-8 \div (-4) = 2$
Positive × Negative OR Negative × Positive = Negative	$8 \times (-4) = -32$ $-8 \times 4 = -32$	Positive ÷ Negative OR Negative ÷ Positive = Negative	$8 \div (-4) = -2$ $-8 \div 4 = -2$

Examples

5. Add or subtract the following real numbers:
    (A) $-18 + 12$
    (B) $-3.64 + (-2.18)$
    (C) $9.37 - 4.25$
    (D) $86 - (-20)$

6. Multiply or divide the following real numbers:
    (A) $\left(\frac{10}{3}\right)\left(-\frac{9}{5}\right)$
    (B) $\frac{-64}{-10}$
    (C) $(2.2)(3.3)$
    (D) $-52 \div 13$

ORDER OF OPERATIONS

The **ORDER OF OPERATIONS** is simply the order in which operations are performed. **PEMDAS** is a common way to remember the order of operations:

1. **P**arentheses
2. **E**xponents
3. **M**ultiplication
4. **D**ivision
5. **A**ddition
6. **S**ubtraction

Multiplication and division, and addition and subtraction, are performed together from left to right. So, performing multiple operations on a set of numbers is a four-step process:

1. P: Calculate expressions inside parentheses, brackets, braces, etc.
2. E: Calculate exponents and square roots.
3. MD: Calculate any remaining multiplication and division in order from left to right.
4. AS: Calculate any remaining addition and subtraction in order from left to right.

Always work from left to right within each step when simplifying expressions.

Examples

7. Simplify: $2(21 - 14) + 6 \div (-2) \times 3 - 10$

8. Simplify: $-(3)^2 + 4(5) + (5 - 6)^2 - 8$

9. Simplify: $\dfrac{(7 - 9)^3 + 8(10 - 12)}{4^2 - 5^2}$

UNITS OF MEASUREMENT

The standard units for the metric and American systems are shown below, along with the prefixes used to express metric units.

Table 2.2. Units and Conversion Factors

DIMENSION	AMERICAN	SI
length	inch/foot/yard/mile	meter
mass	ounce/pound/ton	gram
volume	cup/pint/quart/gallon	liter
force	pound-force	newton
pressure	pound-force per square inch	pascal
work and energy	cal/British thermal unit	joule

Table 2.2. Units and Conversion Factors (continued)

DIMENSION	AMERICAN	SI
temperature	Fahrenheit	kelvin
charge	faraday	coulomb

Table 2.3. Metric Prefixes

PREFIX	SYMBOL	MULTIPLICATION FACTOR
tera	T	1,000,000,000,000
giga	G	1,000,000,000
mega	M	1,000,000
kilo	k	1,000
hecto	h	100
deca	da	10
base unit	--	--
deci	d	0.1
centi	c	0.01
milli	m	0.001
micro	μ	0.000001
nano	n	0.000000001
pico	p	0.000000000001

STUDY TIP

A mnemonic device to help remember the metric system is *King Henry Drinks Under Dark Chocolate Moon* (KHDUDCM).

Units can be converted within a single system or between systems. When converting from one unit to another unit, a conversion factor (a numeric multiplier used to convert a value with a unit to another unit) is used. The process of converting between units using a conversion factor is sometimes known as dimensional analysis.

Table 2.4. Conversion Factors

1 in. = 2.54 cm	1 lb. = 0.454 kg
1 yd. = 0.914 m	1 cal = 4.19 J
1 mi. = 1.61 km	1 degree F = $\frac{9}{5}$°C + 32°C
1 gal. = 3.785 L	1 cm^3 = 1 mL
1 oz. = 28.35 g	1 hr = 3600 s

Examples

10. Convert the following measurements in the metric system.

   (A) 4.25 kilometers to meters

   (B) 8 m^2 to mm^2

11. Convert the following measurements in the American system.
    (A) 12 feet to inches
    (B) 7 yd^2 to ft^2

12. Convert the following measurements in the metric system to the American system.
    (A) 23 meters to feet
    (B) 10 m^2 to yd^2

13. Convert the following measurements in the American system to the metric system.
    (A) 8 in^3 to milliliters
    (B) 16 kilograms to pounds

DECIMALS AND FRACTIONS

Decimals

A DECIMAL is a number that contains a decimal point. A decimal number is an alternative way of writing a fraction. The place value for a decimal includes TENTHS (one place after the decimal), HUNDREDTHS (two places after the decimal), THOUSANDTHS (three places after the decimal), etc.

HELPFUL HINT

To determine which way to move the decimal after multiplying, remember that changing the decimal should always make the final answer smaller.

Table 2.5. Place Values

1,000,000	10^6	millions
100,000	10^5	hundred thousands
10,000	10^4	ten thousands
1,000	10^3	thousands
100	10^2	hundreds
10	10^1	tens
1	10^0	ones
.		decimal
$\frac{1}{10}$	10^{-1}	tenths
$\frac{1}{100}$	10^{-2}	hundredths
$\frac{1}{1000}$	10^{-3}	thousandths

Decimals can be added, subtracted, multiplied, and divided:

■ To add or subtract decimals, line up the decimal point and perform the operation, keeping the decimal point in the same place in the answer.

■ To multiply decimals, first multiply the numbers without the decimal points. Then, sum the number of decimal places to the right of the decimal point in the original numbers and place the decimal

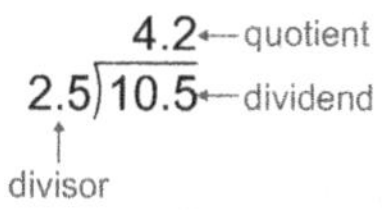

Figure 2.3. Division Terms

Figure 2.3. Division Terms

point in the answer so that there are that many places to the right of the decimal.

- When dividing decimals move the decimal point to the right in order to make the divisor a whole number and move the decimal the same number of places in the dividend. Divide the numbers without regard to the decimal. Then, place the decimal point of the quotient directly above the decimal point of the dividend.

Examples

14. Simplify: $24.38 + 16.51 - 29.87$

15. Simplify: $(10.4)(18.2)$

16. Simplify: $80 \div 2.5$

Fractions

A **FRACTION** is a number that can be written in the form $\frac{a}{b}$, where b is not equal to 0. The a part of the fraction is the **NUMERATOR** (top number) and the b part of the fraction is the **DENOMINATOR** (bottom number).

If the denominator of a fraction is greater than the numerator, the value of the fraction is less than 1 and it is called a **PROPER FRACTION** (for example, $\frac{3}{5}$ is a proper fraction). In an **IMPROPER FRACTION**, the denominator is less than the numerator and the value of the fraction is greater than 1 ($\frac{8}{3}$ is an improper fraction). An improper fraction can be written as a **MIXED NUMBER**, which has a whole number part and a proper fraction part. Improper fractions can be converted to mixed numbers by dividing the numerator by the denominator, which gives the whole number part, and the remainder becomes the numerator of the proper fraction part. (For example, the improper fraction $\frac{25}{9}$ is equal to mixed number $2\frac{7}{9}$ because 9 divides into 25 two times, with a remainder of 7.)

Conversely, mixed numbers can be converted to improper fractions. To do so, determine the numerator of the improper fraction by multiplying the denominator by the whole number, and then adding the numerator. The final number is written as the (now larger) numerator over the original denominator.

Fractions with the same denominator can be added or subtracted by simply adding or subtracting the numerators; the denominator will remain unchanged. To add or subtract fractions with different denominators, find the **LEAST COMMON DENOMINATOR** (**LCD**) of all the fractions. The LCD is the smallest number exactly divisible by each denominator. (For example, the least common denominator of the numbers 2, 3, and 8 is 24.) Once the LCD has been found, each fraction should be written in an equivalent form with the LCD as the denominator.

To multiply fractions, the numerators are multiplied together and denominators are multiplied together. If there are any mixed numbers, they should first be changed to improper fractions. Then, the numerators are multiplied together and the denominators are multiplied together. The fraction can then

HELPFUL HINT

To convert mixed numbers to improper fractions:

$a\frac{m}{n} = \frac{n \times a + m}{n}$

HELPFUL HINT

$\frac{a}{b} \pm \frac{c}{b} = \frac{a \pm c}{b}$

$\frac{a}{b} \times \frac{c}{d} = \frac{ac}{bd}$

$\frac{a}{b} \div \frac{c}{d} = \frac{a}{b} \times \frac{d}{c} = \frac{ad}{bc}$

be reduced if necessary. To divide fractions, multiply the first fraction by the reciprocal of the second.

Any common denominator can be used to add or subtract fractions. The quickest way to find a common denominator of a set of values is simply to multiply all the values together. The result might not be the least common denominator, but it will allow the problem to be worked.

Examples

17. Simplify: $2\frac{3}{5} + 3\frac{1}{4} - 1\frac{1}{2}$

18. Simplify: $\frac{7}{8} \times 3\frac{1}{3}$

19. Simplify: $4\frac{1}{2} \div \frac{2}{3}$

Converting Between Fractions and Decimals

A fraction is converted to a decimal by using long division until there is no remainder and no pattern of repeating numbers occurs.

A decimal is converted to a fraction using the following steps:

- Place the decimal value as the numerator in a fraction with a denominator of 1.
- Multiply the fraction by $\frac{10}{10}$ for every digit in the decimal value, so that there is no longer a decimal in the numerator.
- Reduce the fraction.

Examples

20. Write the fraction $\frac{7}{8}$ as a decimal.

21. Write the fraction $\frac{5}{11}$ as a decimal.

22. Write the decimal 0.125 as a fraction.

FACTORIALS

A **FACTORIAL** of a number n is denoted by $n!$ and is equal to $1 \times 2 \times 3 \times 4 \times \ldots \times n$. Both $0!$ and $1!$ are equal to 1 by definition. Fractions containing factorials can often be simplified by crossing out the portions of the factorials that occur in both the numerator and denominator.

Examples

23. Simplify: $8!$

24. Simplify: $\frac{10!}{7!3!}$

RATIOS

A **RATIO** is a comparison of two numbers and can be represented as $\frac{a}{b}$, $a:b$, or a to b. The two numbers represent a constant relationship, not a specific value: for every a number of items in the first group, there will be b number of items in the second. For example, if the ratio of blue to red candies in a bag is 3:5, the bag will contain 3 blue candies for every 5 red candies. So, the bag might contain 3 blue candies and 5 red candies, or it might contain 30 blue candies and 50 red candies, or 36 blue candies and 60 red candies. All of these values are representative of the ratio 3:5 (which is the ratio in its lowest, or simplest, terms).

To find the "whole" when working with ratios, simply add the values in the ratio. For example, if the ratio of boys to girls in a class is 2:3, the "whole" is five: 2 out of every 5 students are boys, and 3 out of every 5 students are girls.

Examples

25. There are 10 boys and 12 girls in a first-grade class. What is the ratio of boys to the total number of students? What is the ratio of girls to boys?

26. A family spends $600 a month on rent, $400 on utilities, $750 on groceries, and $550 on miscellaneous expenses. What is the ratio of the family's rent to their total expenses?

PROPORTIONS

A **PROPORTION** is an equation which states that two ratios are equal. A proportion is given in the form $\frac{a}{b} = \frac{c}{d}$, where the a and d terms are the extremes and the b and c terms are the means. A proportion is solved using cross-multiplication ($ad = bc$) to create an equation with no fractional components. A proportion must have the same units in both numerators and both denominators.

Examples

27. Solve the proportion for x: $\frac{3x-5}{2} = \frac{x-8}{3}$.

28. A map is drawn such that 2.5 inches on the map equates to an actual distance of 40 miles. If the distance measured on the map between two cities is 17.25 inches, what is the actual distance between them in miles?

29. A factory knows that 4 out of 1000 parts made will be defective. If in a month there are 125,000 parts made, how many of these parts will be defective?

PERCENTAGES

A **PERCENT** (or percentage) means per hundred and is expressed with a percent symbol (%). For example, 54% means 54 out of every 100. A percent can be converted to a decimal by removing the % symbol and moving the decimal point two places to the left, while a decimal can be converted to a percent by moving the decimal point two places to the right and attaching the % sign. A percent can be converted to a fraction by writing the percent as a fraction with 100 as the denominator and reducing. A fraction can be converted to a percent by performing the indicated division, multiplying the result by 100, and attaching the % sign.

The equation for finding percentages has three variables: the part, the whole, and the percent (which is expressed in the equation as a decimal). The equation, as shown below, can be rearranged to solve for any of these variables.

- part = whole × percent
- percent = $\dfrac{\text{part}}{\text{whole}}$
- whole = $\dfrac{\text{part}}{\text{percent}}$

This set of equations can be used to solve percent word problems. All that's needed is to identify the part, whole, and/or percent, and then to plug those values into the appropriate equation and solve.

Examples

30. Change the following values to the indicated form:

   (A) 18% to a fraction

   (B) $\frac{3}{5}$ to a percent

   (C) 1.125 to a percent

   (D) 84% to a decimal

31. In a school of 650 students, 54% of the students are boys. How many students are girls?

Percent Change

Percent change problems involve a change from an original amount. Often percent change problems appear as word problems that include discounts, growth, or markups. In order to solve percent change problems, it's necessary to identify the percent change (as a decimal), the amount of change, and the original amount. (Keep in mind that one of these will be the value being solved for.) These values can then be plugged into the equations below:

HELPFUL HINT
Key terms associated with percent change problems include *discount*, *sales tax*, and *markup*.

- amount of change = original amount × percent change
- percent change = $\dfrac{\text{amount of change}}{\text{original amount}}$
- original amount = $\dfrac{\text{amount of change}}{\text{percent change}}$

Examples

32. An HDTV that originally cost $1,500 is on sale for 45% off. What is the sale price for the item?

33. A house was bought in 2000 for $100,000 and sold in 2015 for $120,000. What was the percent growth in the value of the house from 2000 to 2015?

EXPONENTS AND RADICALS

Exponents

An expression in the form b^n is in an exponential notation where b is the BASE and n is an EXPONENT. To perform the operation, multiply the base by itself the number of times indicated by the exponent. For example, 2^3 is equal to $2 \times 2 \times 2$ or 8.

Table 2.6. Operations with Exponents

RULE	EXAMPLE	EXPLANATION
$a^0 = 1$	$5^0 = 1$	Any base (except 0) to the 0 power is 1.
$a^{-n} = \dfrac{1}{a^n}$	$5^3 = \dfrac{1}{5^3}$	A negative exponent becomes positive when moved from numerator to denominator (or vice versa).
$a^m a^n = a^{m+n}$	$5^3 5^4 = 5^{3+4} = 5^7$	Add the exponents to multiply two powers with the same base.
$(a^m)^n = a^{mn}$	$(5^3)^4 = 5^{3(4)} = 5^{12}$	Multiply the exponents to raise a power to a power.
$\dfrac{a^m}{a^n} = a^{m-n}$	$\dfrac{5^4}{5^3} = 5^{4-3} = 5^1$	Subtract the exponents to divide two powers with the same base.
$(ab)^n = a^n b^n$	$(5 \times 6)^3 = 5^3 6^3$	Apply the exponent to each base to raise a product to a power.
$\dfrac{a^n}{b} = \dfrac{a^n}{b^n}$	$\dfrac{5^3}{6} = \dfrac{5^3}{6^3}$	Apply the exponent to each base to raise a quotient to a power.
$\dfrac{a^{-n}}{b} = \dfrac{b^n}{a}$	$\dfrac{5^{-3}}{6} = \dfrac{6^3}{5}$	Invert the fraction and change the sign of the exponent to raise a fraction to a negative power.
$\dfrac{a^m}{b^n} = \dfrac{b^{-n}}{a^{-m}}$	$\dfrac{5^3}{6^4} = \dfrac{6^{-4}}{5^{-3}}$	Change the sign of the exponent when moving a number from the numerator to denominator (or vice versa).

Examples

34. Simplify: $\dfrac{(10^2)^3}{(10^2)^{-2}}$

35. Simplify: $\dfrac{(x^{-2}y^2)^2}{x^3 y}$

Radicals

RADICALS are expressed as $\sqrt[b]{a}$, where b is called the INDEX and a is the RADICAND. A radical is used to indicate the inverse operation of an exponent: finding the base which can be raised to b to yield a. For example, $\sqrt[3]{125}$ is equal to 5 because $5 \times 5 \times 5$ equals 125. The same operation can be expressed using a fraction exponent, so $\sqrt[b]{a} = a^{\frac{1}{b}}$. Note that when no value is indicated for b, it is assumed to be 2 (square root).

When b is even and a is positive, $\sqrt[b]{a}$ is defined to be the positive real value n such that $n^b = a$ (example: $\sqrt{16} = 4$ only, and not -4, even though $(-4)(-4) = 16$). If b is even and a is negative, $\sqrt[b]{a}$ will be a complex number (example:

$\sqrt{-9} = 3i$). Finally if b is odd, $\sqrt[b]{a}$ will always be a real number regardless of the sign of a. If a is negative, $\sqrt[b]{a}$ will be negative since a number to an odd power is negative (example: $\sqrt[5]{-32} = -2$ since $(-2)^5 = -32$).

$\sqrt[n]{x}$ is referred to as the nth root of x.

- $n = 2$ is the square root
- $n = 3$ is the cube root
- $n = 4$ is the fourth root
- $n = 5$ is the fifth root

The following table of operations with radicals holds for all cases EXCEPT the case where b is even and a is negative (the complex case).

Table 2.7. Operations with Radicals

RULE	EXAMPLE	EXPLANATION
$\sqrt[b]{ac} = \sqrt[b]{a}\sqrt[b]{c}$	$\sqrt[3]{81} = \sqrt[3]{27}\sqrt[3]{3} = 3\sqrt[3]{3}$	The values under the radical sign can be separated into values that multiply to the original value.
$\sqrt[b]{\dfrac{a}{c}} = \dfrac{\sqrt[b]{a}}{\sqrt[b]{c}}$	$\sqrt{\dfrac{4}{81}} = \dfrac{\sqrt{4}}{\sqrt{81}} = \dfrac{2}{9}$	The b-root of the numerator and denominator can be calculated when there is a fraction under a radical sign.
$\sqrt[b]{a^c} = (\sqrt[b]{a})^c = a^{\frac{c}{b}}$	$\sqrt[3]{6^2} = (\sqrt[3]{6})^2 = 6^{\frac{2}{3}}$	The b-root can be written as a fractional exponent. If there is a power under the radical sign, it will be the numerator of the fraction.
$\dfrac{c}{\sqrt[b]{a}} \times \dfrac{\sqrt[b]{a}}{\sqrt[b]{a}} = \dfrac{c\sqrt[b]{a}}{a}$	$\dfrac{5}{\sqrt{2}} \dfrac{\sqrt{2}}{\sqrt{2}} = \dfrac{5\sqrt{2}}{2}$	To rationalize the denominator, multiply the numerator and denominator by the radical in the denominator until the radical has been canceled out.
$\dfrac{c}{b - \sqrt{a}} \times \dfrac{b + \sqrt{a}}{b + \sqrt{a}} = \dfrac{c(b + \sqrt{a})}{b^2 - a}$	$\dfrac{4}{3 - \sqrt{2}} \times \dfrac{3 + \sqrt{2}}{3 + \sqrt{2}} = \dfrac{12 + 4\sqrt{2}}{7}$	To rationalize the denominator, the numerator and denominator are multiplied by the conjugate of the denominator.

Examples

36. Simplify: $\sqrt{48}$

37. Simplify: $\dfrac{6}{\sqrt{8}}$

ABSOLUTE VALUE

The **ABSOLUTE VALUE** of a number means the distance between that number and zero. The absolute value of any number is positive since distance is always positive. The notation for absolute value of a number is two vertical bars:

$\|-27\| = 27$	The distance from -27 to 0 is 27.
$\|27\| = 27$	The distance from 27 to 0 is 27.

Solving equations and simplifying inequalities with absolute values usually requires writing two equations or inequalities, which are then solved separately using the usual methods of solving equations. To write the two equations, set one equation equal to the positive value of the expression inside the absolute value and the other equal to the negative value. Two inequalities can be written in the same manner. However, the inequality symbol should be flipped for the negative value. The formal definition of the absolute value is

$$|x| = \begin{cases} -x, & x < 0 \\ x, & x \geq 0 \end{cases}$$

This is true because whenever x is negative, the opposite of x is the answer (for example, $|-5| = -(-5) = 5$, but when x is positive, the answer is just x. This type of function is called a **PIECE-WISE FUNCTION**. It is defined in two (or more) distinct pieces. To graph the absolute value function, graph each piece separately. When $x < 0$ (that is, when it is negative), graph the line $y = -x$. When $x > 0$ (that is, when x is positive), graph the line $y = x$. This creates a V-shaped graph that is the parent function for absolute value functions.

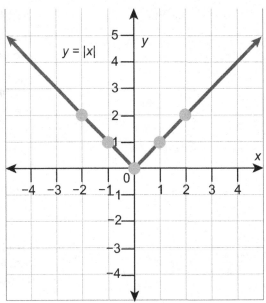

Figure 2.4. Absolute Value Parent Function

Examples

38. Solve for x: $|x - 3| = 27$

39. Solve for r: $\frac{|r - 7|}{5} = 27$

40. Find the solution set for the following inequality: $\left|\frac{3x}{7}\right| \geq 4 - x$.

DESCRIBING SETS OF DATA

Measures of central tendency help identify the center, or most typical, value within a data set. There are three such central tendencies that describe the "center" of the data in different ways. The **MEAN** is the arithmetic average and is found by dividing the sum of all measurements by the number of measurements. The mean of a population is written as μ and the mean of a sample is written as $\bar{x}$.

$$\text{population mean} = \mu = \frac{x_1 + x_2 + \ldots x_N}{N} = \frac{\sum x}{N}$$

$$\text{sample mean} = \overline{x} = \frac{x_1 + x_2 + \ldots x_n}{n} = \frac{\sum x}{n}$$

The data points are represented by x's with subscripts; the sum is denoted using the Greek letter sigma ($\sum$); N is the number of data points in the entire population; and n is the number of data points in a sample set.

The MEDIAN divides the measurements into two equal halves. The median is the measurement right in the middle of an odd set of measurements or the average of the two middle numbers in an even data set. When calculating the median, it is important to order the data values from least to greatest before attempting to locate the middle value. The MODE is simply the measurement that occurs most often. There can be many modes in a data set, or no mode. Since measures of central tendency describe a *center* of the data, all three of these measures will be between the lowest and highest data values (inclusive).

HELPFUL HINT

When the same value is added to each term in a set, the mean increases by that value and the standard deviation is unchanged.

When each term in a set is multiplied by the same value, both the mean and standard deviation will also be multiplied by that value.

Unusually large or small values, called OUTLIERS, will affect the mean of a sample more than the mode. If there is a high outlier, the mean will be greater than the median; if there is a low outlier, the mean will be lower than the median. When outliers are present, the median is a better measure of the data's center than the mean because the median will be closer to the terms in the data set.

The values in a data set can be very close together (close to the mean), or very spread out. This is called the SPREAD or DISPERSION of the data. There are a few MEASURES OF VARIATION (or MEASURES OF DISPERSION) that quantify the spread within a data set. **RANGE** is the difference between the largest and smallest data points in a set:

$$R = \textit{largest data point} - \textit{smallest data point}$$

Notice range depends on only two data points (the two extremes). Sometimes these data points are outliers; regardless, for a large data set, relying on only two data points is not an exact tool.

The understanding of the data set can be improved by calculating QUARTILES. To calculate quartiles, first arrange the data in ascending order and find the set's median (also called quartile 2 or Q2). Then find the median of the lower half of the data, called quartile 1 (Q1), and the median of the upper half of the data, called quartile 3 (Q3). These three points divide the data into four equal groups of data (thus the word *quartile*). Each quartile contains 25% of the data.

INTERQUARTILE RANGE (IQR) provides a more reliable range that is not as affected by extremes. IQR is the difference between the third quartile data point and the first quartile data point and gives the spread of the middle 50% of the data:

$$IQR = Q_3 - Q_1$$

A measure of variation that depends on the mean is STANDARD DEVIATION, which uses every data point in a set and calculates the average distance of each data point from the mean of the data. Standard deviation can be computed for an entire population (written σ) or for a sample of a population (written s):

$$\sigma = \sqrt{\frac{\sum(xi - \mu)^2}{N}} \qquad s = \sqrt{\frac{\sum(xi - \bar{x})^2}{n - 1}}$$

Thus, to calculate standard deviation, the difference between the mean and each data point is calculated. Each of these differences is squared (so that each is positive). The average of the squared values is computed by summing the squares and dividing by N or $(n - 1)$. Then the square root is taken, to "undo" the previous squaring.

The **VARIANCE** of a data set is simply the square of the standard variation:

$$V = \sigma^2 = \frac{1}{N} \sum_{i=1}^{N} (xi - \mu)^2$$

Variance measures how narrowly or widely the data points are distributed. A variance of zero means every data point is the same; a large variance means there are a relatively small amount of data points near the set's mean.

Examples

41. What is the mean of the following data set? {1000, 0.1, 10, 1}

42. What is the median of the following data set? {1000, 10, 1, 0.1}

43. Josey has an average of 81 on four equally weighted tests she has taken in her statistics class. She wants to determine what grade she must receive on her fifth test so that her mean is 83, which will give her a B in the course, but she does not remember her other scores. What grade must she receive on her fifth test?

44. What are the range and interquartile range of the following set? {3, 9, 49, 64, 81, 100, 121, 144, 169}

45. In a group of 7 people, 1 person has no children, 2 people have 1 child, 2 people have 2 children, 1 person has 5 children, and 1 person has 17 children. To the nearest hundredth of a child, what is the standard deviation in this group?

PROBABILITY

Probability describes how likely something is to happen. In probability, an **EVENT** is the single result of a trial, and an **OUTCOME** is a possible event that results from a trial. The collection of all possible outcomes for a particular trial is called the **SAMPLE SPACE**. For example, when rolling a die, the sample space is the numbers $1 - 6$. Rolling a single number, such as 4, would be a single event.

Probability of a Single Event

The probability of a single event occurring is the number of outcomes in which that event occurs (called FAVORABLE EVENTS) divided by the number of items in the sample space (total possible outcomes):

$$P \text{ (an event)} = \frac{\text{number of favorable outcomes}}{\text{total number of possible outcomes}}$$

The probability of any event occurring will always be a fraction or decimal between 0 and 1. It may also be expressed as a percent. An event with 0 probability will never occur and an event with a probability of 1 is certain to occur. The probability of an event not occurring is referred to as that event's COMPLEMENT. The sum of an event's probability and the probability of that event's complement will always be 1.

Examples

46. What is the probability that an even number results when a six-sided die is rolled? What is the probability the die lands on 5?

47. Only 20 tickets were issued in a raffle. If someone were to buy 6 tickets, what is the probability that person would not win the raffle?

48. A bag contains 26 tiles representing the 26 letters of the English alphabet. If 3 tiles are drawn from the bag without replacement, what is the probability that all 3 will be consonants?

Probability of Multiple Events

If events are INDEPENDENT, the probability of one occurring does not affect the probability of the other event occurring. Rolling a die and getting one number does not change the probability of getting any particular number on the next roll. The number of faces has not changed, so these are independent events.

If events are DEPENDENT, the probability of one occurring changes the probability of the other event occurring. Drawing a card from a deck without replacing it will affect the probability of the next card drawn because the number of available cards has changed.

To find the probability that two or more independent events will occur (*A* and *B*), simply multiply the probabilities of each individual event together. To find the probability that one, the other, or both will occur (*A* or *B*), it's necessary to add their probabilities and then subtract their overlap (which prevents the same values from being counted twice).

CONDITIONAL PROBABILITY is the probability of an event occurring given that another event has occurred. The notation $P(B|A)$ represents the probability that event *B* occurs, given that event *A* has already occurred (it is read "probability of *B*, given *A*").

HELPFUL HINT

When drawing objects, the phrase *with replacement* describes independent events, and *without replacement* describes dependent events.

Table 2.8. Probability Formulas

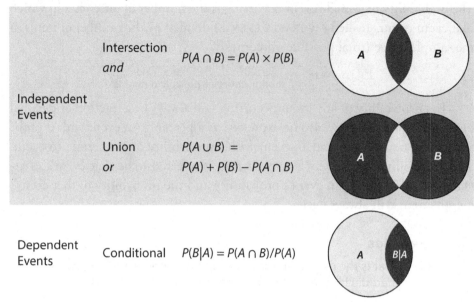

Independent Events	Intersection and	$P(A \cap B) = P(A) \times P(B)$
	Union or	$P(A \cup B) =$ $P(A) + P(B) - P(A \cap B)$
Dependent Events	Conditional	$P(B \mid A) = P(A \cap B)/P(A)$

Two events that are **MUTUALLY EXCLUSIVE** CANNOT happen at the same time. This is similar to disjoint sets in set theory. The probability that two mutually exclusive events will occur is zero. **MUTUALLY INCLUSIVE** events share common outcomes.

Examples

49. A card is drawn from a standard 52-card deck. What is the probability that it is either a queen or a heart?

50. A group of ten individuals is drawing straws from a group of 28 long straws and 2 short straws. If the straws are not replaced, what is the probability, as a percentage, that neither of the first two individuals will draw a short straw?

ARITHMETIC SEQUENCES

ARITHMETIC GROWTH is constant growth, meaning that the difference between any one term in the series and the next consecutive term will be the same constant. This constant is called the **COMMON DIFFERENCE**. Thus, to list the terms in the sequence, one can just add (or subtract) the same number repeatedly. For example, the series {20, 30, 40, 50} is arithmetic since 10 is added each time to get from one term to the next. One way to represent this sequence is using a **RECURSIVE** definition, which basically says: *next term = current term + common difference*. For this example, the recursive definition would be $a_{n+1} = a_n + 10$ because the *next* term a_{n+1} in the sequence is the current term a_n plus 10. In general, the recursive definition of a series is:

$$a_{n+1} = a_n + d, \text{ where } d \text{ is the common difference.}$$

Often, the objective of arithmetic sequence questions is to find a specific term in the sequence or the sum of a certain series of terms. The formulas to use are:

Table 2.9. Formulas for Arithmetic Sequences and Series

FINDING THE *N*TH TERM . . .

$a_n = a_1 + d(n-1)$ $a_n = a_m + d(n-m)$	d = the common difference of the sequence a_n = the nth term in the sequence n = the number of the term a_m = the mth term in the sequence m = the number of the term a_1 = the first term in the sequence

FINDING THE PARTIAL SUM . . .

$S_n = \dfrac{n(a_1 + a_n)}{2}$	S_n = sum of the terms through the nth term a_n = the nth term in the sequence n = the number of the term a_1 = the first term in the sequence

Examples

51. Find the ninth term of the sequence: −57, −40, −23, −6 …

52. If the 23rd term in an arithmetic sequence is 820, and the 5th term is 200, find the common difference between each term.

ANSWER KEY

1. (A) The number is **natural**, **whole**, an **integer**, and **rational**.

    (B) The fraction is **rational**.

    (C) The number is **irrational**. (It cannot be written as a fraction, and written as a decimal is approximately 2.2360679...)

2. (A) $20 = 20 + 0i$ **The real part is 20, and there is no imaginary part.**

    (B) $10 - i = 10 - 1i$ **The real part is 10, and −1i is the imaginary part.**

    (C) $15i = 0 + 15i$ **The real part is 0, and the imaginary part is 15i.**

    A complex number is in the form of $a + bi$, where a is the real part and bi is the imaginary part.

3. (A) **False.** Subtracting the natural number 7 from 2 results in $2 - 7 = -5$, which is an integer, but not a natural number.

    (B) **False.** For example, $(5 - 2\sqrt{3}) + (2 + 2\sqrt{3}) = 7$. The sum of two irrational numbers in this example is a whole number, which is not irrational. The sum of a rational number and an irrational number is sometimes rational and sometimes irrational.

    (C) **True.** Because irrational numbers have decimal parts that are unending and with no pattern, adding a repeating or terminating decimal will still result in an unending decimal without a pattern.

4. (A) **True.** For all real numbers, $a \times (b \times c) = (a \times b) \times c$. Order of multiplication does not change the result.

    (B) **False.** The commutative property does not work for subtraction or division on real numbers. For example, $12 - 5 = 7$, but $5 - 12 = -7$ and $10 \div 2 = 5$, but $2 \div 10 = \frac{1}{5}$.

5. (A) Since $|-18| > |12|$, the answer is negative: $|-18| - |12| = 6$. So the answer is **−6**.

    (B) Adding two negative numbers results in a negative number. Add the values: **−5.82**.

    (C) The first number is larger than the second, so the final answer is positive: **5.12**.

    (D) Change the subtraction to addition, change the sign of the second number, and then add: $86 - (-20) = 86 + (+20) = $ **106**.

6. (A) Multiply the numerators, multiply the denominators, and simplify: $\frac{-90}{15} = $ **−6**.

    (B) A negative divided by a negative is a positive number: **6.4**.

    (C) Multiplying positive numbers gives a positive answer: **7.26**.

    (D) Dividing a negative by a positive number gives a negative answer: **−4**.

7. $2(21 - 14) + 6 \div (-2) \times 3 - 10$

Calculate expressions inside parentheses.

$= 2(7) + 6 \div (-2) \times 3 - 10$

There are no exponents or radicals, so perform multiplication and division from left to right.

$= 14 + 6 \div (-2) \times 3 - 10 = 14 + (-3) \times 3 - 10 = 14 + (-9) - 10$

Perform addition and subtraction from left to right.

$= 5 - 10 = \mathbf{-5}$

8. $-(3)^2 + 4(5) + (5 - 6)^2 - 8$

Calculate expressions inside parentheses.

$= -(3)^2 + 4(5) + (-1)^2 - 8$

Simplify exponents and radicals.

$= -9 + 4(5) + 1 - 8$

Perform multiplication and division from left to right.

$= -9 + 20 + 1 - 8$

Perform addition and subtraction from left to right.

$= 11 + 1 - 8 = 12 - 8 = \mathbf{4}$

9. $\dfrac{(7 - 9)^3 + 8(10 - 12)}{4^2 - 5^2}$

Calculate expressions inside parentheses.

$= \dfrac{(-2)^3 + 8(-2)}{4^2 - 5^2}$

Simplify exponents and radicals.

$= \dfrac{-8 + (-16)}{16 - 25}$

Perform addition and subtraction from left to right.

$= \dfrac{-24}{-9} = \dfrac{\mathbf{8}}{\mathbf{3}}$

10. (A) $4.25 \text{ km} \left(\dfrac{1000 \text{ m}}{1 \text{ km}} \right) = \mathbf{4250 \text{ m}}$

(B) $\dfrac{8 \text{ m}^2}{1} \times \dfrac{1000 \text{ mm}}{1 \text{ m}} \times \dfrac{1000 \text{ mm}}{1 \text{ m}} = \mathbf{8{,}000{,}000 \text{ mm}^2}$

Since the units are square units (m²), multiply by the conversion factor twice, so that both meters cancel.

11. (A) $12 \text{ ft} \left(\dfrac{12 \text{ in}}{1 \text{ ft}} \right) = \mathbf{144 \text{ in}}$

(B) $7 \text{ yd}^2 \left(\dfrac{3 \text{ ft}}{1 \text{ yd}} \right) \left(\dfrac{3 \text{ ft}}{1 \text{ yd}} \right) = \mathbf{63 \text{ ft}^2}$

Since the units are square units (yd²), multiply by the conversion factor twice.

12. (A) $23 \text{ m} \left(\dfrac{3.28 \text{ ft}}{1 \text{ m}} \right) = \mathbf{75.44 \text{ ft}}$

(B) $\dfrac{10 \text{ m}^2}{1} \times \dfrac{1.094 \text{ yd}}{1 \text{ m}} \times \dfrac{1.094 \text{ yd}}{1 \text{ m}} = \mathbf{11.97 \text{ yd}^2}$

13. (A) $8 \text{ in}^3 \left(\frac{16.39 \text{ ml}}{1 \text{ in}^3} \right) = \textbf{131.12 mL}$

    (B) $16 \text{ kg} \frac{2.2 \text{ lb}}{\left(1 \text{ kg} \right)} = \textbf{35.2 lb}$

14. $24.38 + 16.51 - 29.87$

Align the decimals and apply the order of operations left to right.

$$
\begin{aligned}
&24.38 \\
&\underline{+\ 16.51} \\
&= 40.89
\end{aligned}
$$

$$
\begin{aligned}
&40.89 \\
&\underline{-\ 29.87} \\
&= \textbf{11.02}
\end{aligned}
$$

15. $(10.4)(18.2)$

Multiply the numbers ignoring the decimals.

$104 \times 182 = 18{,}928$

The original problem includes two decimal places (one in each number), so move the decimal point in the answer so that there are two places after the decimal point.

$18{,}928 \rightarrow 189.28$

Estimating is a good way to check the answer:

$10.4 \approx 10$, $18.2 \approx 18$, and $10 \times 18 = 180$.

16. $80 \div 2.5$

Move both decimals one place to the right (multiply by 10) so that the divisor is a whole number.

$80 \rightarrow 800$

$2.5 \rightarrow 25$

Divide normally.

$800 \div 25 = 32$

17. $2\frac{3}{5} + 3\frac{1}{4} - 1\frac{1}{2}$

Change each fraction so it has a denominator of 20, which is the LCD of 5, 4, and 2.

$= 2\frac{12}{20} + 3\frac{5}{20} - 1\frac{10}{20}$

Add and subtract the whole numbers together and the fractions together.

$2 + 3 - 1 = 4$

$\frac{12}{20} + \frac{5}{20} - \frac{10}{20} = \frac{7}{20}$

Combine to get the final answer (a mixed number).

$4\frac{7}{20}$

18. $\frac{7}{8} \times 3\frac{1}{3}$

Change the mixed number to an improper fraction.

$3\frac{1}{3} = \frac{10}{3}$

Multiply the numerators together and the denominators together.

$\frac{7}{8}\left(\frac{10}{3}\right) = \frac{7 \times 10}{8 \times 3} = \frac{70}{24}$

Reduce the fraction.

$= \frac{35}{12} = \mathbf{2\frac{11}{12}}$

19. $4\frac{1}{2} \div \frac{2}{3}$

Change the mixed number to an improper fraction.

$4\frac{1}{2} = \frac{9}{2}$

Multiply the first fraction by the reciprocal of the second fraction.

$\frac{9}{2} \div \frac{2}{3} = \frac{9}{2} \times \frac{3}{2} = \frac{27}{4} = \mathbf{6\frac{3}{4}}$

20. Divide the denominator into the numerator using long division.

```
      0.875
   8)7000
    -64
      60
     -56
      40
```

21. Dividing using long division yields a repeating decimal.

```
        0.4545
   11)50000
     -44
       60
      -55
       50
      -44
       60
```

22. Create a fraction with 0.125 as the numerator and 1 as the denominator.

$= \frac{0.125}{1}$

Multiply by $\frac{10}{10}$ three times (one for each numeral after the decimal).

$\frac{0.125}{1} \times \frac{10}{10} \times \frac{10}{10} \times \frac{10}{10} = \frac{125}{1000} = \mathbf{\frac{1}{8}}$

Alternatively, recognize that 0.125 is read "one hundred twenty-five thousandths" and can therefore be written in fraction form as $\frac{125}{1000}$.

23. 8!

Expand the factorial and multiply.

$= 8 \times 7 \times 6 \times 5 \times 4 \times 3 \times 2 \times 1 = \mathbf{40{,}320}$

24. $\frac{10!}{7!3!}$

Expand the factorial.

$= \frac{10 \times 9 \times 8 \times 7!}{7! \times 3 \times 2 \times 1}$

Cross out values that occur in both the numerator and denominator.

$= \frac{10 \times 9 \times 8}{3 \times 2 \times 1}$

Multiply and simplify.

$= \frac{720}{6} = \mathbf{120}$

25. Identify the variables.

number of boys: 10

number of girls: 12

number of students: 22

Write out and simplify the ratio of boys to total students.

number of boys : number of students

$= 10 : 22 = \frac{10}{22} = \mathbf{\frac{5}{11}}$

Write out and simplify the ratio of girls to boys.

number of girls : number of boys

$= 12 : 10 = \frac{12}{10} = \mathbf{\frac{6}{5}}$

26. Identify the variables.

rent $= 600$

utilities $= 400$

groceries $= 750$

miscellaneous $= 550$

total expenses $= 600 + 400 + 750 + 550 = 2300$

Write out and simplify the ratio of rent to total expenses.

rent : total expenses

$= 600 : 2300 = \frac{600}{2300} = \mathbf{\frac{6}{23}}$

27. $\frac{3x - 5}{2} = \frac{x - 8}{3}$.

Cross-multiply.

$3(3x - 5) = 2(x - 8)$

Solve the equation for x.

$9x - 15 = 2x - 16$

$7x - 15 = -16$

$7x = -1$

$x = -\frac{1}{7}$

28. Write a proportion where x equals the actual distance and each ratio is written as inches : miles.

$$\frac{2.5}{40} = \frac{17.25}{x}$$

Cross-multiply and divide to solve for x.

$2.5x = 690$

$x = 276$

The two cities are **276 miles apart**.

29. Write a proportion where x is the number of defective parts made and both ratios are written as defective : total.

$$\frac{4}{1000} = \frac{x}{125,000}$$

Cross-multiply and divide to solve for x.

$1000x = 500,000$

$x = 500$

There are **500 defective parts** for the month.

30. (A) The percent is written as a fraction over 100 and reduced: $\frac{18}{100} = \frac{9}{50}$.

(B) Dividing 5 by 3 gives the value 0.6, which is then multiplied by 100: **60%**.

(C) The decimal point is moved two places to the right: $1.125 \times 100 = $ **112.5%**.

(D) The decimal point is moved two places to the left: $84 \div 100 = $ **0.84**.

31. Identify the variables.

Percent of students who are girls = 100% − 54% = 46%

percent = 46% = 0.46

whole = 650 students

part = ?

Plug the variables into the appropriate equation.

part = whole × percent

= 0.46 × 650 = 299

There are 299 girls.

32. Identify the variables.

original amount = $1,500

percent change = 45% = 0.45

amount of change = ?

Plug the variables into the appropriate equation.

amount of change = original amount × percent change

= 1500 × 0.45 = 675

To find the new price, subtract the amount of change from the original price.

$1500 - 675 = 825$

The final price is $825.

33. Identify the variables.

original amount = $100,000

amount of change = $120,000 - 100,000 = 20,000$

percent change = ?

Plug the variables into the appropriate equation.

$$\text{percent change} = \frac{\text{amount of change}}{\text{original amount}}$$

$$= \frac{20,000}{100,000} = 0.20$$

To find the percent growth, multiply by 100.

$0.20 \times 100 =$ **20%**

34. $\dfrac{(10^2)^3}{(10^2)^{-2}}$

Multiply the exponents raised to a power.

$$= \frac{10^6}{10^{-4}}$$

Subtract the exponent in the denominator from the one in the numerator.

$= 10^{6-(-4)} = 10^{10} =$ **10,000,000,000**

35. $\dfrac{(x^{-2}y^2)^2}{x^3y}$

Multiply the exponents raised to a power.

$$= \frac{x^{-4}y^4}{x^3y}$$

Subtract the exponent in the denominator from the one in the numerator.

$= x^{-4-3}y^{4-1}$

$= x^{-7}y^3$

Move negative exponents to the denominator.

$$= \frac{y^3}{x^7}$$

36. $\sqrt{48}$

Determine the largest square number that is a factor of the radicand (48) and write the radicand as a product using that square number as a factor.

$= \sqrt{16 \times 3}$

Apply the rules of radicals to simplify.

$= \sqrt{16}\,\sqrt{3} =$ **4√3**

37. $\dfrac{6}{\sqrt{8}}$

Apply the rules of radicals to simplify.

$$= \frac{6}{\sqrt{4}\,\sqrt{2}} = \frac{6}{2\sqrt{2}}$$

Multiply by $\dfrac{\sqrt{2}}{\sqrt{2}}$ to rationalize the denominator.

$$= \frac{6}{2\sqrt{2}} \left(\frac{\sqrt{2}}{\sqrt{2}} \right) = \frac{3\sqrt{2}}{2}$$

38. $|x - 3| = 27$

Set the quantity inside the parentheses equal to 27 or −27, and solve:

$$x - 3 = 27 \quad \bigg| \quad x - 3 = -27$$
$$\mathbf{x = 30} \quad \bigg| \quad \mathbf{x = -24}$$

39. $\frac{|r - 7|}{5} = 27$

The first step is to isolate the absolute value part of the equation. Multiplying both sides by 5 gives:

$$|r - 7| = 135$$

If the quantity in the absolute value bars is 135 or −135, then the absolute value would be 135:

$$r - 7 = 135 \quad \bigg| \quad r - 7 = -135$$
$$\mathbf{r = 142} \quad \bigg| \quad \mathbf{r = -128}$$

40. $\left| \frac{3x}{7} \right| \geq 4 - x.$

Simplify the equation.

$$\frac{|3x|}{7} \geq 4 - x$$

$$|3x| \geq 28 - 7x$$

Create and solve two inequalities. When including the negative answer, flip the inequality.

$$3x \geq 28 - 7x$$

$$10x \geq 28$$

$$x \geq \frac{28}{10}$$

$$-(3x) \leq 28 - 7x$$

$$-3x \leq 28 - 7x$$

$$4x \leq 28$$

$$x \leq 7$$

Combine the two answers to find the solution set.

$$\mathbf{\frac{28}{10} \leq x \leq 7}$$

41. Use the equation to find the mean of a sample:

$$\frac{1000 + 0.1 + 10 + 1}{4} = \mathbf{252.78}$$

42. Since there is an even number of data points in the set, the median will be the mean of the two middle numbers. Order the numbers from least to greatest: 0.1, 1, 10, and 1000. The two middle numbers are 1 and 10, and their mean is:

$$\frac{1 + 10}{2} = \mathbf{5.5}$$

43. Even though Josey does not know her test scores, she knows her average. Therefore it can be assumed that each test score was 81, since four scores of 81 would average to 81. To find the score, x, that she needs use the equation for the mean of a sample:

$$\frac{4(81) + x}{5} = 83$$

$$324 + x = 415$$

$$x = \mathbf{91}$$

44. Use the equation for range.

R = largest point − smallest point

$= 169 - 3 = \mathbf{166}$

Place the terms in numerical order and identify Q1, Q2, and Q3.

3

9

$\rightarrow$ Q1 $= \frac{49 + 9}{2} = 29$

49

64

81 $\rightarrow$ Q2

100

121

$\rightarrow$ Q3 $= \frac{121 + 144}{2} = 132.5$

144

169

Find the IQR by subtracting Q1 from Q3.

IQR = Q3 − Q1

$= 132.5 - 29 = \mathbf{103.5}$

45. Create a data set out of this scenario.

{0, 1, 1, 2, 2, 5, 17}

Calculate the population mean.

$$\mu = \frac{x_1 + x_2 + \ldots x_N}{N} = \frac{\sum x}{N}$$

$$\mu = \frac{0 + 1 + 1 + 2 + 2 + 5 + 17}{7} = 4$$

Find the square of the difference of each term and the mean $(x_i - \mu)^2$.

$(0 - 4)^2 = (-4)^2 = 16$

$(1 - 4)^2 = (-3)^2 = 9$

$(1 - 4)^2 = (-3)^2 = 9$

$(2 - 4)^2 = (-2)^2 = 4$

$(2 - 4)^2 = (-2)^2 = 4$

$(5 - 4)^2 = (1)^2 = 1$

$(17 - 4)^2 = (13)^2 = 169$

Plug the sum (Σ) of these squares, 212, into the standard deviation formula.

$$\sigma = \sqrt{\frac{\Sigma(xi - \mu)^2}{N}}$$

$$\sigma = \sqrt{\frac{212}{7}} = \sqrt{30.28} = \mathbf{5.50}$$

46. P(rolling even) = $\frac{\text{number of favorable outcomes}}{\text{total number of possible outcomes}} = \frac{3}{6} = \mathbf{\frac{1}{2}}$

    P(rolling 5) = $\frac{\text{number of favorable outcomes}}{\text{total number of possible outcomes}} = \mathbf{\frac{1}{6}}$

47. P(not winning) = $\frac{\text{number of favorable outcomes}}{\text{total number of possible outcomes}} = \frac{14}{20} = \frac{7}{10}$

    or

    P(not winning) = $1 - $ P(winning) = $1 - \frac{6}{20} = \frac{14}{20} = \mathbf{\frac{7}{10}}$

48. P = $\frac{\text{number of favorable outcomes}}{\text{total number of possible outcomes}} = \frac{\text{number of 3-consonant combinations}}{\text{number of 3-tile combinations}}$

    $= \frac{_{21}C_3}{_{26}C_3} = \frac{1330}{2600} = 0.51 = \mathbf{51\%}$

49. This is a union (*or*) problem.

    $P(A) = $ the probability of drawing a queen $= \frac{1}{13}$

    $P(B) = $ the probability of drawing a heart $= \frac{1}{4}$

    $P(A \cap B) = $ the probability of drawing a heart and a queen $= \frac{1}{52}$

    $P(A \cup B) = P(A) + P(B) - P(A \cap B)$

    $= \frac{1}{13} + \frac{1}{4} - \frac{1}{52} = \mathbf{0.31}$

50. This scenario includes two events, *A* and *B*.

    The probability of the first person drawing a long straw is an independent event:

    $P(A) = \frac{28}{30}$

    The probability the second person draws a long straw changes because one long straw has already been drawn. In other words, it is the probability of event *B* given that event *A* has already happened:

    $P(B|A) = \frac{27}{29}$

    The conditional probability formula can be used to determine the probability of both people drawing long straws:

    $P(A \cap B) = P(A)P(B|A)$

    $= (\frac{28}{30})(\frac{27}{29}) = 0.87$

    There is an **87% chance** that neither of the first two individuals will draw short straws.

51. Identify the variables given.

    $a_1 = -57$

    $d = -57 - (-40) = 17$

    $n = 9$

Plug these values into the formula for the specific term of an arithmetic sequence.

$a_9 = -57 + 17(9 - 1)$

Solve for a_9.

$a_9 = -57 + 17(8)$

$a_9 = -57 + 136$

$\boldsymbol{a_9 = 79}$

52. Idenfity the variables given.

$a_5 = 200$

$a_{23} = 820$

$n = 23$

$m = 5$

$d = ?$

Plug these values into the equation for using one term to find another in an arithmetic sequence.

$a_n = a_m + d(n - m)$

$820 = 200 + d(23 - 5)$

$620 = d(18)$

$\boldsymbol{d = 34.\overline{44}}$

WORD KNOWLEDGE

The AFOQT Word Knowledge section tests vocabulary. Each question will provide a stand-alone word, and five answer choices. The correct answer will be the choice whose meaning most closely matches the definition of the given word. It's a fast-moving section: questions need to be answered in fewer than fifteen seconds. Having a large vocabulary will obviously help with this section, but there are strategies that can be used to determine the meaning of unfamiliar words.

WORD STRUCTURE

In addition to the context of a sentence or passage, an unfamiliar word itself can provide clues about its meaning. A word consists of discrete pieces that determine its meaning; these pieces include word roots, prefixes, and suffixes.

WORD ROOTS are the bases from which many words take their form and meaning. The most common word roots are Greek and Latin, and a broad knowledge of these roots can make it much easier to determine the meaning of words. The root of a word does not always point to the word's exact meaning, but combined with an understanding of the word's place in a sentence, it will often be enough to answer a question about meaning or relationships.

Table 3.1. Common Word Roots

ROOT	MEANING	EXAMPLES
alter	other	alternate, alter ego
ambi	both	ambidextrous
ami, amic	love	amiable
amphi	both ends, all sides	amphibian
anthrop	man, human, humanity	misanthrope, anthropologist
apert	open	aperture
aqua	water	aqueduct, aquarium

Table 3.1. Common Word Roots (continued)

ROOT	MEANING	EXAMPLES
aud	to hear	audience
auto	self	autobiography
bell	war	belligerent, bellicose
bene	good	benevolent
bio	life	biology
ced	yield, go	secede, intercede
cent	one hundred	century
chron	time	chronological
circum	around	circumference
contra, counter	against	contradict
crac, crat	rule, ruler	autocrat, bureaucrat
crypt	hidden	cryptogram, cryptic
curr, curs, cours	to run	precursory
dict	to say	dictator, dictation
dyna	power	dynamic
dys	bad, hard, unlucky	dysfunctional
equ	equal, even	equanimity
fac	to make, to do	factory
form	shape	reform, conform
fort	strength	fortitude
fract	to break	fracture
grad, gress	step	progression
gram	thing written	epigram
graph	writing	graphic
hetero	different	heterogeneous
homo	same	homogeneous
hypo	below, beneath	hypothermia
iso	identical	isolate
ject	throw	projection
logy	study of	biology
luc	light	elucidate
mal	bad	malevolent
meta, met	behind, between	metacognition, behind the thinking
meter, metr	measure	thermometer
micro	small	microbe
mis, miso	hate	misanthrope
mit	to send	transmit

ROOT	MEANING	EXAMPLES
mono	one	monologue
morph	form, shape	morphology
mort	death	mortal
multi	many	multiple
phil	love	philanthropist
port	carry	transportation
pseudo	false	pseudonym
psycho	soul, spirit	psychic
rupt	to break	disruption
scope	viewing instrument	microscope
scrib, scribe	to write	inscription
sect, sec	to cut	section
sequ, secu	follow	consecutive
soph	wisdom, knowledge	philosophy
spect	to look	spectator
struct	to build	restructure
tele	far off	telephone
terr	earth	terrestrial
therm	heat	thermal
vent, vene	to come	convene
vert	turn	vertigo
voc	voice, call	vocalize, evocative

PREFIXES

In addition to understanding the base of a word, it's helpful to know common affixes that change the meaning of words and demonstrate their relationships to other words. PREFIXES are added to the beginning of words and frequently change their meaning (sometimes even to the opposite meaning).

Table 3.2. Common Prefixes

PREFIX	MEANING	EXAMPLES
a, an	without, not	anachronism, anhydrous
ab, abs, a	apart, away from	abscission, abnormal
ad	toward	adhere
agere	act	agent
amphi, ambi	round, both sides	ambivalent
ante	before	antedate, anterior
anti	against	antipathy

Table 3.2. Common Prefixes (continued)

PREFIX	MEANING	EXAMPLES
archos	leader, first, chief	oligarchy
bene	well, favorable	benevolent, beneficent
bi	two	binary, bivalve
caco	bad	cacophony
circum	around	circumnavigate
corpus	body	corporeal
credo	belief	credible
demos	people	demographic
di	two, double	dimorphism, diatomic
dia	across, through	dialectic
dis	not, apart	disenfranchise
dyn	be able	dynamo, dynasty
ego	I, self	egomaniac, egocentric
epi	upon, over	epigram, epiphyte
ex	out	extraneous, extemporaneous
geo	earth	geocentric, geomancy
ideo	idea	ideology, ideation
in	in	induction, indigenous
in, im	not	ignoble, immoral
inter	between	interstellar
lexis	word	lexicography
liber	free, book	liberal
locus	place	locality
macro	large	macrophage
micro	small	micron
mono	one, single	monocle, monovalent
mortis	death	moribund
olig	few	oligarchy
peri	around	peripatetic, perineum
poly	many	polygamy
pre	before	prescient
solus	alone	solitary
subter	under, secret	subterfuge
un	not	unsafe
utilis	useful	utilitarian

Suffixes

Suffixes are added to the end of words, and like prefixes they modify the meaning of the word root. Suffixes also serve an important grammatical function, and can change a part of speech or indicate if a word is plural or related to a plural.

Table 3.3. Common Suffixes

SUFFIX	MEANING	EXAMPLES
able, ible	able, capable	visible
age	act of, state of, result of	wreckage
al	relating to	gradual
algia	pain	myalgia
an, ian	native of, relating to	riparian
ance, ancy	action, process, state	defiance
ary, ery, ory	relating to, quality, place	aviary
cian	processing a specific skill or art	physician
cule, ling	very small	sapling, animalcule
cy	action, function	normalcy
dom	quality, realm	wisdom
ee	one who receives the action	nominee
en	made of, to make	silken
ence, ency	action, state of, quality	urgency
er, or	one who, that which	professor
escent	in the process of	adolescent, senescence
esis, osis	action, process, condition	genesis, neurosis
et, ette	small one, group	baronet, lorgnette
fic	making, causing	specific
ful	full of	frightful
hood	order, condition, quality	adulthood
ice	condition, state, quality	malice
id, ide	connected with, belonging to	bromide
ile	relating to, suited for, capable of	puerile, juvenile
ine	nature of	feminine
ion, sion, tion	act, result, state of	contagion
ish	origin, nature, resembling	impish
ism	system, manner, condition, characteristic	capitalism
ist	one who, that which	artist, flautist

Table 3.3. Common Suffixes (continued)

SUFFIX	MEANING	EXAMPLES
ite	nature of, quality of, mineral product	graphite
ity, ty	state of, quality	captivity
ive	causing, making	exhaustive
ize, ise	make	idolize, bowdlerize
ment	act of, state or, result	containment
nomy	law	autonomy, taxonomy
oid	resembling	asteroid, anthropoid
some	like, apt, tending to	gruesome
strat	cover	strata
tude	state of, condition of	aptitude
um	forms single nouns	spectrum
ure	state of, act, process, rank	rupture, rapture
ward	in the direction of	backward
y	inclined to, tend to	faulty

Examples

1. MONOGRAPH

    (A) a mathematical concept

    (B) a written study of a single subject

    (C) an illness caused by a virus

    (D) a boring piece of art

    (E) a shape formed by straight lines

2. POLYGLOT

    (A) a person who speaks many languages

    (B) a person who loves to travel

    (C) a person who is extremely intelligent

    (D) a person who is unafraid of new places

    (E) a person who makes friends easily

ANSWER KEY

1. **(B)** is correct. The prefix *mono—* means *one*, and the word root *graph* means *written*, so a monograph is a written document about one subject.

2. **(A)** is correct. The prefix *poly—* means *many*, and the suffix *—glot* means *in a language or tongue*.

4

MATH KNOWLEDGE

The Math Knowledge section includes 25 questions to be answered in 22 minutes. The questions cover a broad range of topics, including operations with exponents and radicals, equations and inequalities, and properties of geometric figures. In addition, many of the basic operations tested in the Arithmetic Reasoning section may be needed to answer Math Knowledge questions.

ALGEBRAIC EXPRESSIONS

The foundation of algebra is the **VARIABLE**, an unknown number represented by a symbol (usually a letter such as x or a). Variables can be preceded by a **COEFFICIENT**, which is a constant (i.e., a real number) in front of the variable, such as $4x$ or $-2a$. An **ALGEBRAIC EXPRESSION** is any sum, difference, product, or quotient of variables and numbers (for example $3x^2$, $2x + 7y - 1$, and $\frac{5}{x}$ are algebraic expressions). **TERMS** are any quantities that are added or subtracted (for example, the terms of the expression $x^2 - 3x + 5$ are x^2, $3x$, and 5). A **POLYNOMIAL EXPRESSION** is an algebraic expression where all the exponents on the variables are whole numbers. A polynomial with only two terms is known as a **BINOMIAL**, and one with three terms is a **TRINOMIAL**. A **MONOMIAL** has only one term.

EVALUATING EXPRESSIONS is another way of saying "find the numeric value of an expression if the variable is equal to a certain number." To evaluate the expression, simply plug the given value(s) for the variable(s) into the equation and simplify. Remember to use the order of operations when simplifying:

1. **P**arentheses
2. **E**xponents
3. **M**ultiplication
4. **D**ivision
5. **A**ddition
6. **S**ubtraction

Example

1. If $m = 4$, find the value of the following expression:

$$5(m - 2)^3 + 3m^2 - \frac{m}{4} - 1$$

OPERATIONS WITH EXPRESSIONS

Adding and Subtracting

Expressions can be added or subtracted by simply adding and subtracting LIKE TERMS, which are terms with the same variable part (the variables must be the same, with the same exponents on each variable). For example, in the expressions $2x + 3xy - 2z$ and $6y + 2xy$, the like terms are $3xy$ and $2xy$. Adding the two expressions yields the new expression $2x + 5xy - 2z + 6y$. Note that the other terms did not change; they cannot be combined because they have different variables.

Example

2. If $a = 12x + 7xy - 9y$ and $b = 8x - 9xz + 7z$, what is $a + b$?

Distributing and Factoring

HELPFUL HINT

Operations with polynomials can always be checked by evaluating equivalent expressions for the same value.

Distributing and factoring can be seen as two sides of the same coin. DISTRIBUTION multiplies each term in the first factor by each term in the second factor to get rid of parentheses. FACTORING reverses this process, taking a polynomial in standard form and writing it as a product of two or more factors.

When distributing a monomial through a polynomial, the expression outside the parentheses is multiplied by each term inside the parentheses. Using the rules of exponents, coefficients are multiplied and exponents are added.

When simplifying two polynomials, each term in the first polynomial must multiply each term in the second polynomial. A binomial (two terms) multiplied by a binomial, will require 2×2 or 4 multiplications. For the binomial × binomial case, this process is sometimes called **FOIL**, which stands for first, outside, inside, and last. These terms refer to the placement of each term of the expression: multiply the first term in each expression, then the outside terms, then the inside terms, and finally the last terms. A binomial (two terms) multiplied by a trinomial (three terms), will require 2×3 or 6 products to simplify.

The first term in the first polynomial multiplies each of the three terms in the second polynomial, then the second term in the first polynomial multiplies each of the three terms in the second polynomial. A trinomial (three terms) by a trinomial will require 3×3 or 9 products, and so on.

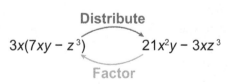

Figure 4.1. Distribution and Factoring

Factoring is the reverse of distributing: the first step is always to remove ("undistribute") the GCF of all the terms, if there is a GCF (besides 1). The GCF is the product of any constants and/or variables that <u>every</u> term shares. (For example, the GCF of $12x^3$, $15x^2$ and $6xy^2$ is $3x$ because

$3x$ evenly divides all three terms.) This shared factor can be taken out of each term and moved to the outside of the parentheses, leaving behind a polynomial where each term is the original term divided by the GCF. (The remaining terms for the terms in the example would be $4x^2$, $5x$, and $2y^2$.) It may be possible to factor the polynomial in the parentheses further, depending on the problem.

Example

3. Expand the following expression: $5x(x^2 - 2c + 10)$

4. Expand the following expression: $(x^2 - 5)(2x - x^3)$

5. Factor the expression $16z^2 + 48z$

6. Factor the expression $6m^3 + 12m^3n - 9m^2$

LINEAR EQUATIONS

An EQUATION states that two expressions are equal to each other. Polynomial equations are categorized by the highest power of the variables they contain: the highest power of any exponent of a linear equation is 1, a quadratic equation has a variable raised to the second power, a cubic equation has a variable raised to the third power, and so on.

Solving Linear Equations

Solving an equation means finding the value or values of the variable that make the equation true. To solve a linear equation, it is necessary to manipulate the terms so that the variable being solved for appears alone on one side of the equal sign while everything else in the equation is on the other side.

The way to solve linear equations is to "undo" all the operations that connect numbers to the variable of interest. Follow these steps:

1. Eliminate fractions by multiplying each side by the least common multiple of any denominators.

2. Distribute to eliminate parentheses, braces, and brackets.

3. Combine like terms.

4. Use addition or subtraction to collect all terms containing the variable of interest to one side, and all terms not containing the variable to the other side.

5. Use multiplication or division to remove coefficients from the variable of interest.

Sometimes there are no numeric values in the equation or there are a mix of numerous variables and constants. The goal is to solve the equation for one of the variables in terms of the other variables. In this case, the answer will be an expression involving numbers and letters instead of a numeric value.

HELPFUL HINT

On multiple-choice tests, it's often easier to plug the possible values into the equation and determine which solution makes the equation true than it is to solve the equation.

Examples

7. Solve for x: $\dfrac{100(x + 5)}{20} = 1$

8. Solve for x: $2(x + 2)^2 - 2x^2 + 10 = 42$

9. Solve the equation for D: $\dfrac{A(3B + 2D)}{2N} = 5M - 6$

Graphs of Linear Equations

The most common way to write a linear equation is **SLOPE-INTERCEPT FORM**, $y = mx + b$. In this equation, m is the slope, which describes how steep the line is, and b is the y-intercept. Slope is often described as "rise over run" because it is calculated as the difference in y-values (rise) over the difference in x-values (run). The slope of the line is also the rate of change of the dependent variable y with respect to the independent variable x. The y-intercept is the point where the line crosses the y-axis, or where x equals zero.

To graph a linear equation, identify the y-intercept and place that point on the y-axis. If the slope is not written as a fraction, make it a fraction by writing it over 1 $\left(\dfrac{m}{1}\right)$. Then use the slope to count up (or down, if negative) the "rise" part of the slope and over the "run" part of the slope to find a second point. These points can then be connected to draw the line.

To find the equation of a line, identify the y-intercept, if possible, on the graph and use two easily identifiable points to find the slope. If the y-intercept is not easily identified, identify the slope by choosing easily identifiable points; then choose one point on the graph, plug the point and the slope values into the equation, and solve for the missing value b.

- standard form: $Ax + By = C$
- $m = -\dfrac{A}{B}$
- x-intercept $= \dfrac{C}{A}$
- y-intercept $= \dfrac{C}{B}$

Another way to express a linear equation is standard form: $Ax + By = C$. In order to graph equations in this form, it is often easiest to convert them to point-slope form. Alternately, it is easy to find the x- or y-intercept from this form, and once these two points are known, a line can be drawn through them. To find the x-intercept, simply make $y = 0$ and solve for x. Similarly, to find the y-intercept, make $x = 0$ and solve for y.

Examples

10. What is the slope of the line whose equation is $6x - 2y - 8 = 0$?

11. Write the equation of the line which passes through the points $(-2, 5)$ and $(-5, 3)$.

12. What is the equation of the following line?

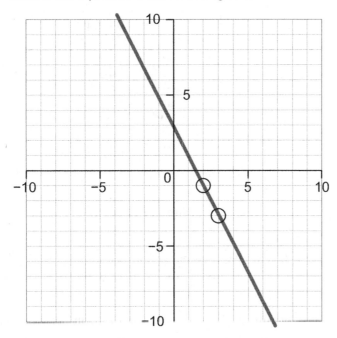

13. What is the equation of the following graph?

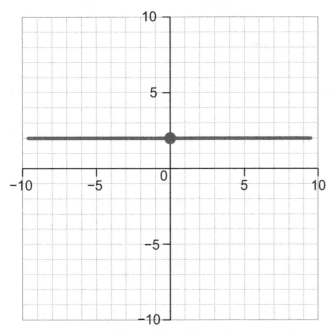

The Distance and Midpoint Formulas

The distance formula finds the distance of a line drawn between two points that terminates at those two points:

$$d = \sqrt{(x_2 - x_1)^2 + (y_2 - y_1)^2}$$

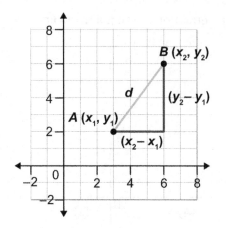

Figure 4.2. The Distance Formula

The distance formula resembles the Pythagorean theorem because it is essentially finding the hypotenuse of the right triangle with legs of length $\Delta x = x_2 - x_1$ and $\Delta y = y_2 - y_1$.

The midpoint formula finds the coordinates of a point exactly in the middle of two other points. To find the midpoint, average the x values and then average the y values. These are the coordinates of the midpoint:

$$\text{Midpoint } M = \left(\frac{x_1 + x_2}{2}, \frac{y_1 + y_2}{2} \right)$$

Examples

14. If $(-3, 8)$ is the midpoint of segment $\overline{AB}$ and point A is at $(-10, -17)$, what are the coordinates of point B?

15. Find the distance between the points $(-10, 50)$ and $(50, 10)$.

Building Equations

In word problems, it is often necessary to translate a verbal description of a relationship into a mathematical equation. No matter the problem, this process can be done using the same steps:

1. Read the problem carefully and identify what value needs to be solved for.

2. Identify the known and unknown quantities in the problem, and assign the unknown quantities a variable.

3. Create equations using the variables and known quantities.

4. Solve the equations.

5. Check the solution: Does it answer the question asked in the problem? Does it make sense?

HELPFUL HINT

Use the acronym STAR to remember word-problem strategies: <u>S</u>earch the problem, <u>T</u>ranslate into an expression or equation, <u>A</u>nswer, and <u>R</u>eview.

Examples

16. A school is holding a raffle to raise money. There is a $3 entry fee, and each ticket costs $5. If a student paid $28, how many tickets did he buy?

17. Kelly is selling shirts for her school swim team. There are two prices: a student price and a nonstudent price. During the first week of the sale, Kelly raised $84 by selling 10 shirts to students and 4 shirts to nonstudents. She earned $185 in the second week by selling 20 shirts to students and 10 shirts to nonstudents. What is the student price for a shirt?

LINEAR INEQUALITIES

Solving Linear Inequalities

An inequality shows the relationship between two expressions, much like an equation. However, the equal sign is replaced with an inequality symbol that expresses the following relationships:

- < less than
- > greater than
- ≤ less than or equal to
- ≥ greater than or equal to

Inequalities are read from left to right. For example, the inequality $x \leq 8$ would be read as "x is less than or equal to 8," meaning x has a value smaller than or equal to 8. The set of solutions of an inequality can be expressed using a number line. The shaded region on the number line represents the set of all the numbers that make an inequality true. One major difference between equations and inequalities is that equations generally have a finite number of solutions, while inequalities generally have infinitely many solutions (an entire interval on the number line containing infinitely many values).

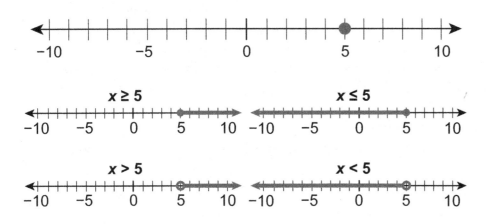

Figure 4.3. Inequalities on a Number Line

Linear inequalities can be solved in the same way as linear equations, with one exception. When multiplying or dividing both sides of an inequality by a negative number, the direction of the inequality sign must reverse—"greater than" becomes "less than" and "less than" becomes "greater than."

Examples

18. Solve for z: $3z + 10 < -z$

19. Solve for x: $2x - 3 > 5(x - 4) - (x - 4)$

Compound Inequalities

Compound inequalities have more than one inequality expression. Solutions of compound inequalities are the sets of all numbers that make *all* the inequalities true. Some compound inequalities may not have any solutions, some will have solutions that contain some part of the number line, and some will have solutions that include the entire number line.

Table 4.1. Unions and Intersections

INEQUALITY	MEANING IN WORDS	NUMBER LINE
$a < x < b$	All values x that are greater than a and less than b	
$a \leq x \leq b$	All values x that are greater than or equal to a and less than or equal to b	
$x < a \text{ or } x > b$	All values of x that are less than a or greater than b	
$x \leq a \text{ or } x \geq b$	All values of x that are less than or equal to a or greater than or equal to b	

Compound inequalities can be written, solved, and graphed as two separate inequalities. For compound inequalities in which the word *and* is used, the solution to the compound inequality will be the set of numbers on the number line where both inequalities have solutions (where both are shaded). For compound inequalities where *or* is used, the solution to the compound inequality will be *all* the shaded regions for *either* inequality.

Examples

20. Solve the compound inequalities: $2x + 4 < -10$ *or* $4(x + 2) > 18$

21. Solve the inequality: $-1 \leq 3(x + 2) - 1 \leq x + 3$

QUADRATIC EQUATIONS

Quadratic equations are degree 2 polynomials; the highest power on the dependent variable is two. While linear functions are represented graphically as lines, the graph of a quadratic function is a PARABOLA. The graph of a parabola has three important components. The VERTEX is where the graph changes direction. In the parent graph $y = x^2$, the origin $(0, 0)$ is the vertex. The AXIS OF SYMMETRY is the vertical line that cuts the graph into two equal halves.

The line of symmetry always passes through the vertex. On the parent graph, the y-axis is the axis of symmetry. The ZEROS or ROOTS of the quadratic are the x-intercepts of the graph.

Forms of Quadratic Equations

Quadratic equations can be expressed in two forms:

- **STANDARD FORM: $y = ax^2 + bx + c$**
  - □ Axis of symmetry: $x = -\frac{b}{2a}$
  - □ Vertex: $(-\frac{b}{2a}, f(-\frac{b}{2a}))$
- **VERTEX FORM: $y = a(x - h)^2 + k$**
  - □ Vertex: (h, k)
  - □ Axis of symmetry: $x = h$

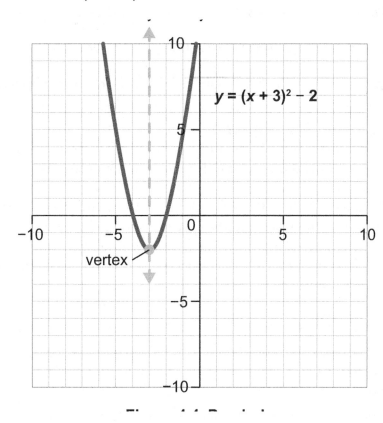

Figure 4.4. Parabola

In both equations, the sign of a determines which direction the parabola opens: if a is positive, then it opens upward; if a is negative, then it opens downward. The wideness or narrowness is also determined by a. If the absolute value of a is less than one (a proper fraction), then the parabola will get wider the closer $|a|$ is to zero. If the absolute value of a is greater than one, then the larger $|a|$ becomes, the narrower the parabola will be.

Equations in vertex form can be converted to standard form by squaring out the $(x - h)^2$ part (using FOIL), distributing the a, adding k, and simplifying the result.

Equations can be converted from standard form to vertex form by COM-
PLETING THE SQUARE. Take an equation in standard form, $y = ax^2 + bc + c$.

1. Move c to the left side of the equation.

2. Divide the entire equation through by a (to make the coefficient of x^2 be 1).

3. Take half of the coefficient of x, square that number, and then add the result to both sides of the equation.

4. Convert the right side of the equation to a perfect binomial squared, $(x + m)^2$.

5. Isolate y to put the equation in proper vertex form.

Examples

22. What is the line of symmetry for $y = -2(x + 3)^2 + 2$?

23. What is the vertex of the parabola $y = -3x^2 + 24x - 27$?

24. Write $y = -3x^2 + 24x - 27$ in vertex form by completing the square.

Solving Quadratic Equations

Solving the quadratic equation $ax^2 + bx + c = 0$ finds x-intercepts of the parabola (by making $y = 0$). These are also called the ROOTS or ZEROS of the quadratic function. A quadratic equation may have zero, one, or two real solutions. There are several ways of finding the zeros. One way is to factor the quadratic into a product of two binomials, and then use the zero product property. (If $m \times n = 0$, then either $m = 0$ or $n = 0$.) Another way is to complete the square and square root both sides. One way that works every time is to memorize and use the QUADRATIC FORMULA:

$$x = \frac{-b \pm \sqrt{b^2 - 4ac}}{2a}$$

The a, b, and c come from the standard form of quadratic equations above. (Note that to use the quadratic equation, the right-hand side of the equation must be equal to zero.)

The part of the formula under the square root radical ($b^2 - 4ac$) is known as the DISCRIMINANT. The discriminant tells how many and what type of roots will result without actually calculating the roots.

Table 4.2. Discriminants

IF $B^2 - 4AC$ IS	THERE WILL BE	AND THE PARABOLA
zero	only 1 real root	has its vertex on the x-axis
positive	2 real roots	has **two** x-intercepts
negative	0 real roots 2 complex roots	has **no** x-intercepts

HELPFUL HINT
With all graphing problems, putting the function into the $y =$ window of a graphing calculator will aid the process of elimination when graphs are examined and compared to answer choices with a focus on properties like axis of symmetry, vertices, and roots of formulas.

25. Find the zeros of the quadratic equation: $y = -(x + 3)^2 + 1$.

26. Find the root(s) for: $z^2 - 4z + 4 = 0$

27. Write a quadratic function that has zeros at $x = -3$ and $x = 2$ that passes through the point $(-2, 8)$.

PROPERTIES OF SHAPES

Basic Definitions

The basic figures from which many other geometric shapes are built are points, lines, and planes. A POINT is a location in a plane. It has no size or shape, but is represented by a dot. It is labeled using a capital letter.

A LINE is a one-dimensional collection of points that extends infinitely in both directions. At least two points are needed to define a line, and any points that lie on the same line are COLINEAR. Lines are represented by two points, such as A and B, and the line symbol: $(\overleftrightarrow{AB})$. Two lines on the same plane will intersect unless they are PARALLEL, meaning they have the same slope. Lines that intersect at a 90 degree angle are PERPENDICULAR.

A LINE SEGMENT has two endpoints and a finite length. The length of a segment, called the measure of the segment, is the distance from A to B. A line segment is a subset of a line, and is also denoted with two points, but with a segment symbol: $\overline{AB}$). The MIDPOINT of a line segment is the point at which the segment is divided into two equal parts. A line, segment, or plane that passes through the midpoint of a segment is called a BISECTOR of the segment, since it cuts the segment into two equal segments.

A RAY has one endpoint and extends indefinitely in one direction. It is defined by its endpoint, followed by any other point on the ray: $\overrightarrow{AB}$. It is important that the first letter represents the endpoint. A ray is sometimes called a half line.

Table 4.3. Basic Geometric Figures

TERM	DIMENSIONS	GRAPHIC	SYMBOL
point	zero		$\cdot A$
line segment	one		$\overline{AB}$
ray	one		$\overrightarrow{AB}$
line	one		$\overleftrightarrow{AB}$
plane	two		Plane M

A **PLANE** is a flat sheet that extends indefinitely in two directions (like an infinite sheet of paper). A plane is a two-dimensional (2D) figure. A plane can always be defined through any three noncollinear points in three-dimensional (3D) space. A plane is named using any three points that are in the plane (for example, plane *ABC*). Any points lying in the same plane are said to be **COPLANAR**. When two planes intersect, the intersection is a line.

Example

28. Which points and lines are not contained in plane *M* in the diagram below?

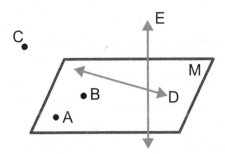

Angles

ANGLES are formed when two rays share a common endpoint. They are named using three letters, with the vertex point in the middle (for example ∠*ABC*, where *B* is the vertex). They can also be labeled with a number or named by their vertex alone (if it is clear to do so). Angles are also classified based on their angle measure. A **RIGHT ANGLE** has a measure of exactly 90°. **ACUTE ANGLES** have measures that are less than 90°, and **OBTUSE ANGLES** have measures that are greater than 90°.

Any two angles that add to make 90° are called **COMPLEMENTARY ANGLES**. A 30° angle would be complementary to a 60° angle. **SUPPLEMENTARY ANGLES** add up to 180°. A supplementary angle to a 60° angle would be a 120° angle; likewise, 60° is the **SUPPLEMENT** of 120°. The complement and supplement of any angle must always be positive. For example, a 140 degree has no complement. Angles that are next to each other and share a common ray are called **ADJACENT ANGLES**. Angles that are adjacent and supplementary are called a **LINEAR PAIR** of angles. Their nonshared rays form a line (thus the *linear* pair). Note that angles that are supplementary do not need to be adjacent; their measures simply need to add to 180°.

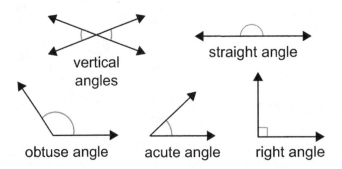

Figure 4.5. Types of Angles

HELPFUL HINT

Angles can be measured in degrees or radians. Use the conversion factor 1 rad = 57.3 degrees to convert between them.

VERTICAL ANGLES are formed when two lines intersect. Four angles will be formed; the vertex of each angle is at the intersection point of the lines. The vertical angles across from each other will be equal in measure. The angles adjacent to each other will be linear pairs and therefore supplementary.

A ray, line, or segment that divides an angle into two equal angles is called an ANGLE BISECTOR.

Examples

29. If angles *M* and *N* are supplementary and $\angle M$ is 30° less than twice $\angle N$, what is the degree measurement of each angle?

30. How many linear pairs of angles are there in the following figure?

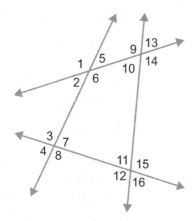

Circles

A CIRCLE is the set of all the points in a plane that are the same distance from a fixed point called the CENTER. The distance from the center to any point on the circle is the RADIUS of the circle. The distance around the circle (the perimeter) is called the CIRCUMFERENCE.

The ratio of a circle's circumference to its diameter is a constant value called pi (π), an irrational number which is commonly rounded to 3.14. The formula to find a circle's circumference is $C = 2\pi r$. The formula to find the enclosed area of a circle is $A = \pi r^2$.

Circles have a number of unique parts and properties:

- The DIAMETER is the largest measurement across a circle. It passes through the circle's center, extending from one side of the circle to the other. The measure of the diameter is twice the measure of the radius.

- A line that cuts across a circle and touches it twice is called a SECANT line. The part of a secant line that lies within a circle is called a CHORD. Two chords within a circle are of equal length if they are are the same distance from the center.

- A line that touches a circle or any curve at one point is TANGENT to the circle or the curve. These lines are always exterior to the circle. A line tangent to a circle and a radius drawn to the point of tangency meet at a right angle (90°).

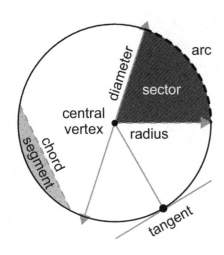

Figure 4.6. Parts of a Circle

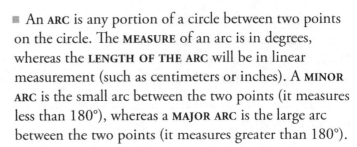

- An **ARC** is any portion of a circle between two points on the circle. The **MEASURE** of an arc is in degrees, whereas the **LENGTH OF THE ARC** will be in linear measurement (such as centimeters or inches). A **MINOR ARC** is the small arc between the two points (it measures less than 180°), whereas a **MAJOR ARC** is the large arc between the two points (it measures greater than 180°).

- An angle with its vertex at the center of a circle is called a **CENTRAL ANGLE**. For a central angle, the measure of the arc intercepted by the sides of the angle (in degrees) is the same as the measure of the angle.

- A **SECTOR** is the part of a circle *and* its interior that is inside the rays of a central angle (its shape is like a slice of pie).

	Area of Sector	Length of an Arc
Degrees	$A = \dfrac{\theta}{360°} \times \pi r^2$	$s = \dfrac{\theta}{360°} \times 2\pi r$
Radians	$A = \dfrac{1}{2} \pi^2 \theta$	$s = r\theta$

- An **INSCRIBED ANGLE** has a vertex on the circle and is formed by two chords that share that vertex point. The angle measure of an inscribed angle is one-half the angle measure of the central angle with the same endpoints on the circle.

- A **CIRCUMSCRIBED ANGLE** has rays tangent to the circle. The angle lies outside of the circle.

- Any angle outside the circle, whether formed by two tangent lines, two secant lines, or a tangent line and a secant line, is equal to half the difference of the intercepted arcs.

- Angles are formed within a circle when two chords intersect in the circle. The measure of the smaller angle formed is half the sum of the two smaller arc measures (in degrees). Likewise, the larger angle is half the sum of the two larger arc measures.

- If a chord intersects a line tangent to the circle, the angle formed by this intersection measures one half the measurement of the intercepted arc (in degrees).

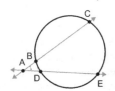

$m\angle A = \frac{1}{2}(\overset{\frown}{CE} - \overset{\frown}{BD})$

Figure 4.7. Angles Outside a Circle

$m\angle A = \frac{1}{2}(\overset{\frown}{CE} - \overset{\frown}{BD})$

Figure 4.7. Angles Outside a Circle

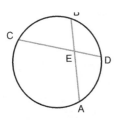

$m\angle E = \frac{1}{2}(\overset{\frown}{AC} + \overset{\frown}{BD})$

Figure 4.8. Intersecting Chords

$m\angle E = \frac{1}{2}(\overset{\frown}{AC} + \overset{\frown}{BD})$

Figure 4.8. Intersecting Chords

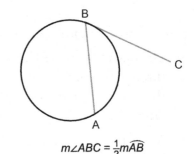

$m\angle ABC = \frac{1}{2}m\overset{\frown}{AB}$

Figure 4.9. Intersecting Chord and Tangent

$m\angle ABC = \frac{1}{2}m\overset{\frown}{AB}$

Figure 4.9. Intersecting Chord and Tangent

Examples

31. Find the area of the sector *NHS* of the circle below with center at *H*:

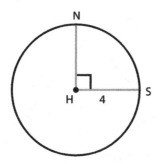

32. In the circle below with center *O*, the minor arc *ACB* measures 5 feet. What is the measurement of *m∠AOB*?

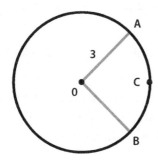

Triangles

Much of geometry is concerned with triangles as they are commonly used shapes. A good understanding of triangles allows decomposition of other shapes (specifically polygons) into triangles for study.

Figure 4.10. Finding the Base and Height of Triangles

Triangles have three sides, and the three interior angles always sum to 180°. The formula for the area of a triangle is $A = \frac{1}{2} bh$ or one-half the product of the base and height (or altitude) of the triangle.

Some important segments in a triangle include the angle bisector, the altitude, and the median. The **ANGLE BISECTOR** extends from the side opposite an angle to bisect that angle. The **ALTITUDE** is the shortest distance from a vertex of the triangle to the line containing the base side opposite that vertex. It is perpendicular to that line and can occur on the outside of the triangle. The **MEDIAN** extends from an angle to bisect the opposite side.

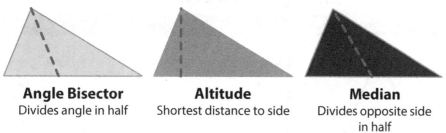

| **Angle Bisector** | **Altitude** | **Median** |
| Divides angle in half | Shortest distance to side | Divides opposite side in half |

Figure 4.11. Important Segments in a Triangle

Figure 4.10. Finding the Base and Height of Triangles

Triangles have two "centers." The CENTROID is where a triangle's three medians meet. The ORTHOCENTER is formed by the intersection of a triangle's three altitudes.

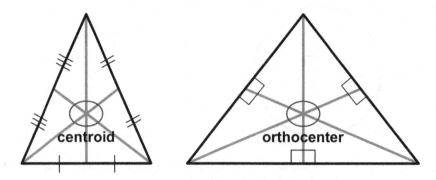

Figure 4.12. Centroid and Orthocenter of a Triangle

Triangles can be classified in two ways: by sides and by angles.

A SCALENE TRIANGLE has no equal sides or angles. An ISOSCELES TRIANGLE has two equal sides and two equal angles, often called BASE ANGLES. In an EQUI-LATERAL TRIANGLE, all three sides are equal as are all three angles. Moreover, because the sum of the angles of a triangle is always 180°, each angle of an equilateral triangle must be 60°.

A RIGHT TRIANGLE has one right angle (90°) and two acute angles. An ACUTE TRIANGLE has three acute angles (all angles are less than 90°). An OBTUSE TRIANGLE has one obtuse angle (more than 90°) and two acute angles.

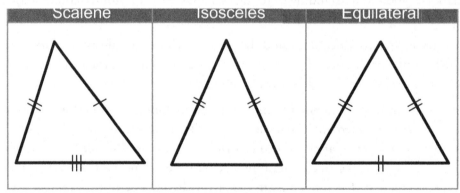

Triangles Based on Angles

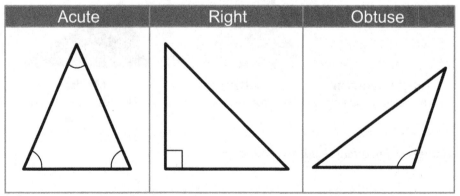

Figure 4.13. Types of Triangles

For any triangle, the side opposite the largest angle will have the longest length, while the side opposite the smallest angle will have the shortest length. The **TRIANGLE INEQUALITY THEOREM** states that the sum of any two sides of a triangle must be greater than the third side. If this inequality does not hold, then a triangle cannot be formed. A consequence of this theorem is the **THIRD-SIDE RULE**: if b and c are two sides of a triangle, then the measure of the third side a must be between the sum of the other two sides and the difference of the other two sides: $c - b < a < c + b$.

Solving for missing angles or sides of a triangle is a common type of triangle problem. Often a right triangle will come up on its own or within another triangle. The relationship among a right triangle's sides is known as the **PYTHAGOREAN THEOREM**: $a^2 + b^2 = c^2$, where c is the hypotenuse and is across from the 90° angle. Right triangles with angle measurements of 90° – 45° – 45° and 90° – 60° – 30° are known as "special" right triangles and have specific relationships between their sides and angles.

HELPFUL HINT

Trigonometric functions can be employed to find missing sides and angles of a triangle.

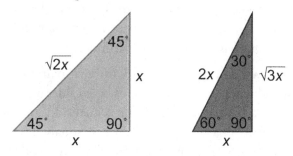

Figure 4.14. Special Right Triangles

Examples

33. Examine and classify each of the following triangles:

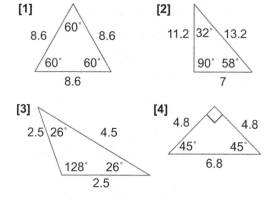

34. What are the minimum and maximum values of x to the nearest hundredth?

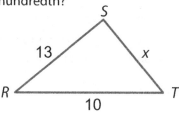

35. Given the diagram, if *XZ* = 100, *WZ* = 80, and *XU* = 70, then *WY* = ?

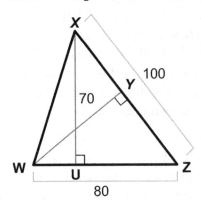

Quadrilaterals

HELPFUL HINT

All squares are rectangles and all rectangles are parallelograms; however, not all parallelograms are rectangles and not all rectangles are squares.

All closed, four-sided shapes are **QUADRILATERALS**. The sum of all internal angles in a quadrilateral is always 360°. (Think of drawing a diagonal to create two triangles. Since each triangle contains 180°, two triangles, and therefore the quadrilateral, must contain 360°.) The **AREA OF ANY QUADRILATERAL** is $A = bh$, where *b* is the base and *h* is the height (or altitude).

A **PARALLELOGRAM** is a quadrilateral with two pairs of parallel sides. A rectangle is a parallelogram with two pairs of equal sides and four right angles. A **KITE** also has two pairs of equal sides, but its equal sides are consecutive. Both a **SQUARE** and a **RHOMBUS** have four equal sides. A square has four right angles, while a rhombus has a pair of acute opposite angles and a pair of obtuse opposite angles. A **TRAPEZOID** has exactly one pair of parallel sides.

Table 4.4 Properties of Parallelograms

TERM	SHAPE	PROPERTIES
Parallelogram		Opposite sides are parallel. Consecutive angles are supplementary. Opposite angles are equal. Opposite sides are equal. Diagonals bisect each other.
Rectangle		All parallelogram properties hold. Diagonals are congruent *and* bisect each other. All angles are right angles.
Square		All rectangle properties hold. All four sides are equal. Diagonals bisect angles. Diagonals intersect at right angles and bisect each other.
Kite		One pair of opposite angles is equal. Two pairs of consecutive sides are equal. Diagonals meet at right angles.

TERM	SHAPE	PROPERTIES
Rhombus	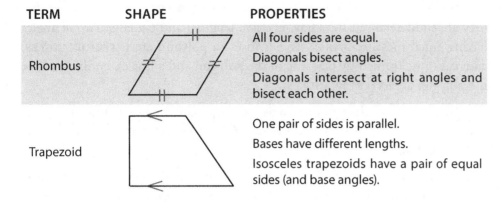	All four sides are equal. Diagonals bisect angles. Diagonals intersect at right angles and bisect each other.
Trapezoid		One pair of sides is parallel. Bases have different lengths. Isosceles trapezoids have a pair of equal sides (and base angles).

Examples

36. In parallelogram *ABCD*, the measure of angle *m* is is $m° = 260°$. What is the measure of $n°$?

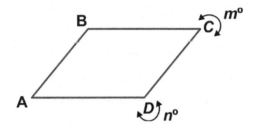

37. A rectangular section of a football field has dimensions of *x* and *y* and an area of 1000 square feet. Three additional lines drawn vertically divide the section into four smaller rectangular areas as seen in the diagram below. If all the lines shown need to be painted, calculate the total number of linear feet, in terms of *x*, to be painted.

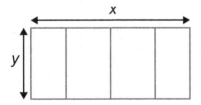

Polygons

Any closed shape made up of three or more line segments is a polygon. In addition to triangles and quadrilaterals, OCTAGONS and HEXAGONS are two common polygons.

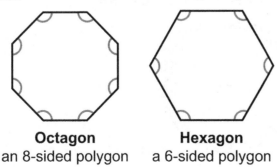

Octagon
an 8-sided polygon

Hexagon
a 6-sided polygon

Figure 4.15. Common Polygons

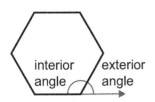

Figure 4.16. Interior and Exterior Angles

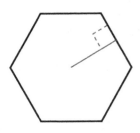

Figure 4.17. Apothem in a Hexagon

The two polygons depicted above are **REGULAR POLYGONS**, meaning that they are equilateral (all sides having equal lengths) and equiangular (all angles having equal measurements). Angles inside a polygon are **INTERIOR ANGLES**, whereas those formed by one side of the polygon and a line extending outside the polygon are **EXTERIOR ANGLES**.

The sum of all the exterior angles of a polygon is always 360°. Dividing 360° by the number of a polygon's sides finds the measure of the polygon's exterior angles.

To determine the sum of a polygon's interior angles, choose one vertex and draw diagonals from that vertex to each of the other vertices, decomposing the polygon into multiple triangles. For example, an octagon has six triangles within it, and therefore the sum of the interior angles is 6 × 180° = 1080°. In general, the formula for finding the sum of the angles in a polygon is *sum of angles = (n − 2) × 180°*, where *n* is the number of sides of the polygon.

To find the measure of a single interior angle in a regular polygon, simply divide the sum of the interior angles by the number of angles (which is the same as the number of sides). So, in the octagon example, each angle is $\frac{1080}{8}$ = 135°.

In general, the formula to find the measure of a regular polygon's interior angles is: *interior angle* = $\frac{(n-2)}{n}$ × 180° where *n* is the number of sides of the polygon.

To find the area of a polygon, it is helpful to know the perimeter of the polygon (*p*), and the **APOTHEM** (*a*). The apothem is the shortest (perpendicular) distance from the polygon's center to one of the sides of the polygon. The formula for the area is: *area* = $\frac{ap}{2}$.

Finally, there is no universal way to find the perimeter of a polygon (when the side length is not given). Often, breaking the polygon down into triangles and adding the base of each triangle all the way around the polygon is the easiest way to calculate the perimeter.

Examples

38. What is the measure of an exterior angle and an interior angle of a regular 400-gon?

39. The circle and hexagon below both share center point T. The hexagon is entirely inscribed in the circle. The circle's radius is 5. What is the area of the shaded area?

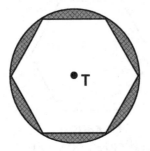

THREE-DIMENSIONAL SHAPES

THREE-DIMENSIONAL SHAPES have depth in addition to width and length. **VOLUME** is expressed as the number of cubic units any shape can hold—that is, what it takes to fill it up. **SURFACE AREA** is the sum of the areas of the two-dimensional figures that are found on its surface. Some three-dimensional shapes also have a unique property called a slant height (ℓ), which is the distance from the base to the apex along a lateral face.

Table 4.5 Three-Dimensional Shapes and Formulas

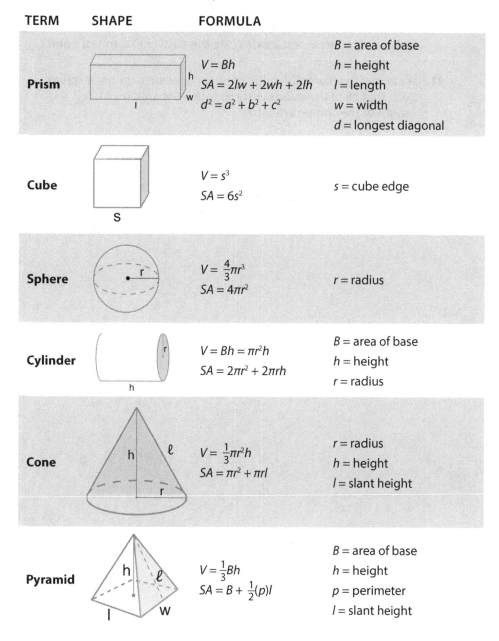

TERM	SHAPE	FORMULA	
Prism		$V = Bh$ $SA = 2lw + 2wh + 2lh$ $d^2 = a^2 + b^2 + c^2$	B = area of base h = height l = length w = width d = longest diagonal
Cube		$V = s^3$ $SA = 6s^2$	s = cube edge
Sphere		$V = \frac{4}{3}\pi r^3$ $SA = 4\pi r^2$	r = radius
Cylinder		$V = Bh = \pi r^2 h$ $SA = 2\pi r^2 + 2\pi rh$	B = area of base h = height r = radius
Cone		$V = \frac{1}{3}\pi r^2 h$ $SA = \pi r^2 + \pi rl$	r = radius h = height l = slant height
Pyramid		$V = \frac{1}{3}Bh$ $SA = B + \frac{1}{2}(p)l$	B = area of base h = height p = perimeter l = slant height

Finding the surface area of a three-dimensional solid can be made easier by using a **NET**. This two-dimensional "flattened" version of a three-dimensional shape shows the component parts that comprise the surface of the solid.

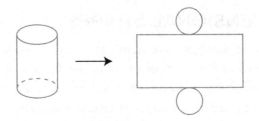

Figure 4.18. Net of a Cylinder

Examples

40. A sphere has a radius *z*. If that radius is increased by *t*, by how much is the surface area increased? Write the answer in terms of *z* and *t*.

41. A cube with volume 27 cubic meters is inscribed within a sphere such that all of the cube's vertices touch the sphere. What is the length of the sphere's radius?

ANSWER KEY

1. $5(m-2)^3 + 3m^2 - \frac{m}{4} - 1$

    Plug the value 4 in for m in the expression.

    $= 5(4-2)^3 + 3(4)^2 - \frac{4}{4} - 1$

    Calculate all the expressions inside the parentheses.

    $= 5(2)^3 + 3(4)^2 - \frac{4}{4} - 1$

    Simplify all exponents.

    $= 5(8) + 3(16) - \frac{4}{4} - 1$

    Perform multiplication, division, addition, and subtraction from left to right.

    $= 40 + 48 - 1 - 1 = \mathbf{86}$

2. The only like terms in both expressions are $12x$ and $8x$, so these two terms will be added, and all other terms will remain the same.

    $a + b = (12x + 8x) + 7xy - 9y - 9xz + 7z = \mathbf{20x + 7xy - 9y - 9xz + 7z}$

3. $5x(x^2 - 2c + 10)$

    Distribute and multiply the term outside the parentheses to all three terms inside the parentheses.

    $(5x)(x^2) = 5x^3$

    $(5x)(-2c) = -10xc$

    $(5x)(10) = 50x$

    $= \mathbf{5x^3 - 10xc + 50x}$

4. $(x^2 - 5)(2x - x^3)$

    Apply FOIL: first, outside, inside, and last.

    $(x^2)(2x) = 2x^3$

    $(x^2)(-x^3) = -x^5$

    $(-5)(2x) = -10x$

    $(-5)(-x^3) = 5x^3$

    Combine like terms and put them in order.

    $= 2x^3 - x^5 - 10x + 5x^3 = \mathbf{-x^5 + 7x^3 - 10x}$

5. $16z^2 + 48z$

    Both terms have a z, and 16 is a common factor of both 16 and 48. So the greatest common factor is $16z$. Factor out the GCF.

    $16z^2 + 48z = \mathbf{16z(z + 3)}$

6. $6m^3 + 12m^3n - 9m^2$

    All the terms share the factor m^2, and 3 is the greatest common factor of 6, 12, and 9. So, the GCF is $3m^2$.

$$6m^3 + 12m^3n - 9m^2 = \mathbf{3m^2(2m + 4mn - 3)}$$

7. $\frac{100(x + 5)}{20} = 1$

Multiply both sides by 20 to cancel out the denominator.

$(20)(\frac{100(x + 5)}{20}) = (1)(20)$

$100(x + 5) = 20$

Distribute 100 through the parentheses.

$100x + 500 = 20$

"Undo" the +500 by subtracting 500 on both sides of the equation to isolate the variable term.

$100x = -480$

"Undo" the multiplication by 100 by dividing by 100 on both sides to solve for x.

$x = \frac{-480}{100} = \mathbf{-4.8}$

8. $2(x + 2)^2 - 2x^2 + 10 = 42$

Eliminate the exponents on the left side.

$2(x + 2)(x + 2) - 2x^2 + 10 = 42$

Apply FOIL.

$2(x^2 + 4x + 4) - 2x^2 + 10 = 42$

Distribute the 2.

$2x^2 + 8x + 8 - 2x^2 + 10 = 42$

Combine like terms on the left-hand side.

$8x + 18 = 42$

Isolate the variable. "Undo" +18 by subtracting 18 on both sides.

$8x = 24$

"Undo" multiplication by 8 by dividing both sides by 8.

$\mathbf{x = 3}$

9. $\frac{A(3B + 2D)}{2N} = 5M - 6$

Multiply both sides by 2N to clear the fraction, and distribute the A through the parentheses.

$3AB + 2AD = 10MN - 12N$

Isolate the term with the D in it by moving 3AB to the other side of the equation.

$2AD = 10MN - 12N - 3AB$

Divide both sides by 2A to get D alone on the right-hand side.

$\mathbf{D = \frac{(10MN - 12N - 3AB)}{2A}}$

10. $6x - 2y - 8 = 0$

Rearrange the equation into slope-intercept form by solving the equation for y.

$-2y = -6x + 8$

$y = \frac{-6x + 8}{-2}$

$y = 3x - 4$

The slope is 3, the value attached to x.

$\boldsymbol{m = 3}$

11. $(-2, 5)$ and $(-5, 3)$

Calculate the slope.

$m = \frac{3 - 5}{(-5) - (-2)} = \frac{-2}{-3} = \frac{2}{3}$

To find b, plug into the equation $y = mx + b$ the slope for m and a set of points for x and y.

$5 = \frac{2}{3}(-2) + b$

$5 = \frac{-4}{3} + b$

$b = \frac{19}{3}$

Replace m and b to find the equation of the line.

$\boldsymbol{y = \frac{2}{3}x + \frac{19}{3}}$

12. The y-intercept can be identified on the graph as $(0, 3)$.

$b = 3$

To find the slope, choose any two points and plug the values into the slope equation. The two points chosen here are $(2, -1)$ and $(3, -3)$.

$m = \frac{(-3) - (-1)}{3 - 2} = \frac{-2}{1} = -2$

Replace m with -2 and b with 3 in $y = mx + b$.

$\boldsymbol{y = -2x + 3}$

13. The line has a rise of 0 and a run of 1, so the slope is $\frac{0}{1} = 0$. There is no x-intercept. The y-intercept is $(0, 2)$, meaning that the b-value in the slope-intercept form is 2.

$\boldsymbol{y = 0x + 2,\ \text{or}\ y = 2}$

14. Identify the given variables.

$A = (x_1, y_1) = (-10, -17)$

$B = (x_2, y_2)$

$M = (-3, 8)$

Use the midpoint formula to find point B.

$M_x = \frac{x_2 + x_1}{2}$

$-3 = \frac{x_2 + (-10)}{2}$

$x_2 = 4$

$M_y = \frac{y_2 + y_1}{2}$

$$8 = \frac{y_2 + (-17)}{2}$$

$$y_2 = 33$$

B = (4, 33)

15. Identify the given variables.

$(x_1, y_1) = (-10, 50)$

$(x_2, y_2) = (50, 10)$

Plug these values into the distance formula and solve.

$$d = \sqrt{(x_2 - x_1)^2 + (y_2 - y_1)^2}$$

$$d = \sqrt{(50 - (-10))^2 + (10 - 50)^2}$$

$$d = \sqrt{(60)^2 + (-40)^2}$$

$$d = \sqrt{3600 + 1600}$$

$$d = \sqrt{5200}$$

$d \approx 72.11$

16. Identify the quantities.

Number of tickets $= x$

Cost per ticket $= 5$

Cost for x tickets $= 5x$

Total cost $= 28$

Entry fee $= 3$

Set up equations. The total cost for x tickets will be equal to the cost for x tickets plus the $3 flat fee.

$5x + 3 = 28$

Solve the equation for x.

$5x + 3 = 28$

$5x = 25$

$x = 5$

The student bought **5 tickets**.

17. Assign variables.

Student price $= s$

Nonstudent price $= n$

Create two equations using the number of shirts Kelly sold and the money she earned.

$10s + 4n = 84$

$20s + 10n = 185$

Solve the system of equations using substitution.

$10s + 4n = 84$

$10n = -20s + 185$

$n = -2s + 18.5$

$10s + 4(-2s + 18.5) = 84$

$10s - 8s + 74 = 84$

$2s + 74 = 84$

$2s = 10$

$s = 5$

The student cost for shirts is **$5**.

18. $3z + 10 < -z$

Collect nonvariable terms to one side.

$3z < -z - 10$

Collect variable terms to the other side.

$4z < -10$

Isolate the variable.

$z < -2.5$

19. $2x - 3 > 5(x - 4) - (x - 4)$

Distribute 5 through the parentheses and -1 through the parentheses.

$2x - 3 > 5x - 20 - x + 4$

Combine like terms.

$2x - 3 > 4x - 16$

Collect x-terms to one side, and constant terms to the other side.

$-2x > -13$

Divide both sides by -2; since dividing by a negative, reverse the direction of the inequality.

$x < 6.5$

20. $2x + 4 < -10$ *or* $4(x + 2) > 18$

Solve each inequality independently.

$2x < -14$	$4x + 8 > 18$
$x < -7$	$4x > 10$
	$x > 2.5$

The solution to the original compound inequality is **the set of all x for which $x < -7$ or $x > 2.5$.**

21. $-1 \leq 3(x + 2) - 1 \leq x + 3$

Break up the compound inequality into two inequalities.

$-1 \leq 3(x + 2) - 1$ *and* $3(x + 2) - 1 \leq x + 3$

Solve separately.

$-1 \leq 3x + 6 - 1$	$3x + 6 - 1 \leq x + 3$
$-6 \leq 3x$	$2x \leq -2$
$-2 \leq x$ and	$x \leq -1$

The only values of x that satisfy *both* inequalities are the values between -2 and -1 (inclusive).

$-2 \leq x \leq -1$

22. This quadratic is given in vertex form, with $h = -3$ and $k = 2$. The vertex of this equation is $(-3, 2)$. The line of symmetry is the vertical line that passes through this point. Since the x-value of the point is -3, the line of symmetry is **$x = -3$**.

23. $y = -3x^2 + 24x - 27$?

This quadratic equation is in standard form. Use the formula for finding the x-value of the vertex.

$x = -\dfrac{b}{2a}$ where $a = -3, b = 24$

$x = -\dfrac{24}{2(-3)} = 4$

Plug $x = 4$ into the original equation to find the corresponding y-value.

$y = -3(4)^2 + 24(4) - 27 = 21$

The vertex is at **$(4, 21)$**.

24. $y = -3x^2 + 24x - 27$

Move c to the other side of the equation.

$y + 27 = -3x^2 + 24x$

Divide through by a (-3 in this example).

$\dfrac{y}{-3} - 9 = x^2 - 8x$

Take half of the new b, square it, and add that quantity to both sides.

$\dfrac{1}{2}(-8) = -4$. Squaring it gives $(-4)^2 = 16$.

$\dfrac{y}{-3} - 9 + 16 = x^2 - 8x + 16$

Simplify the left side, and write the right side as a binomial squared.

$\dfrac{y}{-3} + 7 = (x - 4)^2$

Subtract 7, and then multiply through by -3 to isolate y.

$y = -3(x - 4)^2 + 21$

25. **Method 1**: Make $y = 0$; isolate x by square rooting both sides:

Make $y = 0$.

$0 = -(x + 3)^2 + 1$

Subtract 1 from both sides.

$-1 = -(x + 3)^2$

Divide by -1 on both sides.

$1 = (x + 3)^2$

Square root both sides. Don't forget to write plus OR minus 1.

$(x + 3) = \pm 1$

Write two equations using $+1$ and -1.

$(x + 3) = 1$ or $(x + 3) = -1$

Solve both equations. These are the zeros.

$x = -2$ or $x = -4$

Method 2: Convert vertex form to standard form, and then use the quadratic formula.

Put the equation in standard form by distributing and combining like terms.

$y = -(x + 3)^2 + 1$

$y = -(x^2 + 6x + 9) + 1$

$y = -x^2 - 6x - 8$

Find the zeros using the quadratic formula.

$x = \dfrac{-b \pm \sqrt{(b^2 - 4ac)}}{2a}$

$x = \dfrac{-(-6) \pm \sqrt{(-6)^2 - 4(-1)(-8)}}{2(-1)}$

$x = \dfrac{6 \pm \sqrt{36 - 32}}{-2}$

$x = \dfrac{6 \pm \sqrt{4}}{-2}$

$x = -4, -2$

26. This polynomial can be factored in the form $(z - 2)(z - 2) = 0$, so the only root is $z = 2$. There is only one x-intercept, and the vertex of the graph is *on* the x-axis.

27. If the quadratic has zeros at $x = -3$ and $x = 2$, then it has factors of $(x + 3)$ and $(x - 2)$. The quadratic function can be written in the factored form $y = a(x + 3)(x - 2)$. To find the a-value, plug in the point $(-2, 8)$ for x and y:

$8 = a(-2 + 3)(-2 - 2)$

$8 = a(-4)$

$a = -2$

The quadratic function is **$y = -2(x + 3)(x - 2)$**.

28. Points A and B and line D are all on plane M. Point C is above the plane, and line E cuts through the plane and thus does not lie on plane M. The point at which line E intersects plane M is on plane M but the line as a whole is not.

29. Set up a system of equations.

$\angle M + \angle N = 180°$

$\angle M = 2\angle N - 30°$

Use substitution to solve for $\angle N$.

$\angle M + \angle N = 180°$

$(2\angle N - 30°) + \angle N = 180°$

$3\angle N - 30° = 180°$

$3\angle N = 210°$

$\boldsymbol{\angle N = 70°}$

Solve for $\angle M$ using the original equation.

$\angle M + \angle N = 180°$

$\angle M + 70° = 180°$

$\boldsymbol{\angle M = 110°}$

30. Any two adjacent angles that are supplementary are linear pairs, so there are 16 linear pairs in the figure ($\angle 1$ and $\angle 5$, $\angle 2$ and $\angle 6$, $\angle 5$ and $\angle 6$, $\angle 2$ and $\angle 1$, and so on).

31. Identify the important parts of the circle.

    $r = 4$

    $\angle NHS = 90°$

    Plug these values into the formula for the area of a sector.

    $A = \dfrac{\theta}{360°} \times \pi r^2 = \dfrac{90}{360} \times \pi (4)^2$

    Plug these values into the formula for the area of a sector (continued).

    $= \dfrac{1}{4} \times 16\pi = \boldsymbol{4\pi}$

32. Identify the important parts of the circle.

    $r = 3$

    length of $\overset{\frown}{ACB} = 5$

    Plug these values into the formula for the length of an arc and solve for θ.

    $s = \dfrac{\theta}{360°} \times 2\pi r$

    $5 = \dfrac{\theta}{360} \times 2\pi (3)$

    $\dfrac{5}{6\pi} = \dfrac{\theta}{360}$

    $\theta = 95.5°$

    $\boldsymbol{m\angle AOB = 95.5°}$

33. **Triangle 1 is an equilateral triangle** (all 3 sides are equal, and all 3 angles are equal)

    Triangle 2 is a scalene, right triangle (all 3 sides are different, and there is a 90° angle)

    Triangle 3 is an obtuse, isosceles triangle (there are 2 equal sides and, consequently, 2 equal angles)

Triangle 4 is a right, isosceles triangle (there are 2 equal sides and a 90° angle)

34. The sum of two sides is 23 and their difference is 3. To connect the two other sides and enclose a space, x must be less than the sum and greater than the difference (that is, $3 < x < 23$). Therefore, **x's minimum value to the nearest hundredth is 3.01 and its maximum value is 22.99.**

35. $WZ = b_1 = 80$

    $XU = h_1 = 7.0$

    $XZ = b_2 = 100$

    $WY = h_2 = ?$

    The given values can be used to write two equation for the area of $\triangle WXZ$ with two sets of bases and heights.

    $A = \frac{1}{2}bh$

    $A_1 = \frac{1}{2}(80)(70) = 2800$

    $A_2 = \frac{1}{2}(100)(h_2)$

    Set the two equations equal to each other and solve for WY.

    $2800 = \frac{1}{2}(100)(h_2)$

    $h_2 = 56$

    $WY = 56$

36. Find $\angle C$ using the fact that the sum of $\angle C$ and m is 360°.

    $260° + m\angle C = 360°$

    $m\angle C = 100°$

    Solve for $\angle D$ using the fact that consecutive interior angles in a quadrilateral are supplementary.

    $m\angle C + m\angle D = 180°$

    $100° + m\angle D = 180°$

    $m\angle D = 80°$

    Solve for n by subtracting $m\angle D$ from 360°.

    $m\angle D + n = 360°$

    $n = 280°$

37. Find equations for the area of the field and length of the lines to be painted (L) in terms of x and y.

    $A = 1000 = xy$

    $L = 2x + 5y$

    Substitute to find L in terms of x.

    $y = \frac{1000}{x}$

    $L = 2x + 5y$

    $L = 2x + 5\left(\frac{1000}{x}\right)$

$$L = 2x + \frac{5000}{x}$$

38. The sum of the exterior angles is 360°. Dividing this sum by 400 gives $\frac{360°}{400} = \mathbf{0.9°}$. Since an interior angle is supplementary to an exterior angle, all the interior angles have measure $180 - 0.9 = \mathbf{179.1°}$. Alternately, using the formula for calculating the interior angle gives the same result:

$$\textit{interior angle} = \frac{400 - 2}{400} \times 180° = 179.1°$$

39. The area of the shaded region will be the area of the circle minus the area of the hexagon. Use the radius to find the area of the circle.

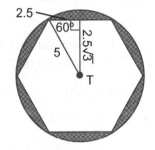

$$A_c = \pi r^2$$
$$= \pi(5)^2 = 25\pi$$

To find the area of the hexagon, draw a right triangle from the vertex, and use special right triangles to find the hexagon's apothem. Then, use the apothem to calculate the area.

$$a = 2.5\sqrt{3}$$
$$A_H = \frac{ap}{2}$$
$$= \frac{(2.5\sqrt{3})(30)}{2} = 64.95$$

Subtract the area of the hexagon from the circle to find the area of the shaded region.

$$= A_c - A_H$$
$$= 25\pi - 64.95 \approx \mathbf{13.59}$$

40. Write the equation for the area of the original sphere.

$$SA_1 = 4\pi z^2$$

Write the equation for the area of the new sphere.

$$SA_2 = 4\pi(z + t)^2 = 4\pi(z^2 + 2zt + t^2) = 4\pi z^2 + 8\pi zt + 4\pi t^2$$

To find the difference between the two, subtract the original from the increased surface area.

$$A_2 - A_1 = 4\pi z^2 + 8\pi zt + 4\pi t^2 - 4\pi z^2 = \mathbf{4\pi t^2 + 8\pi zt}$$

41. Since the cube's volume is 27, each side length is equal to $\sqrt[3]{27} = 3$. The long diagonal distance from one of the cube's vertices to its opposite vertex will provide the sphere's diameter:

$$d = \sqrt{3^2 + 3^2 + 3^2} = \sqrt{27} = 5.2$$

Half of this length is the radius, which is **2.6 meters**.

PARAGRAPH COMPREHENSION

The AFOQT Paragraph Comprehension section includes short reading passages followed by questions about those passages. The passages will cover simple, easy-to-understand topics, and no outside knowledge will be needed to answer the questions. The sections below will introduce the types of questions that are included in the Paragraph Comprehension section and explain how to answer them.

THE MAIN IDEA

The **MAIN IDEA** of a text describes the author's main topic and general concept; it also generalizes the author's point of view about a subject. It is contained within and throughout the text. The reader can easily find the main idea by considering how the main topic is addressed throughout a passage. In the reading test, the expectation is not only to identify the main idea but also to differentiate it from a text's theme and to summarize the main idea clearly and concisely.

The main idea is closely connected to topic sentences and how they are supported in a text. Questions may deal with finding topic sentences, summarizing a text's ideas, or locating supporting details. The sections and practice examples that follow detail the distinctions between these aspects of text.

Identifying the Main Idea

To identify the main idea, first identify the topic. The difference between these two things is simple: the **TOPIC** is the overall subject matter of a passage; the main idea is what the author wants to say about that topic. The main idea covers the author's direct perspective about a topic, as distinct from the **THEME**, which is a generally true idea that the reader might derive from a text. Most of the time, fiction has a theme, whereas nonfiction has a main idea. This is the case because in a nonfiction text, the author speaks more directly to the audience about a topic—his or her perspective is more visible. For example, the following

HELPFUL HINT

The author's perspective on the subject of the text and how he or she has framed the argument or story hints at the main idea. For example, if the author framed the story with a description, image, or short anecdote, this suggests a particular idea or point of view.

passage conveys the topic as well as what the author wants to communicate about that topic.

The "shark mania" of recent years can be largely pinned on the sensationalistic media surrounding the animals: from the release of *Jaws* in 1975 to the week of ultra-hyped shark feeding frenzies and "worst shark attacks" countdowns known as Shark Week, popular culture both demonizes and fetishizes sharks until the public cannot get enough. Swimmers and beachgoers may look nervously for the telltale fin skimming the surface, but the reality is that shark bites are extremely rare and they are almost never unprovoked. Sharks attack people at very predictable times and for very predictable reasons. Rough surf, poor visibility, or a swimmer sending visual and physical signals that mimic a shark's normal prey are just a few examples.

Of course, some places are just more dangerous to swim. Shark attack "hot spots," such as the coasts of Florida, South Africa, and New Zealand try a variety of solutions to protect tourists and surfers. Some beaches employ "shark nets," meant to keep sharks away from the beach, though these are controversial because they frequently trap other forms of marine life as well. Other beaches use spotters in helicopters and boats to alert beach officials when there are sharks in the area. In addition, there is an array of products that claim to offer personal protection from sharks, ranging from wetsuits in different colors to devices that broadcast electrical signals in an attempt to confuse the sharks' sensory organs. At the end of the day, though, beaches like these remain dangerous, and swimmers must assume the risk every time they paddle out from shore.

HELPFUL HINT
Readers should identify the topic of a text and pay attention to how the details about it relate to one another. A passage may discuss, for example, topic similarities, characteristics, causes, and/or effects.

The author of this passage has a clear topic: sharks and the relationship between humans and sharks. In order to identify the main idea of the passage, the reader must ask what the author wants to say about this topic, what the reader is meant to think or understand. The author makes sure to provide information about several different aspects of the relationship between sharks and humans, and points out that humans must respect sharks as dangerous marine animals, without sensationalizing the risk of attack. This conclusion results from looking at the various pieces of information the author includes as well as the similarities between them. The passage describes sensationalistic media, then talks about how officials and governments try to protect beaches, and ends with the observation that people must take personal responsibility. These details clarify what the author's main idea is. Summarizing that main idea by focusing on the connection between the different details helps the reader draw a conclusion.

Examples

The art of the twentieth and twenty-first centuries demonstrates several aspects of modern societal advancement. A primary example is the advent and ascendancy of technology: New technologies have developed new avenues for art making, and the globalization brought about by the Internet has both diversified the art world and brought it together simultaneously. Even as artists are able to engage in a global conversation about the categories and characteristics of art, creating a more uniform understanding, they can now express themselves in a diversity of ways for a diversity of audiences. The result has been a rapid change in how art is made and consumed.

1. This passage is primarily concerned with
   (A) the importance of art in the twenty-first century.
   (B) the use of art to communicate overarching ideals to diverse communities.
   (C) the importance of technology to art criticism.
   (D) the change in understanding and creation of art in the modern period.
   (E) the desire of artists to diversify the media with which art is created.

2. Which of the following best describes the main idea of the passage?
   (A) Modern advances in technology have diversified art making and connected artists to distant places and ideas.
   (B) Diversity in modern art is making it harder for art viewers to understand and talk about that art.
   (C) The use of technology to discuss art allows us to create standards for what art should be.
   (D) Art making before the invention of technology such as the Internet was disorganized and poorly understood.
   (E) Art making in the twenty-first century is dependent on the use of technology in order to meet current standards.

Topic and Summary Sentences

Identifying the main idea requires understanding the structure of a piece of writing. In a short passage of one or two paragraphs, the topic and summary sentences quickly relate what the paragraphs are about and what conclusions the author wants the reader to draw. These sentences function as bookends to a paragraph or passage, telling readers what to think and keeping the passage tied tightly together.

Generally, the TOPIC SENTENCE is the first, or very near the first, sentence in a paragraph. It is a general statement that introduces the topic, clearly and specifically directing the reader to access any previous experience with that topic.

The SUMMARY SENTENCE, on the other hand, frequently—but not always!—comes at the end of a paragraph or passage, because it wraps up all the ideas presented. This sentence provides an understanding of what the author wants to say about the topic and what conclusions to draw about it. While a topic sentence acts as an introduction to a topic, allowing the reader to activate his or her own ideas and experiences, the summary statement asks the reader to accept the author's ideas about that topic. Because of this, a summary sentence helps the reader quickly identify a piece's main idea.

HELPFUL HINT

A **summary** is a very brief restatement of the most important parts of an argument or text. Building a summary begins with the most important idea in a text. A longer summary also includes supporting details. The text of a summary should be much shorter than the original.

Examples

Altogether, Egypt is a land of tranquil monotony. The eye commonly travels either over a waste of waters, or over a green plain unbroken by elevations. The hills which inclose (*sic*) the Nile valley have level tops, and sides that are bare of trees, or shrubs, or flowers, or even mosses. The sky is generally cloudless. No fog or mist enwraps the distance in mystery; no rainstorm sweeps across the scene; no rainbow spans the empyrean; no shadows chase each other over the landscape. There is an entire absence of picturesque scenery. A single broad river, unbroken within the limits of Egypt even by a rapid, two flat strips of green plain at its side, two low lines of straight-topped hills beyond them, and a boundless open space where the river divides itself into half a dozen sluggish branches before reaching the sea, constitute Egypt, which is by nature a southern Holland—"weary, stale, flat and unprofitable."

—from *Ancient Egypt* by George Rawlinson

3. Which of the following best explains the general idea and focus indicated by the topic sentence?

(A) Egypt is a boring place without much to do.

(B) The land of Egypt is undisturbed; the reader will read on to find out what makes it so dull.

(C) Egypt is a peaceful place; its people live with a sense of predictability.

(D) The land of Egypt is quiet; the reader wants to know what is missing.

(E) The reader is curious about how people survive in an area of worn out uniformity.

4. Which of the following best states what the author wants the reader to understand after reading the summary sentence?

(A) There is not much to get excited about while visiting Egypt.

(B) Egypt is a poverty-stricken wasteland.

(C) The land of Egypt is worn out from overuse.

(D) The land of Egypt lacks anything fresh or inspiring.

(E) Egypt is so flat and worn down it is not worth visiting.

SUPPORTING DETAILS

Between a topic sentence and a summary sentence, the rest of a paragraph is built with SUPPORTING DETAILS. Supporting details come in many forms; the purpose of the passage dictates the type of details that will support the main idea. A persuasive passage may use facts and data or detail specific reasons for the author's opinion. An informative passage will primarily use facts about the topic to support the main idea. Even a narrative passage will have supporting details—specific things the author says to develop the story and characters.

The most important aspect of supporting details is exactly what the term states: They support the main idea. Examining the various supporting details and how they work with one another will solidify how the author views a topic and what the main idea of the passage is. Supporting details are key to understanding a passage.

Identifying Supporting Details

How can the reader identify the most important pieces of information in a passage? Supporting details build an argument and contain the concepts upon which the main idea rests. While supporting details will help the reader determine the main idea, it is actually easier to find the most important supporting details by first understanding the main idea; the pieces that make up the main argument then become clear.

SIGNAL WORDS—transitions and conjunctions—explain to the reader how one sentence or idea is connected to another. These words and phrases can be anywhere in a sentence, and it is important to understand what each signal word means. Signal words can add information, provide counterarguments, create organization in a passage, or draw conclusions. Some common signal words include *in particular*, *in addition*, *besides*, *contrastingly*, *therefore*, and *because*.

Examples

The war is inevitable—and let it come! I repeat it, sir, let it come! It is in vain, sir, to extenuate the matter. Gentlemen may cry, "Peace! Peace!"—but there is no peace. The war is actually begun! The next gale that sweeps from the north will bring to our ears the clash of resounding arms! Our brethren are already in the field! Why stand we here idle? What is it that gentlemen wish? What would they have? Is life so dear, or peace so sweet, as to be purchased at the price of chains and slavery? Forbid it, Almighty God! I know not what course others may take; but as for me, give me liberty or give me death!

—from "Give Me Liberty or Give Me Death" speech by Patrick Henry

5. In the fourth sentence of the text, the word *but* signals

    (A) an example.

    (B) a consequence.

    (C) an exception.

    (D) a reason.

    (E) a counterargument.

6. What argument does the author use to support his main point?

    (A) Life in slavery is not the goal of the country.

    (B) To die bravely is worthwhile.

    (C) Life without freedom is intolerable.

    (D) The cost of going to war is too great.

    (E) People cannot live in peace without going to war.

Evaluating Supporting Details

Besides using supporting details to help understand a main idea, the reader must evaluate them for relevance and inconsistency. An author selects details to help organize a passage and support its main idea. Sometimes, the author's bias results in details left out that don't directly support the main idea or that support an opposite idea. The reader has to be able to notice not only what the author says but also what the author leaves out.

To understand how a supporting detail relates to the main idea, the purpose of the passage should be discerned: what the author is trying to communicate and what the author wants from the reader. Every passage has a specific goal, and each paragraph in a passage is meant to support that goal. For each supporting detail, the position in the text, the signal words, and the specific content work together to alert the reader to the relationship between the supporting ideas and the main idea.

Close reading involves noticing the striking features of a text. For example, does a point made in the text appeal to the reader's sense of justice? Does a description seem rather exaggerated or overstated? Do certain words—such as *agonizing*—seem emotive? Are rhetorical questions being used to lead the reader to a certain conclusion?

Though the author generally includes details that support the text's main idea, the reader must decide how those details relate to one another as well as find any gaps in the support of the author's argument. This is particularly important in a persuasive piece of writing, when an author may allow bias to show through. Discovering the author's bias and how the supporting details reveal that bias is also key to understanding a text.

Examples

In England in the 'fifties came the Crimean War, with the deep stirring of national feeling which accompanied it, and the passion of gratitude and admiration which was poured forth on Miss Florence Nightingale for her work on behalf of our wounded soldiers. It was universally felt that there was work for women, even in war—the work of cleansing, setting in order, breaking down red tape, and soothing the vast sum of human suffering which every war is bound to cause. Miss Nightingale's work in war was work that never had been done until women came forward to do it, and her message to her countrywomen was educate yourselves, prepare, make ready; never imagine that your task can be done by instinct, without training and preparation. Painstaking study, she insisted, was just as necessary as a preparation for women's work as for men's work; and she bestowed the whole of the monetary gift offered her by the gratitude of the nation to form training-schools for nurses at St. Thomas's and King's College Hospitals.

—from *Women's Suffrage: A Short History of a Great Movement* by Millicent Garrett Fawcett

7. Which of the following best states the bias of the passage?

    (A) Society underestimates the capacity of women.

    (B) Generally, women are not prepared to make substantial contributions to society.

    (C) If women want power, they need to prove themselves.

    (D) One strong woman cannot represent all women.

    (E) The strength of women is their ability to take care of others.

8. Which of the following best summarizes what the author left out of the passage?

(A) Women can fight in wars.

(B) Other women should be recognized.

(C) Women need to stop wasting time giving speeches at conventions and start proving themselves.

(D) Without the contributions of women, society suffers.

(E) Women are the ones who get the important work done.

DRAWING CONCLUSIONS

Reading text begins with making sense of the explicit meanings of information or a narrative. Understanding occurs as the reader draws conclusions and makes logical inferences. To draw a conclusion, the reader considers the details or facts. He or she then comes to a conclusion—the next logical point in the thought sequence. For example, in a Hemingway story, an old man sits alone in a café. A young waiter says that the café is closing, but the old man continues to drink. The waiter starts closing up, and the old man signals for a refill. Based on these details, the reader might conclude that the old man has not understood the young waiter's desire for him to leave.

An inference is distinguished from a conclusion drawn. An **INFERENCE** is an assumption the reader makes based on details in the text as well as his or her own knowledge. It is more of an educated guess that extends the literal meaning. Inferences begin with the given details; however, the reader uses the facts to determine additional facts. What the reader already knows informs what is being suggested by the details of decisions or situations in the text. Returning to the example of the Hemingway story, the reader might infer that the old man is lonely, enjoys being in the café, and is reluctant to leave.

When reading fictional text, inferring character motivations is essential. The actions of the characters move the plot forward; a series of events is understood by making sense of why the characters did what they did. Hemingway includes contrasting details as the young waiter and an older waiter discuss the old man. The older waiter sympathizes with the old man; both men have no one at home and experience a sense of emptiness in life, which motivates them to seek the café.

Another aspect of understanding text is connecting it to other texts. Readers may connect the Hemingway story about the old man in the café to other Hemingway stories about individuals struggling to deal with loss and loneliness in a dignified way. They can extend their initial connections to people they know or their personal experiences. When readers read a persuasive text, they often connect the arguments made to counterarguments and opposing evidence of which they are aware. They use these connections to infer meaning.

HELPFUL HINT

When considering a character's motivations, the reader should ask what the character wants to achieve, what the character will get by accomplishing this, and what the character seems to value the most.

HELPFUL HINT

Conclusions are drawn by thinking about how the author wants the reader to feel. A group of carefully selected facts can cause the reader to feel a certain way.

Examples

I believe it is difficult for those who publish their own memoirs to escape the imputation of vanity; nor is this the only disadvantage under which they labor: it is also their misfortune, that what is uncommon is rarely, if ever, believed, and what is obvious we are apt to turn from with disgust, and to charge the writer with impertinence. People generally think those memoirs only worthy to be read or remembered which abound in great or striking events, those, in short, which in a high degree excite either admiration or pity: all others they consign to contempt and oblivion. It is therefore, I confess, not a little hazardous in a private and obscure individual, and a stranger too, thus to solicit the indulgent attention of the public; especially when I own I offer here the history of neither a saint, a hero, nor a tyrant. I believe there are few events in my life, which have not happened to many: it is true the incidents of it are numerous; and, did I consider myself an European, I might say my sufferings were great: but when I compare my lot with that of most of my countrymen, I regard myself as a *particular favorite of Heaven*, and acknowledge the mercies of Providence in every occurrence of my life. If then the following narrative does not appear sufficiently interesting to engage general attention, let my motive be some excuse for its publication. I am not so foolishly vain as to expect from it either immortality or literary reputation. If it affords any satisfaction to my numerous friends, at whose request it has been written, or in the smallest degree promotes the interests of humanity, the ends for which it was undertaken will be fully attained, and every wish of my heart gratified. Let it therefore be remembered, that, in wishing to avoid censure, I do not aspire to praise.

—from *The Interesting Narrative of the Life of Olaudah Equiano, or Gustavus Vassa, The African* by Olaudah Equiano

9. Which of the following best explains the primary motivation of the narrator?

   (A) He wants his audience to know that he is not telling his story out of vanity.

   (B) He is hoping people will praise his courage.

   (C) He wants to give credit to God for protecting him.

   (D) He is honoring the wishes of his friends.

   (E) He is not seeking personal notoriety; he is hoping people will be influenced by his story and the human condition will improve.

10. Given the details of what the narrator says he is *not*, as well as what he claims his story is *not*, it can be inferred that his experience was

   (A) a story that could lead to his success.

   (B) an amazing story of survival and struggle that will be unfamiliar to many readers.

   (C) an adventure that will thrill the audience.

   (D) a narrow escape from suffering.

   (E) an interesting story that is worthy of publication.

UNDERSTANDING THE AUTHOR

Many questions on the Paragraph Comprehension section will ask for an interpretation of an author's intentions and ideas. This requires an examination of the author's perspective and purpose as well as the way the author uses language to communicate these things.

In every passage, an author chooses words, structures, and content with specific purpose and intent. With this in mind, the reader can begin to comprehend why an author opts for particular words and structures and how these ultimately relate to the content.

The Author's Purpose

The author of a passage sets out with a specific goal in mind: to communicate a particular idea to an audience. The AUTHOR'S PURPOSE is determined by asking why the author wants the reader to understand the passage's main idea. There are four basic purposes to which an author can write: narrative, expository, technical, and persuasive. Within each of these general purposes, the author may direct the audience to take a clear action or respond in a certain way.

The purpose for which an author writes a passage is also connected to the structure of that text. In a NARRATIVE, the author seeks to tell a story, often to illustrate a theme or idea the reader needs to consider. In a narrative, the author uses characteristics of storytelling, such as chronological order, characters, and a defined setting, and these characteristics communicate the author's theme or main idea.

In an EXPOSITORY passage, on the other hand, the author simply seeks to explain an idea or topic to the reader. The main idea will probably be a factual statement or a direct assertion of a broadly held opinion. Expository writing can come in many forms, but one essential feature is a fair and balanced representation of a topic. The author may explore one detailed aspect or a broad range of characteristics, but he or she mainly seeks to prompt a decision from the reader.

Similarly, in TECHNICAL writing, the author's purpose is to explain specific processes, techniques, or equipment in order for the reader to use that process or equipment to obtain a desired result. Writing like this employs chronological or spatial structures, specialized vocabulary, and imperative or directive language.

In PERSUASIVE writing, though the reader is free to make decisions about the message and content, the author actively seeks to convince him or her to accept an opinion or belief. Much like expository writing, persuasive writing is presented in many organizational forms, but the author will use specific techniques, or RHETORICAL STRATEGIES, to build an argument. Readers can identify these strategies in order to clearly understand what an author wants them to believe, how the author's perspective and purpose may lead to bias, and whether the passage includes any logical fallacies.

Common rhetorical strategies include the appeals to ethos, logos, and pathos. An author uses these to build trust with the reader, explain the logical points of his or her argument, and convince the reader that his or her opinion is the best option.

An ETHOS—ETHICAL—APPEAL uses balanced, fair language and seeks to build a trusting relationship between the author and the reader. An author

HELPFUL HINT
Reading persuasive text requires an awareness of what the author believes about the topic.

HELPFUL HINT
Readers should consider how different audiences will react to a text. For example, how a slave owner's reactions to the narrative of Olaudah Equiano (on page 89) will differ from a slave trader's.

might explain his or her credentials, include the reader in an argument, or offer concessions to an opposing argument.

A LOGOS—LOGICAL—APPEAL builds on that trust by providing facts and support for the author's opinion, explaining the argument with clear connections and reasoning. At this point, the reader should beware of logical fallacies that connect unconnected ideas and build arguments on incorrect premises. With a logical appeal, an author strives to convince the reader to accept an opinion or belief by demonstrating that not only is it the most logical option but it also satisfies his or her emotional reaction to a topic.

A PATHOS—EMOTIONAL—APPEAL does not depend on reasonable connections between ideas; rather, it seeks to remind the reader, through imagery, strong language, and personal connections, that the author's argument aligns with his or her best interests.

Many persuasive passages seek to use all three rhetorical strategies to best appeal to the reader.

Clues will help the reader determine many things about a passage, from the author's purpose to the passage's main idea, but understanding an author's purpose is essential to fully understanding the text.

Examples

Evident truth. Made so plain by our good Father in Heaven, that all *feel* and *understand* it, even down to brutes and creeping insects. The ant, who has toiled and dragged a crumb to his nest, will furiously defend the fruit of his labor, against whatever robber assails him. So plain, that the most dumb and stupid slave that ever toiled for a master, does constantly *know* that he is wronged. So plain that no one, high or low, ever does mistake it, except in a plainly *selfish* way; for although volume upon volume is written to prove slavery a very good thing, we never hear of the man who wishes to take the good of it, *by being a slave himself.*

Most governments have been based, practically, on the denial of the equal rights of men, as I have, in part, stated them; *ours* began, by *affirming* those rights. *They* said, some men are too *ignorant*, and *vicious*, to share in government. Possibly so, said we; and, by your system, you would always keep them ignorant and vicious. We proposed to give *all* a chance; and we expected the weak to grow stronger, the ignorant, wiser; and all better, and happier together.

We made the experiment; and the fruit is before us. Look at it. Think of it. Look at it, in its aggregate grandeur, of extent of country, and numbers of population, of ship, and steamboat.

—fragment from Abraham Lincoln's speech on slavery

11. The author's purpose is to

(A) explain ideas.

(B) narrate a story.

(C) describe a situation.

(D) persuade to accept an idea.

(E) define a problem.

12. To achieve his purpose, the author primarily uses
- **(A)** concrete analogies.
- **(B)** logical reasoning.
- **(C)** emotional appeals.
- **(D)** images.
- **(E)** figurative language.

The Audience

The structure, purpose, main idea, and language of a text all converge on one target: the intended audience. An author makes decisions about every aspect of a piece of writing based on that audience, and readers can evaluate the writing through the lens of that audience. By considering the probable reactions of an intended audience, readers can determine many things: whether or not they are part of that intended audience; the author's purpose for using specific techniques or devices; the biases of the author and how they appear in the writing; and how the author uses rhetorical strategies. While readers evaluate each of these things separately, identifying and considering the intended audience adds depth to the understanding of a text and helps highlight details with more clarity.

Several aspects identify the text's intended audience. First, when the main idea of the passage is known, the reader considers who most likely cares about that idea, benefits from it, or needs to know about it. Many authors begin with the main idea and then determine the audience in part based on these concerns.

Then the reader considers language. The author tailors language to appeal to the intended audience, so the reader can narrow down a broad understanding of that audience. The figurative language John Steinbeck uses in his novel *The Grapes of Wrath* reveals the suffering of the migrant Americans who traveled to California to find work during the Great Depression of the 1930s. Steinbeck spoke concretely to the Americans who were discriminating against the migrants. Instead of finding work in the "land of milk and honey," migrants faced unbearable poverty and injustice. The metaphor that gives the novel its title is "and in the eyes of the people there is the failure; and in the eyes of the hungry there is a growing wrath. In the souls of the people the grapes of wrath are filling and growing heavy, growing heavy for the vintage." Steinbeck used the image of ripening grapes, familiar to those surrounded by vineyards, to condemn this harsh treatment, provide an education of the human heart, and inspire compassion in his audience. Readers who weren't directly involved in the exodus of people from Oklahoma to the West, could have little difficulty grasping the meaning of Steinbeck's language in the description: "66 is the path of a people in flight, refugees from dust and shrinking land, from the thunder of tractors and invasion, from the twisting winds that howl up out of Texas, from floods that bring no richness to the land and steal what little richness is there."

HELPFUL HINT
When reading a persuasive text, students should maintain awareness of what the author believes about the topic.

Examples

In the following text, consideration should be made for how an English political leader of 1729 might have reacted.

It is a melancholy object to those, who walk through this great town, or travel in the country, when they see the streets, the roads and cabin-doors crowded with beggars of the female sex, followed by three, four, or six children, all in rags, and importuning every passenger for an alms. These mothers instead of being able to work for their honest livelihood, are forced to employ all their time in strolling to beg sustenance for their helpless infants who, as they grow up, either turn thieves for want of work, or leave their dear native country, to fight for the Pretender in Spain, or sell themselves to the Barbados.

I shall now therefore humbly propose my own thoughts, which I hope will not be liable to the least objection.

I have been assured by a very knowing American of my acquaintance in London, that a young healthy child well nursed, is, at a year old, a most delicious nourishing and wholesome food, whether stewed, roasted, baked, or boiled; and I make no doubt that it will equally serve in a fricassee.

I do therefore humbly offer it to public consideration, that of the hundred and twenty thousand children, already computed, twenty thousand may be reserved for breed, whereof only one fourth part to be males; which is more than we allow to sheep, black cattle, or swine, and my reason is, that these children are seldom the fruits of marriage, a circumstance not much regarded by our savages, therefore, one male will be sufficient to serve four females. That the remaining hundred thousand may, at a year old, be offered in sale to the persons of quality and fortune, through the kingdom, always advising the mother to let them suck plentifully in the last month, so as to render them plump, and fat for a good table. A child will make two dishes at an entertainment for friends, and when the family dines alone, the fore or hind quarter will make a reasonable dish, and seasoned with a little pepper or salt, will be very good boiled on the fourth day, especially in winter.

> —from *A Modest Proposal for Preventing the Children of Poor People in Ireland From Being a Burden on Their Parents or Country, and for Making Them Beneficial to the Public* by Jonathan Swift

13. Which of the following best states the central idea of the passage?

    (A) Irish mothers are not able to support their children.

    (B) The Irish people lived like savages.

    (C) The people of England are quality people of fortune.

    (D) The poverty of the Irish forces their children to become criminals.

    (E) The kingdom of England has exploited the weaker country of Ireland to the point that the Irish people cannot support their families.

14. The author's use of phrases like "humbly propose," "liable to the least objection," "wholesome food" suggests which of the following purposes?

    (A) to inform people about the attitudes of the English

    (B) to use satire to reveal the inhumane treatment of the Irish

    (C) to persuade people to survive by any means

    (D) to express his admiration of the Irish people

    (E) to narrate the struggles of the English people

Tone and Mood

Two important aspects of the communication between author and audience occur subtly. The TONE of a passage describes the author's attitude toward the topic, distinct from the MOOD, which is the pervasive feeling or atmosphere in a passage that provokes specific emotions in the reader. The distinction between these two aspects lies once again in the audience: the mood influences the reader's emotional state in response to the piece, while the tone establishes a relationship between the audience and the author. Does the author intend to instruct the audience? Is the author more experienced than the audience, or does he or she wish to convey a friendly or equal relationship? In each of these cases, the author uses a different tone to reflect the desired level of communication.

DICTION, or word choice, primarily determines mood and tone in a passage. Many readers make the mistake of thinking about the ideas an author puts forth and using those alone to determine particularly tone; a much better practice is to separate specific words from the text and look for patterns in connotation and emotion. By considering categories of words used by the author, the reader can discover both the overall emotional atmosphere of a text and the attitude of the author toward the subject.

Every word has not only a literal meaning but also a CONNOTATIVE MEANING, relying on the common emotions, associations, and experiences an audience might associate with that word. The following words are all synonyms: *dog*, *puppy*, *cur*, *mutt*, *canine*, *pet*. Two of these words—*dog* and *canine*—are neutral words, without strong associations or emotions. Two others—*pet* and *puppy*—have positive associations. The last two—*cur* and *mutt*—have negative associations. A passage that uses one pair of these words versus another pair activates the positive or negative reactions of the audience.

HELPFUL HINT

To determine the author's tone, students should examine what overall feeling they are experiencing.

HELPFUL HINT

To decide the connotation of a word, the reader examines whether the word conveys a positive or negative association in the mind. Adjectives are often used to influence the feelings of the reader, such as in the phrase "an ambitious attempt to achieve."

Examples

Day had broken cold and grey, exceedingly cold and grey, when the man turned aside from the main Yukon trail and climbed the high earth-bank, where a dim and little-travelled trail led eastward through the fat spruce timberland. It was a steep bank, and he paused for breath at the top, excusing the act to himself by looking at his watch. It was nine o'clock. There was no sun nor hint of sun, though there was not a cloud in the sky. It was a clear day, and yet there seemed an intangible *pall* over the face of things, a subtle gloom that made the day dark, and that was due to the absence of sun. This fact did not worry the man. He was used to the lack of sun. It had been days since he had seen the sun, and he knew that a few more days must pass before that cheerful orb, due south, would just peep above the sky-line and dip immediately from view.

—from "To Build a Fire" by Jack London

15. Which of the following best describes the mood of the passage?

    (A) exciting and adventurous

    (B) fierce and determined

    (C) bleak and forbidding

    (D) grim yet hopeful

    (E) intense yet filled with fear

16. The connotation of the words intangible *pall* is

    (A) a death-like covering.

    (B) a vague sense of familiarity.

    (C) an intimation of communal strength.

    (D) an understanding of the struggle ahead.

    (E) a refreshing sense of possibility.

MEANING OF WORDS AND PHRASES

HELPFUL HINT

Look in the Word Knowledge chapter to learn more strategies for determining the meaning of unfamiliar words.

Vocabulary-in-context questions ask about the meaning of specific words in the passage. The questions will ask which answer choice is most similar in meaning to the specified word, or which answer choice could be substituted for that word in the passage.

When a reader is confronted with unfamiliar words, the passage itself can help clarify their meaning. Often, identifying the tone or main idea of the passage can help eliminate answer choices. For example, if the tone of the passage is generally positive, try eliminating the answer choices with a negative connotation. Or, if the passage is about a particular occupation, rule out words unrelated to that topic.

Passages may also provide specific context clues that can help determine the meaning of a word.

One type of context clue is a **DEFINITION**, or **DESCRIPTION**, **CLUE**. Sometimes, authors use a difficult word, then include *that is* or *which is* to signal that they are providing a definition. An author also may provide a synonym or restate the idea in more familiar words:

> Teachers often prefer teaching students with intrinsic motivation; these students have an internal desire to learn.

The meaning of *intrinsic* is restated as an *internal desire*.

Similarly, authors may include an **EXAMPLE CLUE**, providing an example phrase that clarifies the meaning of the word:

> Teachers may view extrinsic rewards as efficacious; however, an individual student may not be interested in what the teacher offers. For example, a student who is diabetic may not feel any incentive to work when offered a sweet treat.

Efficacious is explained with an example that demonstrates how an extrinsic reward may not be effective.

Another commonly used context clue is the **CONTRAST**, or **ANTONYM**, **CLUE**. In this case, authors indicate that the unfamiliar word is the opposite of a familiar word:

> In contrast to intrinsic motivation, extrinsic motivation is contingent on teachers offering rewards that are appealing.

The phrase "in contrast" tells the reader that *extrinsic* is the opposite of *intrinsic*.

Examples

17. One challenge of teaching is finding ways to incentivize, or to motivate, learning.

Which of the following is the meaning of *incentivize* as used in the sentence?

(A) encourage

(B) determine

(C) challenge

(D) improve

(E) dissuade

18. If an extrinsic reward is extremely desirable, a student may become so apprehensive he or she cannot focus. The student may experience such intense pressure to perform that the reward undermines its intent.

Which of the following is the meaning of *apprehensive* as used in the sentence?

(A) uncertain

(B) distracted

(C) anxious

(D) forgetful

(E) resentful

ANSWER KEY

1. (A) is incorrect. The focus of the passage is what the art of the twentieth and twenty-first centuries demonstrates.

    (B) is incorrect. Although the passage mentions a diversity of audiences, it discusses the artists expressing themselves, not attempting to communicate overarching ideals.

    (C) is incorrect. The passage discusses how new technologies have "developed new avenues for art making," but nothing about criticism.

    (D) is correct. The art of the modern period reflects the new technologies and globalization possible through the Internet.

    (E) is incorrect. The passage mentions the diversity of ways artists express themselves, not the media specifically.

2. **(A) is correct.** According to the text, technology and the Internet have "diversified the art world and brought it together simultaneously."

    (B) is incorrect. The passage explains that the global conversation about art has created a more uniform understanding.

    (C) is incorrect. The passage indicates that artists now engage in a global conversation about art, but this is one detail in the passage. The main idea of the passage concerns the advances in art in the twentieth and twenty-first centuries.

    (D) is incorrect. The invention of technology and the Internet have diversified art; however, that does not mean it was disorganized previously.

    (E) is incorrect. Technology is a means to an end; art is not dependent on it.

3. (A) is incorrect. The word *monotony* does suggest the idea of being bored; however, the focus is the land of Egypt, not what people have to do. In addition, tranquility is part of the general idea.

    (B) is correct. This option indicates both the main idea and what the reader will focus on while reading.

    (C) is incorrect. This option leaves out what the focus will be.

    (D) is incorrect. This option leaves out the general idea of monotony.

    (E) is incorrect. This option is inaccurate; the topic sentence does not suggest anything about survival.

4. (A) is incorrect. The summary describes the place, not a visit to the place.

    (B) is incorrect. The word *unprofitable* suggests that the land of Egypt is unrewarding, not poverty stricken.

    (C) is incorrect. The reason the land is stale and weary may not be due to overuse. This summary describes; it does not explain the reasons the land is worn.

    (D) is correct. The words *weary*, *stale*, and *unprofitable* suggest a lack of freshness or anything that stimulates enthusiasm.

(E) is incorrect. The first part of the sentence is correct, but the summary sentence does not indicate that Egypt is not worth visiting.

5. (A) is incorrect. The author includes an example that the war has begun when he says "Our brethren are already in the field!" The word *but* does not signal this example.

    (B) is incorrect. The phrase "but there is no peace" is a fact, not a consequence.

    (C) is incorrect. In order to be an exception, the word *but* would have to be preceded by a general point or observation. In this case, *but* is preceded by a demand for peace.

    (D) is incorrect. *But* does not introduce a reason in this text; it introduces a contradictory point.

    (E) is correct. The argument or claim that the country should be at peace precedes the word *but*. *But* counters the demand for peace with the argument that there is no peace; the war has begun.

6. (A) is incorrect. The main point is that the country has to go to war with England to be free. The author does not support his point with a discussion of the goals of the country.

    (B) is incorrect. This does not relate to the main point of going to war.

    (C) is correct. The author indicates that life is not so dear, nor peace so sweet, "as to be purchased at the price of chains and slavery."

    (D) is incorrect. This is inaccurate. The author insists that the cost of not fighting for freedom is too great.

    (E) is incorrect. Those who opposed going to war believed that Americans could find a way to live peacefully, without a war; the author's main point is the opposite.

7. **(A) is correct.** The author is suggesting that the work Florence Nightingale did had not been done before women came forward. Up till that point, what a woman could do had not been recognized.

    (B) is incorrect. This fact may have been true at the time this text was written, but only because educational opportunities were not available to women, and women were not encouraged to develop their abilities. Including this fact reveals the bias that women should be granted opportunities to train and to contribute.

    (C) is incorrect. This option does not apply; Florence Nightingale did more than prove herself.

    (D) is incorrect. The fact that Florence Nightingale donated the money awarded her to the training of women indicates that other women were preparing themselves to contribute.

    (E) is incorrect. This may or may not be true. It does not matter what kind of strength women have; the bias is that the strength of women wasn't really known.

8. (A) is incorrect. "It was universally felt that there was work for women, even in war" suggests that women had much to offer and didn't need to be sheltered; however, "there was work" does not mean the author thought women should engage in combat.

(B) is incorrect. Since the passage is specifically about Florence Nightingale, nothing in it suggests the author included information about what other women did.

(C) is incorrect. Information about women's suffrage conventions is unrelated to the topic of the paragraph.

(D) is correct. The author emphasizes that "Miss Nightingale's work in war was work that never had been done until women came forward to do it."

(E) is incorrect. The author shows the importance of Miss Nightingale's work, but that does not suggest it was the only important work being done.

9. (A) is incorrect. That motive is how the passage begins, but it is not his primary motive.

(B) is incorrect. He says he does not aspire to praise, and he does not suggest that he was courageous.

(C) is incorrect. He does state that the "mercies of Providence" were always with him; however, that acknowledgement is not his primary motive.

(D) is incorrect. Although he says that he wrote it at the request of friends, the story is meant to improve humanity.

(E) is correct. In the passage "If it…in the smallest degree promotes the interests of humanity, the ends for which it was undertaken will be fully attained, and every wish of my heart gratified," the narrator's use of the word *humanity* could mean he wants to improve the human condition or he wants to increase human benevolence, or brotherly love.

10. (A) is incorrect. The narrator says that what is obvious in his story is what people "are apt to turn from with disgust, and to charge the writer with impertinence." The narrator is telling a story that his audience couldn't disagree with and might consider rude.

(B) is correct. By saying "what is uncommon is rarely, if ever, believed, and what is obvious we are apt to turn from with disgust," the narrator suggests that his experience wasn't common or ordinary and could cause disgust.

(C) is incorrect. The reader can infer that the experience was horrific; it will inspire disgust, not excitement.

(D) is incorrect. The narrator admits he suffered; he indicates that he narrowly escaped death. This is not an inference.

(E) is incorrect. By saying "If then the following narrative does not appear sufficiently interesting to engage general attention, let my motive be some excuse for its publication," the narrator makes clear that he does not think his narrative is interesting, but he believes his motive to help humanity makes it worthy of publication.

11. (A) is incorrect. The injustice of slavery in America is made clear, but only to convince the audience that slavery cannot exist in America.

(B) is incorrect. The author briefly mentions the narrative of America in terms of affirming the equal rights of all people, but he does not tell a story or relate the events that led to slavery.

(C) is incorrect. The author does not describe the conditions of slaves or the many ways their human rights are denied.

(D) is correct. The author provides logical reasons and evidence that slavery is wrong, that it violates the American belief in equal rights.

(E) is incorrect. Although the author begins with a short definition of evident truth, he is simply laying the foundation for his persuasive argument that slavery violates the evident truth Americans believe.

12. (A) is incorrect. The author mentions the ant's willingness to defend what is his but does not make an explicit and corresponding conclusion about the slave; instead, he says, "So plain, that the most dumb and stupid slave that ever toiled for a master, does constantly *know* that he is wronged." The implied parallel is between the ant's conviction about being wronged and the slave knowing he is wronged.

(B) is correct. The author uses logic when he points out that people who claim slavery is good never wish "to take the good of it, *by being a slave.*" The author also points out that the principle of our country is to give everyone, including the "ignorant," opportunity; then he challenges his listeners to look at the fruit of this principle, saying, "Look at it, in its aggregate grandeur, of extent of country, and numbers of population, of ship, and steamboat."

(C) is incorrect. The author relies on logic and evidence, and makes no emotional appeals about the suffering of slaves.

(D) is incorrect. The author does offer evidence of his point with an image of the grandeur of America, but his primary appeal is logic.

(E) is incorrect. Initially, the author uses hyperbole when he says, "Evident truth. Made so plain by our good Father in Heaven, that all *feel* and *understand* it, even down to brutes and creeping insects." However, the author's primary appeal is logos.

13. (A) is incorrect. This is a fact alluded to in the passage, not a central idea.

(B) is incorrect. Although the author does refer to the Irish as savages, the reader recognizes that the author is being outrageously satirical.

(C) is incorrect. The author does say "That the remaining hundred thousand may, at a year old, be offered in sale to the persons of quality and fortune, through the kingdom," referring to the English. However, this is not the central idea; the opposite is, given that this is satire.

(D) is incorrect. The author does mention children growing up to be thieves, but this is not the central idea.

(E) is correct. The author is hoping to use satire to shame England.

14. (A) is incorrect. The author's subject is the poverty of the Irish, and his audience is the English who are responsible for the suffering of the Irish.

(B) is correct. The intended meaning of a satire sharply contradicts the literal meaning. Swift's proposal is not humble; it is meant to humble the arrogant. He expects the audience to be horrified. The children would make the worst imaginable food.

(C) is incorrect. The author is not serious. His intent is to shock his English audience.

(D) is incorrect. The author is expressing sympathy for the Irish.

(E) is incorrect. It is the Irish people who are struggling.

15. (A) is incorrect. The man is on some adventure as he turns off the main trail, but the context is one of gloom and darkness, not excitement.

(B) is incorrect. The cold, dark day is fierce, and the man may be determined; however, the overall mood of the entire passage is one of grim danger.

(C) is correct. The man is oblivious to the gloom and darkness of the day, which was "exceedingly cold and grey."

(D) is incorrect. The atmosphere is grim, and there is no indication the man is hopeful about anything. He is aware only of his breath and steps forward.

(E) is incorrect. The cold, grey scene of a lone man walking off the trail is intense, but "this fact did not worry the man."

16. **(A) is correct.** Within the context of the sentence "It was a clear day, and yet there seemed an intangible *pall* over the face of things, a subtle gloom that made the day dark," the words *gloom* and *dark* are suggestive of death; the words *over the face* suggest a covering.

(B) is incorrect. The word *intangible* can mean a vague sense, but there is nothing especially familiar about a clear day that is dark, with no sunlight.

(C) is incorrect. The word *intangible* suggests intimation; however, from the beginning, the author shows the man alone, and reports, "the man turned aside from the main Yukon trail."

(D) is incorrect. A struggle may be indicated by the darkness and gloom, but the man has no understanding of this possibility. The text refers to the darkness, saying, "This fact did not worry the man. He was used to the lack of sun."

(E) is incorrect. The man is hiking this trail for some possibility, but he is not refreshed; he is pausing to catch his "breath at the top, excusing the act to himself by looking at his watch."

17. **(A) is correct.** The word *incentivize* is defined immediately with the synonym *motivate*, or *encourage*.

(B) is incorrect. *Determine* is not a synonym for *motivate*. In addition, the phrase "to determine learning" does not make sense in the sentence.

(C) is incorrect. *Challenge* is not a synonym for motivate.

(D) is incorrect. *Improve* is closely related to motivation, but it is not the best synonym provided.

(E) is incorrect. *Dissuade* is an antonym for motivate.

18. (A) is incorrect. Nothing in the sentence suggests the student is uncertain.

(B) is incorrect. *Distracted* is related to the clue "focus" but does not address the clue "pressure to perform."

(C) is correct. The reader can infer that the pressure to perform is making the student anxious.

(D) is incorrect. Nothing in the sentence suggests the student is forgetful.

(E) is incorrect. The clues describe the student as feeling pressured but do not suggest the student is resentful.

SITUATIONAL JUDGMENT TEST

The Situational Judgment test evaluates the judgment and decision-making ability of candidates dealing with interpersonal situations. Candidates are presented with fifty multiple-choice questions to answer in thirty-five minutes. Each question presents a scenario that junior officers are likely to encounter in their careers. The scenario will be followed by five possible actions that could be taken in response. Candidates will need to pick the MOST effective and LEAST effective course of action to resolve the situation.

The candidates' responses to the questions on this test are not judged as right or wrong; rather, the responses provide the officer recruitment board with an idea of how candidates value the significance of communication, integrity, and resource management, and how they exercise leadership characteristics. There is no minimum passing score for this test. The score is a self-composite score and is not combined with any other AFOQT subtest.

Candidates cannot study and memorize answers for this test. To answer questions correctly, they must understand how military personnel demonstrate leadership qualities, enforce established standards, and produce results. While candidates will have to rely on their own personal values and experiences, there are some general strategies that can help in choosing the most effective answer. Consider the following guidelines:

- Do not ignore a situation, confront it.
- Attempt to solve situations at the appropriate level; do not escalate situations to superior officers.
- Deal directly with those involved in a situation—do not involve supervisors, subordinates, or peers unless absolutely necessary. In situations involving lower enlisted members, always consult the member's first noncommissioned officer in the chain of command.
- If the situation involves classified information, ensure that it is secured in accordance with appropriate regulations and guidelines.

- Do not spread details of the situation to others during casual conversation.
- Counsel the individual(s) in a private setting, not in front of peers or other junior officers.

Examples

Situation I. As a new first lieutenant in a flight, you notice that the technical sergeant consistently relies on one airman to complete tasks. It is obvious that this airman is very energetic and gets quick results. There are a total of three airmen of the same rank and experience, and the other two either act busy on their computers or say they have personal appointments. You have noticed this many times during the past month.

Possible actions:

(A) Meet with the master sergeant, supervisor of the technical sergeant, and discuss what you observed.

(B) Talk to the technical sergeant, explaining what you have noticed. Do this to understand why only one airman gets all the work.

(C) As officer of the flight, direct all tasks yourself to show the technical sergeant how to delegate work.

(D) Talk with the other flight leaders in the unit and see if they have the same problem.

(E) Do nothing, stay away from the technical sergeant's responsibilities.

    1. Select the MOST EFFECTIVE action (A – E) in response to the situation.

    2. Select the LEAST EFFECTIVE action (A – E) in response to the situation.

Situation II. In performance of your administrative duties, you send numerous daily emails. You are working on a special project with close-hold information. In a rush to leave your office to meet with the commander, you realize you emailed pertinent information about this project to someone not involved with the special project. No classified information was included in the email.

Possible actions:

(A) Leave the office so you are not late to the meeting with the commander.

(B) During your meeting with the commander, explain your mistake and ask for his or her directive.

(C) Direct your master sergeant or senior enlisted member to email the unintended recipient so you can make the commander meeting.

(D) Immediately call or email the unintended recipient, stating that the email was sent in error and tell him or her to delete it before opening.

(E) Send the email to the correct recipient. No further action is necessary since no classified information was transmitted.

    1. Select the MOST EFFECTIVE action (A – E) in response to the situation.

    2. Select the LEAST EFFECTIVE action (A – E) in response to the situation.

Situation III. As a maintenance officer, you are responsible for maintaining the operational readiness of six airplanes. An upcoming training mission is scheduled in three days that will require all six airplanes. Currently, only five airplanes are fully operational. The sixth airplane is partially mission capable (meaning it needs maintenance of some type, but the limited capability may or may not affect the requirement of the training mission). The pending maintenance tasks to make the sixth airplane fully mission capable would typically require twelve hours of maintenance time. The technical sergeant informed you yesterday that the maintainers were scheduled to have the next two days off prior to the mission.

Possible actions:

(A) Inform the commander that the sixth aircraft will not be ready for the mission.

(B) Meet with the maintainers and tell them they have to work until the aircraft is mission capable.

(C) Since the aircraft is partially mission capable, direct that the aircraft is flown at the current readiness level in the upcoming mission.

(D) Meet with the master sergeant and maintainers to determine how to meet the mission requirements.

(E) Devise a plan of action to schedule the maintenance (personnel, time, and equipment) and meet with the master sergeant to direct that the aircraft be fixed in time for the mission.

    1. Select the MOST EFFECTIVE action (A – E) in response to the situation.

    2. Select the LEAST EFFECTIVE action (A – E) in response to the situation.

Answer Key

Situation I

(A) Discussing the issue with the technical sergeant's supervisor before talking with the technical sergeant him- or herself escalates the problem before you understand the reasoning behind the situation. Also, by escalating the issue, you pass the problem to another person before attempting to address it yourself.

(B) Discussing the issue with the technical sergeant directly is the **most effective** course of action. This identifies what you perceive as a problem and allows the technical sergeant to address the reasoning behind his or her decisions. As a new officer to the flight, you are establishing a work ethic standard to spread down to the airman level.

(C) By assigning all tasks to the airmen directly, you are overstepping your boundaries and undermining the leadership of the technical sergeant before understanding the problem. The airmen may notice your style of leadership and lose respect for both you and the technical sergeant.

(D) Discussing the issues with other flight leaders may cause rumors to spread throughout the squadron, which can lead to a decrease in unit morale.

(E) If you do nothing to understand and correct the perceived issue, it will not improve and will likely continue to cause friction between you and the leadership of the flight. This is the **least effective** course of action.

Situation II

(A) Since the information on the special project is close hold (although not classified), time is of the essence to correct the problem. It is better to be late for the meeting and to explain to the commander that you had a time-sensitive issue to attend to.

(B) There are two reasons why this is the **least effective** solution. One—there is no need to escalate the issue without trying to correct the wrongdoing. The commander is not the right person to resolve this seemingly minimal situation. Two—you should correct the problem before leaving to attend the meeting. The worst thing that could happen is that the commander will instruct you not to be late again.

(C) If the master sergeant or other senior enlisted member is available and you explained briefly what happened, this would be a satisfactory course of action. You will save time when you delegate the task to a responsible individual in the office who understands the importance of document and information control, and you can make the meeting with the commander on time.

(D) By correcting the situation yourself, you are not burdening anyone else with the responsibility to correct your problem. You save time that would be required to explain to another individual what happened and how you want it resolved. If a senior enlisted member is available, it could be delegated easily (answer C), but this is the **most effective** response.

(E) Although the correct recipient will receive the email, you do not correct the problem, which is that an unintended individual received the email. Even though the project was not classified, it was close hold, meaning only a select few individuals should have received information about it.

Situation III

(A) This situation needs to be resolved at the flight level, not escalated to the commander level. Arbitrarily removing an aircraft from a mission may be detrimental to the success of the mission. Taskings for a specific number of aircraft are identified for a reason.

(B) This action oversteps the senior enlisted leadership of the flight by not discussing the situation with the enlisted leadership before directing the maintainers' schedule. Quite often the senior enlisted leadership has more insight to individual personnel issues than the officers and must be informed of any changes before the lower enlisted.

(C) Junior maintenance officers will not have the authority to approve this option. Mission readiness of aircraft may also involve the safety of other personnel, in which case, commanders will retain authority for such a decision. This is the **least effective** selection due to safety concerns.

(D) For resource management (personnel, time, and equipment), the lower-ranking personnel will not be involved in the decision-making process.

(E) This is the **most effective** solution. Explaining the situation and requirements to the flight senior enlisted leadership emphasizes the importance of sacrifice for military personnel. During this meeting, the two of you can agree on your plan of action, and the enlisted leadership can provide insight on any unforeseen circumstances that may preclude mission accomplishment.

7

SELF-DESCRIPTION INVENTORY

The Self Description Inventory (SDI) is a well-known personality assessment used by the US military as a means of personnel selection. A personality test is a standardized, scientific instrument intended to reveal an individual's characteristics or mental and emotional construct. (Note that the terms *instrument*, *survey*, *assessment*, and *inventory* have the same meaning and are used interchangeably.) The SDI is a 220-item computerized or paper-and-pencil-formatted test with a time limit of forty minutes.

This test aims to measure five personality traits known as the "Big Five": extraversion, agreeableness, conscientiousness, neuroticism, and openness. In broad terms, each attribute determines typical features of personality. For example, an extrovert (having the quality of extraversion) is commonly labeled as being affable, confident, talkative, and outgoing. Agreeableness is generally connected with being approachable, empathetic, cooperative, and easygoing. Conscientiousness is linked with being success-driven, methodical, reliable, accountable, and diligent. Traits that characterize neuroticism include anxiety, hopelessness, and irritability. Lastly, individuals who score high on openness tend to be interested in scientific activities, and are intellectually inquisitive and thoughtful.

Research shows a relationship between temperament and occupational-based outcomes such as productivity, job performance, collaboration, and leadership. The purpose of the SDI is to measure the overall personality of an individual to determine his or her "fit" for the job at hand.

It is important to work quickly but to answer all statements thoroughly. Do not waste time deciding what your response ought to be. There are no right or wrong answers or high/low scores to calculate. Give your first impression of how closely each statement represents you from the scale ranging from *Strongly Agree* to *Strongly Disagree*. If you strongly agree with a statement, choose A on the scale; if you strongly disagree with a statement, choose E. If your response is somewhere in between, choose B, C, or D (Agree, Neutral, Disagree). Ultimately, your responses are compared with others in your age and sex category.

Below are examples of the kinds of statements on the inventory.

Example

A	B	C	D	E
Strongly Agree	Agree	Neutral	Disagree	Strongly Disagree

1. I can be aloof and cold.
2. I get nervous easily.
3. I am helpful and unselfish.
4. I am full of energy.
5. I am easily angered.
6. I am a quick learner.
7. I can be tense.
8. I am inventive.
9. I can be moody.
10. I remain calm in stressful situations.

PHYSICAL SCIENCE

T he AFOQT Physical Science section covers topics in chemistry, physics, earth science, and space science. Candidates will have 10 minutes to answer 20 multiple choice questions.

CHEMISTRY

Atoms and Elements

An ATOM is the smallest particle of an element that is still identifiable as a part of that element; if you break down an atom any further, it is no longer an identifiable element.

An atom is made up of several subatomic particles. The three most important are PROTONS; which have a positive charge; ELECTRONS, which have a negative charge; and NEUTRONS, which are neutral. The protons and neutrons of an atom are located at its center in the nucleus; the electrons move in orbitals around the nucleus. Protons and neutrons both have mass that is measured in atomic mass units (amu); the mass of an electron is so negligible that it is usually not considered.

Electrons orbit the nucleus in increasing energy levels called SHELLS. Only the electrons in the outermost, or VALENCE, shell are involved in chemical reactions. Atoms that are close to having a completely full or empty shell will be the most reactive and will easily give electrons (if the shell is almost empty) or receive electrons (if the shell is almost full). Atoms with full valence shells, which include the noble gases, are nonreactive. The space taken up by orbiting electrons is large relative to the size of the nucleus. Thus, the nucleus is only a small portion of the total amount of space an atom takes up, even though it contains most of an atom's mass.

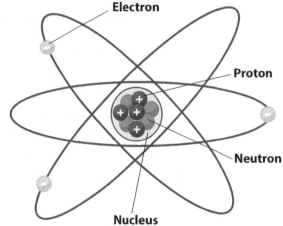

Figure 8.1. Atomic Structure

All atoms of the same ELEMENT have the same number of protons (called that element's ATOMIC NUMBER). For example, all carbon atoms have six protons. There are approximately 109 known elements; eighty-eight of these occur naturally on the earth, while the others are synthesized (manufactured). The elements are grouped together on the periodic table, and each has its own one- or two-letter symbol.

The PERIODIC TABLE OF ELEMENTS is a chart that arranges the chemical elements in an easy-to-understand way. Each element is listed in order of increasing atomic number and aligned so that the elements exhibit similar qualities. Each row in the table is known as a period, and each column is called a group.

Elements in the periodic table exhibit trends across periods and groups:

- Elements within a group have the same outer electron arrangement. The number of the main group corresponds to the number of valence electrons in those elements; however, most of the transition elements contain two electrons in their valence shells.

- The horizontal rows correspond to the number of occupied electron shells of the atom.

- The elements set below the main table are the lanthanides (upper row) and actinides. They also usually have two electrons in their outer shells.

- In general, the elements increase in mass from left to right and from top to bottom.

While all atoms in an element have the same number of protons, they can have different numbers of neutrons and electrons. Atoms of the same element with different numbers of neutrons are called ISOTOPES and can have different masses. Atoms of the same element that have different numbers of electrons are called IONS and will have a charge. Positive ions are called cations, and negative ions are called anions. If an atom has the same number of protons and electrons, it is neutral.

When two or more atoms join together they form a MOLECULE. For example, O_3 (ozone) contains three oxygen atoms bound together, and H_2O (water) contains two hydrogen atoms and one oxygen. Water is considered a COMPOUND because it is made by combining two or more different elements. Atoms can be joined together by different types of bonds. In a COVALENT BOND, the atoms share electrons. In an IONIC BOND, two ions with opposite charges are attracted to each other and bind together. Chemical formulas are used to represent the atomic composition of a molecule. For example, one molecule of water contains two hydrogen atoms (H) and one oxygen atom (O), so its chemical formula is H_2O.

Examples

1. The smallest unit of an element is a(n)

    (A) molecule

    (B) atom

    (C) proton

    (D) ion

    (E) nucleus

Figure 8.2. The Periodic Table

Legend: Alkali Metal · Alkaline Earth Metals · Transition Metal · Basic Metal · Metalloid · Nonmetal · Halogen · Noble Gas · Lanthanide · Actinide

Key: Atomic Number / Symbol / Name / Atomic Mass

Group	1	2	3	4	5	6	7	8	9	10	11	12	13	14	15	16	17	18
	1 H Hydrogen 1.008																	2 He Helium 4.0026
	3 Li Lithium 6.941	4 Be Beryllium 9.0122											5 B Boron 10.81	6 C Carbon 12.011	7 N Nitrogen 14.007	8 O Oxygen 15.999	9 F Fluorine 18.998	10 Ne Neon 20.180
	11 Na Sodium 22.990	12 Mg Magnesium 24.305											13 Al Aluminum 26.982	14 Si Silicon 28.085	15 P Phosphorus 30.974	16 S Sulfur 32.06	17 Cl Chlorine 35.45	18 Ar Argon 39.948
	19 K Potassium 39.098	20 Ca Calcium 40.078	21 Sc Scandium 44.956	22 Ti Titanium 47.867	23 V Vanadium 50.942	24 Cr Chromium 51.996	25 Mn Manganese 54.938	26 Fe Iron 55.845	27 Co Cobalt 58.933	28 Ni Nickel 58.963	29 Cu Copper 63.546	30 Zn Zinc 65.38	31 Ga Gallium 69.723	32 Ge Germanium 72.64	33 As Arsenic 74.922	34 Se Selenium 78.971	35 Br Bromine 79.904	36 Kr Krypton 83.798
	37 Rb Rubidium 85.468	38 Sr Strontium 87.62	39 Y Yttrium 88.906	40 Zr Zirconium 91.224	41 Nb Niobium 92.906	42 Mo Molybdenum 254	43 Tc Technetium 98	44 Ru Ruthenium 101.07	45 Rh Rhodium 102.91	46 Pd Palladium 106.42	47 Ag Silver 107.87	48 Cd Cadmium 112.41	49 In Indium 114.82	50 Sn Tin 118.71	51 Sb Antimony 121.76	52 Te Tellurium 127.60	53 I Iodine 126.90	54 Xe Xenon 121.29
	55 Cs Caesium 132.91	56 Ba Barium 137.33	57-71	72 Hf Hafnium 178.49	73 Ta Tantalum 183.84	74 W Tungsten 183.84	75 Re Rhenium 186.21	76 Os Osmium 190.23	77 Ir Iridium 192.22	78 Pt Platinum 195.08	79 Au Gold 196.97	80 Hg Mercury 200.59	81 Tl Thallium 204.38	82 Pb Lead 207.2	83 Bi Bismuth 208.98	84 Po Polonium 209	85 At Astatine 210	86 Rn Radon 222
	87 Fr Francium 223.020	88 Ra Radium 226	89-103	104 Rf Rutherfordium 267	105 Db Dubnium 268	106 Sg Seaborgium 271	107 Bh Bohrium 272	108 Hs Hassium 277	109 Mt Meitnerium 276	110 Ds Darmstadtium 281	111 Rg Roentgenium 280	112 Cn Copernicium 285	113 Uut Ununtrium Unknown	114 Fl Flerovium 254	115 Uup Ununpentium Unknown	116 Lv Livermorium 291	117 Uus Ununseptium Unknown	118 Uuo Ununoctium Unknown

Lanthanide:

57 La Lanthanium 138.905	58 Ce Cerium 140.12	59 Pr Praseodymium 140.91	60 Nd Neodymium 144.24	61 Pm Promethium 144.913	62 Sm Samarium 150.36	63 Eu Europium 151.96	64 Gd Gadolinium 157.25	65 Tb Terbium 158.33	66 Dy Dysprosium 152.50	67 Ho Holmium 154.930	68 Er Erbium 167.259	69 Tm Thulium 168.934	70 Yb Ytterbium 173.065	71 Lu Lutetium 174.967

Actinide:

89 Ac Actinium 227.028	90 Th Thorium 232.038	91 Pa Protactinium 231.036	92 U Uranium 238.029	93 Np Neptunium 237.048	94 Pu Plutonium 244.064	95 Am Americium 243.061	96 Cm Curium 247.070	97 Bk Berkelium 247.070	98 Cf Californium 251.080	99 Es Einsteinium 254	100 Fm Fermium 257.095	101 Md Mendelevium 258.1	102 No Nobelium 259.101	103 Lr Lawrencium 262

2. The identity of an element is determined by
   (A) the number of its protons
   (B) the number of its electrons
   (C) its charge
   (D) its atomic mass
   (E) the number of its valence electrons

Compounds and Mixtures

Substances that contain more than one type of element are called COMPOUNDS (so, a molecule that contains more than one element is also a compound). Compounds made up of identical molecules are called pure substances. Water, for example, is a pure substance made up only of identical water molecules.

A MIXTURE consists of two or more substances that are not chemically bonded. Mixtures are generally placed in one of two categories. The components in a HOMOGENEOUS MIXTURE are uniformly distributed; examples include salt water and air. In a HETEROGENEOUS MIXTURE, the components are not uniformly distributed. Vegetable soup, for example, is heterogeneous, as are rocks and soil.

A uniform, or homogeneous, mixture of different molecules is called a SOLUTION. If the solution is a liquid, the material being dissolved is the SOLUTE, and the liquid it is being dissolved in is called the SOLVENT. Both solids and gases can dissolve in liquids. A SATURATED SOLUTION has reached a point of maximum concentration; no more solute will dissolve in it.

Example

3. A coffee solution is produced when a teaspoon of dry coffee crystals is dissolved in a cup of hot water. The original crystals are classified as a
   (A) reactant.
   (B) product.
   (C) solute.
   (D) solvent.
   (E) mixture.

States of Matter

The physical states of matter are generally grouped into three main STATES.

SOLIDS are rigid; they maintain their shape and have strong intermolecular forces. In solids, the molecules are closely packed together, and solid materials usually have a high density. In the majority of solids, called crystalline solids, the ions or molecules are packed into a crystal structure that is highly ordered.

LIQUIDS cannot maintain their own shape; they conform to their containers but contain forces strong enough to keep molecules from dispersing into spaces. GASES have indefinite shape; they disperse rapidly through space due to random movement of particles and are able to occupy any volume. They are held together by weak forces.

Two other states of matter include LIQUID CRYSTALS, which can maintain their shape as well as be made to flow, and PLASMAS, gases in which electrons have been stripped from their nuclei.

Changes in temperature and pressure can cause matter to change states. Generally, adding energy (in the form of heat) changes a substance to a higher energy state (e.g., solid to liquid). Transitions from a high to lower energy state (e.g., liquid to solid) release energy. Each of these changes has a specific name:

- solid to liquid: melting
- liquid to solid: freezing
- liquid to gas: evaporation
- gas to liquid: condensation
- solid to gas: sublimation
- gas to solid: deposition

Example

4. Which of the following describes the process that causes water droplets to form on the outside of a cold glass of water on a hot day?

(A) melting

(B) deposition

(C) evaporation

(D) sublimation

(E) condensation

Chemical Reactions

A CHEMICAL REACTION occurs when there is a conversion of one set of chemical substances to another set. Chemical reactions are caused primarily by a change in bonding structure in these substances due to the exchange of electrons.

In a chemical reaction, the starting substances are called the REAGENTS or REACTANTS, and the ending substances are called the PRODUCTS. In the reaction below, the reactants sodium hydroxide (NaOH) and iron sulfate ($FeSO_4$) react to form the products sodium sulfate (Na_2SO_4) and iron hydroxide ($Fe(OH)_2$). Note the COEFFICIENT of 2 in front of the sodium hydroxide reactant: for every one mole of the other reactants and products, the reaction requires two moles of sodium hydroxide.

$$2NaOH + FeSO_4 \rightarrow Na_2SO_4 + Fe(OH)_2$$

This reaction is known as a DOUBLE DISPLACEMENT REACTION because the ions in each reagent are displaced and trade places to form two new products. In a SINGLE DISPLACEMENT REACTION, a lone atom or molecule displaces an ion in the second reagent, creating two new products, as shown below:

$$MgCl_2 + 2Na \rightarrow Mg + 2NaCl$$

In a SYNTHESIS REACTION, two compounds combine to form a single product:

$$C + O_2 \rightarrow CO_2$$

The opposite reaction, when a single reactant breaks down into two or more products, is called a DECOMPOSITION REACTION.

Finally, a COMBUSTION REACTION occurs when oxygen is reacted in the presence of heat to a combustible compound, usually an organic compound. The products of a combustion reaction are always water and carbon dioxide. For example, the reaction of methane with oxygen will proceed as follows:

$$CH_4 + 2O_2 \rightarrow CO_2 + 2H_2O$$

In OXIDATION/REDUCTION REACTIONS (also called redox reactions), electrons are transferred between atoms. In a redox reaction, the total number of electrons shared by the reactants does not change—they are simply shifted around. An element is OXIDIZED when it loses its electrons, and the element that gains those electrons is now REDUCED. Therefore, the element that does the oxidizing is known as the REDUCING AGENT because it has given electrons, or has reduced, a different element in the reaction. The same thing happens with the reduced element. It is called the OXIDIZING AGENT because it has taken electrons from a different element. In the reaction below, copper is reduced and silver is oxidized.

$$Cu_{(s)} + 2AgNO_{3(aq)} \rightarrow 2Ag_{(s)} + Cu(NO_3)_{2(aq)}$$

Example

5. Which type of chemical reaction takes place when kerosene reacts with oxygen to light a lamp?

   (A) oxidation

   (B) neutralization

   (C) combustion

   (D) sublimation

   (E) synthesis

Properties of Matter

MATTER is commonly defined as anything that takes up space and has mass. MASS is the quantity of matter something possesses (e.g., how much of something there is); it is usually measured in grams (g) or kilograms (kg). In addition to mass, it is possible to measure many other properties of matter, including weight, volume, density, and reactivity. These properties fall into one of two categories: EXTRINSIC PROPERTIES are directly related to the amount of material being measured (e.g., mass and volume), while INTRINSIC PROPERTIES are those that are independent of the quantity of matter present (e.g., density and specific gravity).

Matter can undergo two types of change: chemical and physical. A CHEMICAL CHANGE occurs when an original substance is transformed into a new substance with different properties. An example would be the burning of wood, which produces ash and smoke. Transformations that do not produce new substances, such as cutting a piece of wood or melting ice, are called PHYSICAL CHANGES.

Example

6. Which of the following is not a physical change?

    (A) melting of aspirin

    (B) lighting a match

    (C) putting sugar in tea

    (D) boiling antifreeze

    (E) slicing bread

Acids and Bases

There are a number of different technical definitions for acids and bases. In general, an ACID can be defined as a substance that produces hydrogen ions (H^+) in solution, while a BASE produces hydroxide ions (OH^-). Acidic solutions, which include common liquids like orange juice and vinegar, share a set of distinct characteristics: they have a sour taste and react strongly with metals. Bases, such as bleach and detergents, will taste bitter and have a slippery texture.

The acidity or basicity of a solution is described using its **pH** value, which is the negative log of the concentration of hydrogen ions. A neutral solution, which has the same concentration of hydrogen and hydroxide ions, has a pH of 7. Bases have a pH between 7 and 14, and acids have a pH between 0 and 7. Note that the pH scale is exponential, so a solution with a pH of 2 has 100 times more hydrogen ions than one with a pH of 4. A STRONG ACID ionizes completely in solution, meaning it releases all of its H^+ ions and will have a pH close to 1.

pH scale

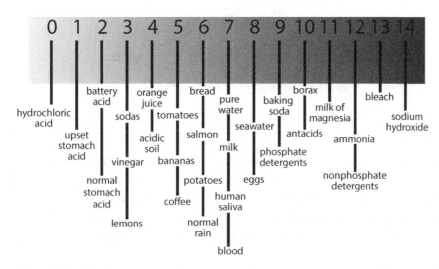

Figure 8.3. pH Scale

A **BUFFER** is any solution that exhibits very little change in its pH when small amounts of an acid or base are added to it. An acidic buffer solution is simply one with a pH of less than 7. Often a weak acid and one of its salts are combined to create an acidic buffer. Other times a weak base can be combined with one of its salts to create an alkaline buffer. Any solution with a pH greater than 7 would be known as an alkaline buffer solution.

Example

7. Which substance can be used to neutralize an acid spill?
    (A) sodium bicarbonate
    (B) citric acid
    (C) cat litter
    (D) water
    (E) vinegar

PHYSICS

Force and Motion

To study motion, it is necessary to understand the concept of scalars and vectors. **SCALARS** are measurements that have a quantity but no direction. **VECTORS**, in contrast, have both a quantity and a direction. **DISTANCE** is a scalar: it describes how far an object has traveled along a path. Distance can have values such as 54 m or 16 miles. **DISPLACEMENT** is a vector: it describes how far an object has traveled from its starting position. A displacement value will indicate direction, such as 54 m east or –16 miles.

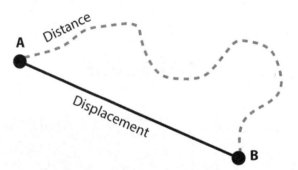

Figure 8.4. Distance versus Displacement

SPEED describes how quickly something is moving. It is found by dividing distance by time, and so it is a scalar value. **VELOCITY** is the rate at which an object changes position. Velocity is found by dividing displacement by time, meaning it is a vector value. An object that travels a certain distance and then returns to its starting point has a velocity of zero because its final position did not change. Its speed, however, can be found by dividing the total distance it traveled by the time it took to make the trip. **ACCELERATION** is how quickly an object changes velocity.

A push or pull that causes an object to move or change direction is called a **FORCE**. Forces can arise from a number of different sources. **GRAVITY** is the attraction of one mass to another mass. For example, the earth's gravitational field pulls objects toward it, and the sun's gravitational field keeps planets in motion around it. Electrically charged objects will also create a field that will cause other charged objects in that field to move. Other forces include **TENSION**,

HELPFUL HINT

The normal force balances out gravity in resting objects. When a book rests on a table, gravity pulls down on it, and the normal force pushes up, canceling each other out and holding the book still.

which is found in ropes pulling or holding up an object; FRICTION, which is created by two objects moving against each other; and the NORMAL FORCE, which occurs when an object is resting on another object. The BUOYANT force is the upward force experienced by floating objects.

An object that is at rest or moving with a constant speed has a net force of zero, meaning all the forces acting on it cancel each other out. Such an object is said to be at EQUILIBRIUM. Isaac Newton proposed three LAWS OF MOTION that govern forces:

- **NEWTON'S FIRST LAW**: An object at rest stays at rest, and an object in motion stays in motion, unless acted on by a force.

- **NEWTON'S SECOND LAW**: Force is equal to the mass of an object multiplied by its acceleration ($F = ma$).

- **NEWTON'S THIRD LAW**: For every action, there is an equal and opposite reaction.

The laws of motion have made it possible to build SIMPLE MACHINES, which take advantage of the rules of motion to make work easier to perform. Simple machines include the inclined plane, wheel and axle, pulley, screw, wedge, and lever.

Lever   Inclined Plane   Wedge

Pulley   Wheel and Axle   Screw

Figure 8.5. Simple Machines

Examples

8. What term describes the speed and direction of a moving soccer ball?

   (A) velocity

   (B) acceleration

   (C) mass

   (D) force

   (E) displacement

9. The resistance to motion caused by one object rubbing against another object is
   (A) inertia
   (B) friction
   (C) velocity
   (D) gravity
   (E) tension

Energy and Matter

ENERGY is the capacity of an object to do work. In other words, it is the capacity of an object to cause some sort of movement or change. There are two kinds of energy: kinetic and potential. KINETIC ENERGY is the energy possessed by objects in motion, and POTENTIAL ENERGY is possessed by objects that have the potential to be in motion due to their position. Potential energy is defined in relation to a specific point. For example, a book held 10 feet off the ground has more potential energy than a book held 5 feet off the ground, because it has the potential to fall farther (i.e., to do more work).

HELPFUL HINT

Like matter, energy is always conserved. It can be changed from one form to another, but it can never be created or destroyed.

Kinetic energy can be turned into potential energy, and vice versa. In the example above, dropping one of the books turns potential energy into kinetic energy. Conversely, picking up a book and placing it on a table turns kinetic energy into potential energy.

There are several types of potential energy. The energy stored in a book placed on a table is GRAVITATIONAL POTENTIAL ENERGY; it is derived from the pull of the earth's gravity on the book. ELECTRIC POTENTIAL ENERGY is derived from the interaction between positive and negative charges. Because opposite charges attract each other, and like charges repel, energy can be stored when opposite charges are moved apart or when like charges are pushed together. Similarly, compressing a spring stores ELASTIC POTENTIAL ENERGY. Energy is also stored in chemical bonds as CHEMICAL POTENTIAL ENERGY.

TEMPERATURE is the special name given to the kinetic energy of all the atoms or molecules in a substance. While it might look like a substance is not in motion, in fact, its atoms are constantly spinning and vibrating. The more energy the atoms have, the higher the substance's temperature. HEAT is the movement of energy from one substance to another. Energy will spontaneously move from high-energy (high-temperature) substances to low-energy (low-temperature) substances.

This energy can be transferred by radiation, convection, or conduction. RADIATION does not need a medium; the sun radiates energy to the earth through the vacuum of space. CONDUCTION occurs when two substances are in contact with each other. When a pan is placed on a hot stove, the heat energy is conducted from the stove to the pan and then to the food in the pan. CONVECTION transfers energy through circular movement of air or liquids. For example, a convection oven transfers heat through circular movement caused by hot air rising and cold air sinking.

Example

10. Which of the following has the least amount of kinetic energy?

   (A) a plane flying through the sky

   (B) a plane sitting on the runway

   (C) a ladybug flying toward a flower

   (D) a meteorite falling to the earth

   (E) a car moving with a constant velocity

Waves

Energy can also be transferred through WAVES, which are repeating pulses of energy. Waves that travel through a medium, like ripples on a pond or compressions in a Slinky, are called MECHANICAL WAVES. Waves that vibrate up and down (like the ripples on a pond) are TRANSVERSE WAVES, and those that travel through compression (like the Slinky) are LONGITUDINAL WAVES. Mechanical waves will travel faster through denser mediums; for example, sound waves will move faster through water than through air.

Waves can be described using a number of different properties. A wave's highest point is called its CREST, and its lowest point is the TROUGH. A wave's midline is halfway between the crest and trough; the AMPLITUDE describes the distance between the midline and the crest (or trough). The distance between crests (or troughs) is the WAVELENGTH. A wave's PERIOD is the time it takes for a wave to go through one complete cycle, and the number of cycles a wave goes through in a specific period of time is its FREQUENCY.

SOUND is a special type of longitudinal wave created by vibrations. Our ears are able to interpret these waves as particular sounds. The frequency, or rate, of

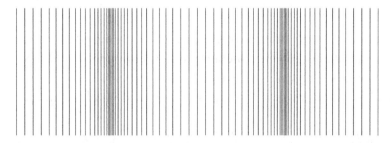

Longitudinal Wave

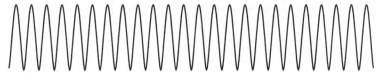

Transverse Wave

Figure 8.6. Types of Waves

the vibration determines the sound's PITCH. LOUDNESS depends on the amplitude, or height, of a sound wave.

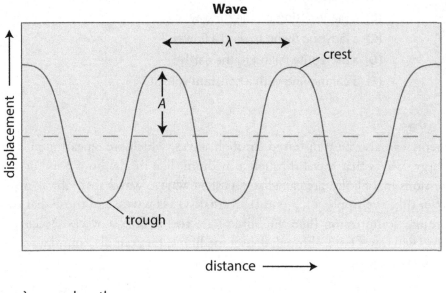

Figure 8.7 Parts of a Wave

The DOPPLER EFFECT is the difference in perceived pitch caused by the motion of the object creating the wave. For example, as an ambulance approaches, the siren's pitch will appear to increase to the observer and then to decrease as the ambulance moves away. This occurs because sound waves are compressed as the ambulance approaches an observer and are spread out as the ambulance moves away from the observer.

ELECTROMAGNETIC WAVES are composed of oscillating electric and magnetic fields and thus do not require a medium to travel through. The electromagnetic spectrum classifies the types of electromagnetic waves based on their frequency. These include radio waves, microwaves, X-rays, and visible light.

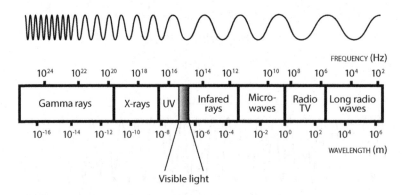

Figure 8.8. The Electromagnetic Spectrum

The study of light is called OPTICS. Because visible light is a wave, it will display similar properties to other waves. It will REFLECT, or bounce off, surfaces, which can be observed by shining a flashlight on a mirror. Light will also

REFRACT, or bend, when it travels between substances. This effect can be seen by placing a pencil in water and observing the apparent bend in the pencil.

Curved pieces of glass called LENSES can be used to bend light in a way that affects how an image is perceived. Some microscopes, for example, make objects appear larger through the use of specific types of lenses. Eyeglasses also use lenses to correct poor vision.

The frequency of a light wave is responsible for its COLOR, with red/orange colors having a lower frequency than blue/violet colors. White light is a blend of all the frequencies of visible light. Passing white light through a prism will bend each frequency at a slightly different angle, separating the colors and creating a RAINBOW. Sunlight passing through raindrops can undergo this effect, creating large rainbows in the sky.

HELPFUL HINT
The order of the colors in the spectrum of light can be remembered using **ROY G. BIV**: Red – Orange – Yellow – Green – Blue – Indigo – Violet.

Examples

11. Which type of wave is a longitudinal wave?
    (A) ocean wave
    (B) light wave
    (C) sound wave
    (D) X-ray wave
    (E) microwave

12. Which of the following scenarios demonstrates refraction?
    (A) a rainbow during a rainstorm
    (B) an echo in a cave
    (C) a candle appearing in a mirror
    (D) the Doppler effect
    (E) an increase in radio volume

Electricity and Magnetism

ELECTRIC CHARGE is created by a difference in the balance of protons and electrons, which creates a positively or negatively charged object. Charged objects create an electric field that spreads outward from the object. Other charged objects in that field will experience a force: objects that have opposite charges will be ATTRACTED to each other, and objects with the same charge will be REPELLED, or pushed away, from each other.

Because protons cannot leave the nucleus, charge is created by the movement of electrons. Materials that conduct electrons well are called CONDUCTORS, and those that do not conduct electricity well are INSULATORS. Static electricity, or ELECTROSTATIC charge, occurs when a surface has a buildup of charges. For example, if a student rubs a balloon on her head, the friction will cause electrons to move from her hair to the balloon. This creates a negative charge on the balloon and a positive charge on her hair; the resulting attraction will cause her hair to move toward the balloon.

ELECTRICITY is the movement of electrons through a conductor, and an electric CIRCUIT is a closed loop through which electricity moves. Circuits include a VOLTAGE source, which powers the movement of electrons known as CURRENT (measured in AMPERES or AMPS). Sources of voltage include batteries, generators, and wall outlets (which are in turn powered by electric power stations). Other elements, such as lights, computers, and microwaves, can then be connected to the circuit to be powered by its electricity. Elements in a circuit that resist the flow of electrons are called RESISTORS. Resistance is measured in Ohms (Ω).

MAGNETS are created by the alignment of spinning electrons within a substance. This alignment will occur naturally in some substances, including iron, nickel, and cobalt, all of which can be used to produce PERMANENT MAGNETS. The alignment of electrons creates a MAGNETIC FIELD, which, like an electric or gravitational field, can act on other objects. Magnetic fields have a north and a south pole that act similarly to electric charges: opposite poles will attract, and same poles will repel each other. However, unlike electric charge, which can be either positive or negative, a magnetic field ALWAYS has two poles. If a magnet is cut in half, the result is two magnets, each with a north and a south pole.

Electricity and magnetism are closely related. A moving magnet creates an electric field, and a moving charged particle will create a magnetic field. A specific kind of TEMPORARY MAGNET known as an electromagnet can be made by coiling a wire around a metal object and running electricity through it. A magnetic field will be created when the wire contains a current but will disappear when the flow of electricity is stopped.

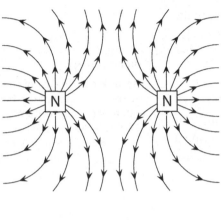

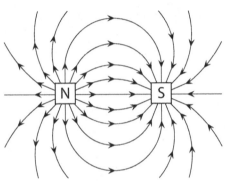

Figure 8.9. Magnetic Field Lines

Examples

13. What part of the atom flows through a circuit to power a light bulb?
    (A) protons
    (B) neutrons
    (C) electrons
    (D) nucleus
    (E) ions

14. Which metal attracts magnets?
    (A) iron
    (B) copper
    (C) silver
    (D) gold
    (E) platinum

EARTH AND SPACE SCIENCE

Astronomy

Astronomy is the study of space. Our PLANET, Earth, is just one out of a group of planets that orbit the SUN, which is the star at the center of our SOLAR SYSTEM.

Other planets in our solar system include Mercury, Venus, Mars, Jupiter, Saturn, Uranus, and Neptune. Every planet, except Mercury and Venus, has **MOONS**, or naturally occurring satellites that orbit a planet. Our solar system also includes **ASTEROIDS** and **COMETS**, small rocky or icy objects that orbit the Sun. Many of these are clustered in the asteroid belt, which is located between the orbits of Mars and Jupiter.

Figure 8.10. The Solar System

Our solar system is a small part of a bigger star system called a galaxy. (Our galaxy is called the Milky Way.) **GALAXIES** consist of stars, gas, and dust held together by gravity and contain millions of **STARS**, which are hot balls of plasma and gases. The universe includes many types of stars, including supergiant stars, white dwarfs, giant stars, and neutron stars. Stars form in nebulas, which are large clouds of dust and gas. When very large stars collapse, they create **BLACK HOLES**, which have a gravitational force so strong that light cannot escape.

Earth, the moon, and the sun interact in a number of ways that impact life on our planet. When the positions of the three align, eclipses occur. A **LUNAR ECLIPSE** occurs when Earth lines up between the moon and the sun; the moon moves into the shadow of Earth and appears dark in color. A **SOLAR ECLIPSE** occurs when the moon lines up between Earth and the sun; the moon covers the sun, blocking sunlight.

The cycle of day and night and the seasonal cycle are determined by the earth's motion. It takes approximately 365 days, or one year, for Earth to revolve around the sun. While Earth is revolving around the sun, it is also rotating on its axis, which takes approximately twenty-four hours, or one day. As the planet rotates, different areas alternately face toward the sun and away from the sun, creating night and day.

The earth's axis is not directly perpendicular to its orbit, meaning the planet tilts on its axis. The seasons are caused by this tilt. When the Northern Hemisphere is tilted toward the sun, it receives more sunlight and experiences summer. At the same time that the Northern Hemisphere experiences summer, the Southern Hemisphere, which receives less direct sunlight, experiences winter.

HELPFUL HINT

The phrase *My Very Educated Mother Just Served Us Noodles* can help students remember the order of the planets: **Me**rcury – **V**enus – **E**arth – **M**ars – **J**upiter – **S**aturn – **U**ranus – **N**eptune.

As the earth revolves, the Northern Hemisphere will tilt away from the sun and move into winter, while the Southern Hemisphere tilts toward the sun and moves into summer.

> **Example**
>
> **15.** What term describes what occurs when the moon moves between the earth and the sun?
> - **(A)** aurora
> - **(B)** lunar eclipse
> - **(C)** black hole
> - **(D)** solar eclipse
> - **(E)** seasons

Geology

GEOLOGY is the study of the minerals and rocks that make up the earth. A **MINERAL** is a naturally occurring, solid, inorganic substance with a crystalline structure. There are several properties that help identify a mineral, including color, luster, hardness, and density. Examples of minerals include talc, diamonds, and topaz.

Although a **ROCK** is also a naturally occurring solid, it can be either organic or inorganic and is composed of one or more minerals. Rocks are classified based on their method of formation. The three types of rocks are igneous, sedimentary, and metamorphic. **IGNEOUS** rocks are the result of tectonic processes that bring **MAGMA**, or melted rock, to the earth's surface; they can form either above or below the surface. **SEDIMENTARY** rocks are formed from the compaction of rock fragments that results from weathering and erosion. Lastly, **METAMORPHIC ROCKS** form when extreme temperature and pressure cause the structure of pre-existing rocks to change.

The rock cycle describes how rocks form and break down. Typically, the cooling and solidification of magma as it rises to the surface creates igneous rocks. These rocks are then subject to **WEATHERING**, the mechanical and/or chemical processes by which rocks break down. During **EROSION** the resulting sediment is deposited in a new location. As sediment is deposited, the resulting compaction creates new sedimentary rocks. As new layers are added, rocks and minerals are forced closer to the earth's core where they are subjected to heat and pressure, resulting in metamorphic rock. Eventually, they will reach their melting point and return to magma, starting the cycle over again. This process takes place over hundreds of thousands or even millions of years.

PALEONTOLOGY, the study of the history of life on Earth, is sometimes also considered part of geology. Paleontologists study the **ROCK RECORD**, which retains biological history through **FOSSILS**, the preserved remains and traces of ancient life. Fossils can be used to learn about the evolution of life on the planet, particularly bacteria, plants, and animals that have gone extinct. Throughout Earth's history, there have been five documented catastrophic events that caused major extinctions. For each mass extinction, there are several theories about the cause but no definitive answers. Theories about what triggered mass extinctions

HELPFUL HINT

Luster describes how light reflects off the surface of a mineral. Terms to describe luster include *dull*, *metallic*, *pearly*, and *waxy*.

include climate change, ice ages, asteroid and comet impacts, and volcanic activity.

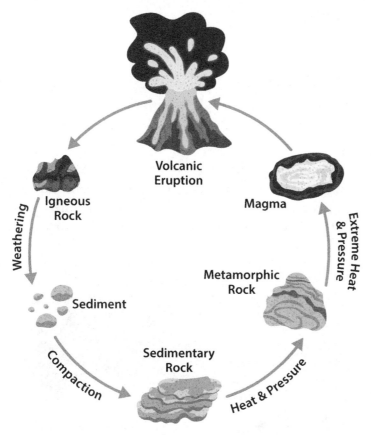

Figure 8.11. The Rock Cycle

The surface of the earth is made of large plates that float on the less dense layer beneath them. These TECTONIC PLATES make up the lithosphere, the planet's surface layer. Over 200 million years ago, the continents were joined together in one giant landmass called Pangea. Due to continental drift, or the slow movement of tectonic plates, the continents gradually shifted to their current positions.

The boundaries where plates meet are the locations for many geologic features and events. Mountains are formed when plates collide and push land upward, and trenches form when one plate is pushed beneath another. In addition, the friction created by plates sliding past each other is responsible for most EARTHQUAKES.

VOLCANOES, which are vents in the earth's crust that allow molten rock to reach the surface, frequently occur along the edges of tectonic plates. However, they can also occur at hotspots located far from plate boundaries.

The outermost layer of the earth, which includes tectonic plates, is called the LITHOSPHERE. Beneath the lithosphere are, in order, the ASTHENOSPHERE, MESOSPHERE, and core. The CORE includes two parts: the outer core is a liquid layer, and the inner core is composed of solid iron. It is believed the inner core spins at a rate slightly different from the rest of the planet, which creates the earth's magnetic field.

Example

16. The type of rock that forms when lava cools and solidifies is

   (A) igneous

   (B) sedimentary

   (C) metamorphic

   (D) sandstone

   (E) marble

Hydrology

The earth's surface includes many bodies of water that together form the **HYDRO-SPHERE**. The largest of these are the bodies of salt water called **OCEANS**. There are five oceans: the Arctic, Atlantic, Indian, Pacific, and Southern. Together, the oceans account for 71 percent of the earth's surface and 97 percent of the earth's water.

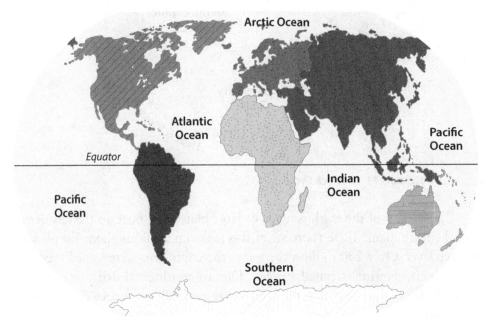

Figure 8.12. The Earth's Oceans

Oceans are subject to cyclic rising and falling water levels at shorelines called **TIDES**, which are the result of the gravitational pull of the moon and sun. The oceans also experience **WAVES**, which are caused by the movement of energy through the water.

Other bodies of water include **LAKES**, which are usually freshwater, and **SEAS**, which are usually saltwater. **RIVERS** and **STREAMS** are moving bodies of water that flow into lakes, seas, and oceans. The earth also contains **GROUNDWATER**, or water that is stored underground in rock formations called aquifers.

Much of the earth's water is stored as ice. The North and South Poles are usually covered in large sheets of ice called **POLAR ICE**. **GLACIERS** are large masses of ice and snow that move. Over long periods of time, they scour Earth's surface, creating features such as lakes and valleys. Large chunks of ice that break off from glaciers are called **ICEBERGS**.

The **WATER CYCLE** is the circulation of water throughout the earth's surface, atmosphere, and hydrosphere. Water on the earth's surface **EVAPORATES**, or changes from a liquid to a gas, and becomes water vapor. Plants also release water vapor through **TRANSPIRATION**. Water vapor in the air then comes together to form **CLOUDS**. When it cools, this water vapor condenses into a liquid and falls from the sky as **PRECIPITATION**, which includes rain, sleet, snow, and hail. Precipitation replenishes groundwater and the water found in features such as lakes and rivers, thus starting the cycle over again.

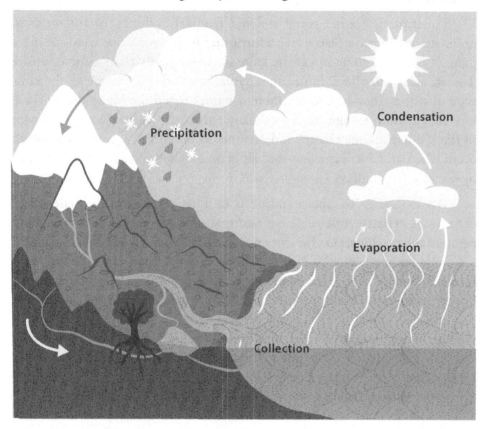

Figure 8.13. The Water Cycle

Example

17. During the water cycle, groundwater is replenished by

   (A) transpiration

   (B) glaciers

   (C) lakes

   (D) evaporation

   (E) precipitation

Meteorology

Above the surface of Earth is the mass of gases called the **ATMOSPHERE**. The atmosphere includes the troposphere, which is closest to the earth, followed by the stratosphere, mesosphere, and thermosphere. The outermost layer of the atmosphere is the exosphere, which is located 6,200 miles above the surface. Generally, temperature in the atmosphere decreases with altitude. The **OZONE**

HELPFUL HINT

Between each layer, a boundary exists where conditions change. This boundary takes the first part of the name of the previous layer followed by *pause*. For example, the boundary between the troposphere and stratosphere is called the *tropopause*.

LAYER, which captures harmful radiation from the sun, is located in the stratosphere.

The humidity, or amount of water vapor in the air, and the temperature are two major atmospheric conditions that determine WEATHER, the day-to-day changes in atmospheric conditions. A warm front occurs when warm air moves over a cold air mass, causing the air to feel warmer and more humid. A cold front occurs when cold air moves under a warm air mass, causing a drop in temperature.

Sometimes, weather turns violent. Tropical cyclones, or HURRICANES, originate over warm ocean water. Hurricanes have destructive winds of more than 74 miles per hour and create large storm surges that can cause extensive damage along coastlines. Hurricanes, typhoons, and cyclones are all the same type of storm; they just have different names based on where the storm is located. Hurricanes originate in the Atlantic or Eastern Pacific Ocean, typhoons in the Western Pacific Ocean, and cyclones in the Indian Ocean. TORNADOES occur when unstable warm and cold air masses collide and a rotation is created by fast-moving winds.

The long-term weather conditions in a geographic location are called CLIMATE. A CLIMATE ZONE is a large area that experiences similar average temperature and precipitation. The three major climate zones, based on temperature, are the polar, temperate, and tropical zones. Each climate zone is subdivided into subclimates that have unique characteristics. The tropical climate zone (warm temperatures) can be subdivided into tropical wet, tropical wet and dry, semiarid, and arid. The temperate climate zones (moderate temperatures) include Mediterranean, humid subtropical, marine West Coast, humid continental, and subarctic. The polar climate zones (cold temperatures) include tundra, highlands, nonpermanent ice, and ice cap. Polar climates are cold and experience prolonged, dark winters due to the tilt of the earth's axis.

HELPFUL HINT

Most of Earth's atmosphere is composed of nitrogen (78 percent) and oxygen (21 percent). Other elements and compounds including argon, water, carbon dioxide, and methane make up the remaining 1 percent.

Example

18. Which gas is found in large quantities in Earth's atmosphere?
    (A) carbon monoxide
    (B) bromine
    (C) nitrogen
    (D) fluorine
    (E) argon

ANSWER KEY

1.   (A) is incorrect. A molecule is the simplest form of a compound, consisting of two or more atoms.

     (B) is correct. An atom is the smallest unit of an element.

     (C) is incorrect. A proton is a positively charged particle in the nucleus of an atom.

     (D) is incorrect. An ion is an electrically charged atom or group of atoms.

     (E) is incorrect. The nucleus is the portion of an atom that contains the protons and neutrons. The nucleus on its own is not an element.

2.   **(A) is correct.** The number of protons in an atom determines which element it is.

     (B) is incorrect. The number of electrons determines the charge of an atom but not its element. Atoms with the same number of electrons can be different elements.

     (C) is incorrect. An atom may carry a charge, but it does not determine what element it is.

     (D) is incorrect. Atomic mass is the sum of the mass of an atom's protons and neutrons. Atoms with the same atomic mass may be different elements.

     (E) is incorrect. The number of valence electrons determines an atom's reactivity, not its identity as an element.

3.   (A) is incorrect. Reactants are the molecules that react in a chemical reaction.

     (B) is incorrect. Products are formed after a chemical reaction.

     (C) is correct. The solute is the material that dissolves in a solution.

     (D) is incorrect. The solvent is the material the solute dissolves into. In this example, the hot water is the solvent.

     (E) is incorrect. The combination of the coffee and the water is a mixture.

4.   (A is incorrect. Melting is the process of solids becoming liquid.

     (B) is incorrect. Deposition is the process of gases becoming solid.

     (C) is incorrect. Evaporation is the process of liquids becoming gas.

     (D) is incorrect. Sublimation is the process of solids becoming gas.

     (E) is correct. The water droplets form when gaseous water in the air comes in contact with the cold glass and condenses into liquid water.

5.   (A) is incorrect. Oxidation is a chemical change in which a substance loses electrons, as happens when iron is exposed to oxygen and rusts.

     (B) is incorrect. Neutralization is a chemical reaction that occurs when an acid and a base react to form a salt and water.

     (C) is correct. Combustion is a chemical reaction that produces carbon dioxide and water. Burning lamp oil (fuel) is combustion.

(D) is incorrect. Sublimation is a physical change that takes place when matter transitions from a solid to a gas.

(E) is incorrect. In a synthesis reaction, two or more reactants combine to form a single product.

6.   (A) is incorrect. Melting is a change in state, which is a physical change.

(B) is correct. Lighting a match results in combustion, a chemical reaction.

(C) is incorrect. Putting sugar in tea forms a solution, which is a physical change.

(D) is incorrect. Boiling is a change in state, which is a physical change.

(E) is incorrect. Slicing bread changes the shape of the material, which is a physical change.

7.   **(A) is correct.** Sodium bicarbonate, which is a base, will neutralize an acid.

(B) is incorrect. Citric acid neutralizes a base spill.

(C) is incorrect. Cat litter may absorb an acid, but it will not neutralize it.

(D) is incorrect. Water is neutral and therefore will not neutralize an acid.

(E) is incorrect. Vinegar is an acid and thus will not neutralize another acid.

8.   **(A) is correct.** Velocity is the speed of an object in a certain direction.

(B) is incorrect. Acceleration describes how quickly an object's velocity is changing.

(C) is incorrect. Mass refers to the amount of matter in an object.

(D) is incorrect. A force causes an object to change speed or direction.

(E) is incorrect. Displacement describes how far an object has moved from its starting point.

9.   (A) is incorrect. Inertia is an object's tendency not to change position or direction unless an outside force acts upon it.

(B) is correct. Friction occurs when motion is impeded because one object is rubbing against another object.

(C) is incorrect. Velocity is the rate at which an object is displaced from its original position.

(D) is incorrect. Gravity is a force that attracts objects to one another.

(E) is incorrect. Tension is the force caused by pulling an object or hanging an object from a rope.

10. (A) is incorrect. A plane flying through the sky would have kinetic energy because of its mass and velocity.

(B) is correct. Something that is not moving has zero velocity; therefore, it has no kinetic energy.

(C) is incorrect. Even though it has a low mass and a low velocity, a ladybug does have a small amount of kinetic energy.

(D) is incorrect. A meteorite falling toward the earth would have a large amount of kinetic energy because of its mass and velocity.

(E) is incorrect. A moving car will have some amount of kinetic energy.

11. (A) is incorrect. Waves on the surface of the ocean are transverse waves.

(B) is incorrect. Light waves are transverse waves.

(C) is correct. Sound waves are longitudinal waves because the vibrations travel in the same direction as the energy.

(D) is incorrect. X-rays are electromagnetic waves, which are transverse.

(E) is incorrect. Microwaves are electromagnetic waves, which are transverse.

12. **(A) is correct.** The light of the sun hits rain droplets and bends into a band of colors. The bending of waves is refraction.

(B) is incorrect. Echo is an example of sound reflection.

(C) is incorrect. A mirror is used to show light reflection.

(D) is incorrect. The Doppler effect describes the change in pitch caused by moving sources of sound waves.

(E) is incorrect. The perceived volume of a sound wave relates to its amplitude.

13. (A) is incorrect. Protons remain in the nucleus of an atom.

(B) is incorrect. Neutrons remain in the nucleus of an atom.

(C) is correct. Electrons are negatively charged subatomic particles that exist outside the nucleus of an atom. A power source forces moving electrons through a circuit.

(D) is incorrect. The nucleus is the part of an atom that contains protons and neutrons.

(E) is incorrect. An ion is a charged atom or molecule. The movement of only electrons creates electricity.

14. **(A) is correct.** Magnets readily attract iron.

(B) is incorrect. Not all metals are attracted to magnets; copper is not.

(C) is incorrect. Silver is not attracted to magnets.

(D) is incorrect. Gold is not attracted to magnets.

(E) is incorrect. Platinum is not attracted to magnets.

15. (A) is incorrect. An aurora occurs when particles from the solar wind are trapped in the earth's magnetic field.

(B) is incorrect. A lunar eclipse is when the earth moves between the moon and the sun, blocking moonlight.

(C) is incorrect. A black hole is a massive star with a gravitational field so strong that light cannot escape.

(D) is correct. When the moon moves between the earth and the sun, a solar eclipse occurs, blocking sunlight from the planet.

(E) is incorrect. The seasons are caused by the tilt of the earth's axis.

16. **(A) is correct.** Igneous rocks form when liquid rock cools and solidifies.

    (B) is incorrect. Sedimentary rocks form when sediments are cemented together.

    (C) is incorrect. Metamorphic rocks form when igneous or sedimentary rocks are exposed to extreme temperature and/or pressure to the point that the rocks are changed physically or chemically.

    (D) is incorrect. Sandstone is a type of sedimentary rock.

    (E) is incorrect. Marble is a type of metamorphic rock.

17. (A) is incorrect. Transpiration is the process through which water is released by plants as vapor.

    (B) is incorrect. Glaciers are large masses of ice; they do not contribute to the groundwater supply.

    (C) is incorrect. Lakes are large bodies of water; they do not contribute to the groundwater supply.

    (D) is incorrect. Evaporation is the process through which water becomes water vapor in the air.

    (E) is correct. Precipitation such as rain and snow seep into the ground to add to the groundwater supply.

18. (A) is incorrect. Carbon monoxide is a rare gas.

    (B) is incorrect. Bromine is a rare gas.

    (C) is correct. Nitrogen makes up 78 percent of Earth's atmosphere.

    (D) is incorrect. Fluorine is a rare gas.

    (E) is incorrect. Argon is found in only small amounts in Earth's atmosphere.

9

TABLE READING

The table reading section of the AFOQT gauges a candidate's ability to visually process information provided in a table. The test will present a series of tables, each of which is followed by a set of questions. The questions will provide a column and a row, and the candidate needs only to find the value in the cell of the table that corresponds to the given column and row.

Candidates must process the information quickly—only seven minutes are given to answer forty multiple-choice questions. The score from this test is used in combination with other scores to determine eligibility for Air Force training as a Pilot, Combat Systems Officer (CSO), and Air Battle Manager (ABM). Candidates taking the test are not allowed to have a straight edge or any additional devices to assist in aligning a row or column when answering the questions.

STRATEGIES

The strategy for Table Reading questions is simple: for each question on the test, identify the column value and the row value, and then find the value where that column and row meet. Lastly, find the correct value in the list of answer choices.

	Column 1	Column 2	Column 3	Column 4
Row 1				
Row 2				
Row 3				
Row 4				
Row 5				

Figure 9.1. Table

The best strategy to prepare for the AFOQT Table Reading test is simply to practice reading and identifying values in a table. Use a timer when practicing and aim to take no more than ten seconds per question. This will allow for a few minutes at the end of the section to check answers.

HELPFUL HINT
Don't be afraid to use your hands and fingers to mark columns or to hide rows as you work.

The tables will cover a variety of topics. Several will have an *x*-value for each column and a *y*-value for each row. For these tables, the questions will simply be a list of paired (x, y) values. Other tables will cover topics like measurements, prices, or locations, and may be related to a military topic (although no outside knowledge will be needed to answer the questions).

Example

x-value

		0	2	4	6	8	10
	0	0.25	3.21	5.67	0.34	12.00	4.23
	2	4.03	102.36	87.94	0.06	14.08	8.01
y-value	**4**	56.91	15.05	0.87	115.35	48.74	0.11
	6	12.12	0.44	15.49	122.80	0.78	5.21
	8	89.47	144.12	1.06	6.49	66.28	0.52
	10	15.28	4.69	100.38	0.51	34.76	0.81

	x	*y*	**(A)**	**(B)**	**(C)**	**(D)**	**(E)**
1.	4	2	15.05	87.94	0.06	15.49	66.28
2.	2	8	48.74	89.47	144.12	0.44	14.08

ANSWER KEY

1. (B)

2. (C)

INSTRUMENT COMPREHENSION

The questions on the Instrument Comprehension section of the AFOQT test candidates' ability to understand basic cockpit instruments. The test includes twenty-five questions with a five-minute time limit, so questions need to be answered quickly. Each multiple-choice question will show two figures: an artificial horizon and a compass. The artificial horizon will show the attitude of the aircraft, providing information on the aircraft's pitch and bank. The compass displays heading information. The answer choices will show four aircraft silhouettes, one of which matches the attitude and heading shown in the question.

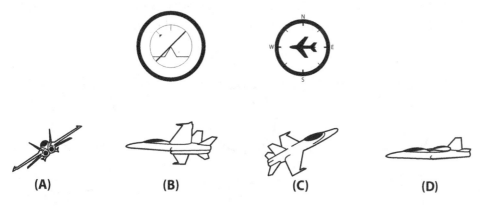

Figure 10.1. Instrument Comprehension Example Problem

In the example above, the artificial horizon shows that the plane is in level flight and banking right. The compass gives the plane's heading as west. These instrument readings correspond to plane B. Plane A is in level flight, but is banking left and heading north. Plane C is banking right, but is climbing and heading east. Finally, plane D is in level flight headed west, but is not banking.

READING THE ARTIFICIAL HORIZON

The artificial horizon is a representation of the attitude of the aircraft, which includes the aircraft's pitch and bank. Pitch is the nose up or down attitude of the plane in relation to the horizon, while bank (or roll) is the relationship of the line drawn from wingtip to wingtip and the horizon. The instrument display will include an aircraft in its center that remains fixed and a line representing the horizon that moves to show the relationship of the plane to the horizon. The instrument also includes an arrow that shows the aircraft's bank.

To read the instrument, start by determining pitch, which describes the attitude of the plane's nose relative to the horizon. If the horizon line passes through the aircraft depiction in the center of the instrument, the plane is level. If it is below, the plane is climbing, and the nose will be higher than the tail. If the horizon is above the aircraft depiction, the plane is descending and the nose will be lower than the tail. If the horizon is at an angle, reference the point in the center of the horizon line from left to right on the instrument and compare it to the aircraft depiction. The farther the horizon line is from the center of the instrument, the more the airplane is pitched.

Next, determine the bank, or relative wing level (low or high). Bank can be determined by referencing the tilt of the horizon. If the horizon is higher on the right, the plane is turning right, and the answer will show the right wing low. Conversely, if the horizon is higher on the left, the plane is turning left, and the answer will show the left wing down. The wings will be opposite the horizon. A level horizon means there is no bank, and the wings will also be level.

HELPFUL HINT

Remember, the wings and the horizon will be opposite. If the horizon is lower on the left, the right wing of the airplane in the answer will be lower.

The arrow shown on the artificial horizon can also be used to determine pitch. If the arrow is centered in the display, the plane is not banking. The arrow will be left of center if the plane is banking right, and right of center if the plane is banking left.

| Descending | Climbing | Level flight |
| Banking left | No bank | Banking right |

Figure 10.2. The Artifical Horizon

The pitch of the airplane in the answers can be identified by referencing an imagined line between the nose and tail of the plane. If the line is level, the plane is flying straight and level. If the line is higher at the nose, the plane is climbing. If the line is lower at the nose, the plane is descending. Pitch can be a little harder to determine if the plane is oriented directly in or out of the picture, but close examination will show if the nose is higher, lower, or even with the tail.

Next, determine bank angle by looking at the relative position of the wings. One wing will be higher or lower than the other, or both wings will be even.

READING THE COMPASS

The compass figure displays heading information. The compass display will show an arrow or a plane that points in the direction the aircraft is traveling and will include the four cardinal directions (north, south, east, and west) and the four intercardinal directions (northeast, northwest, southeast, and southwest).

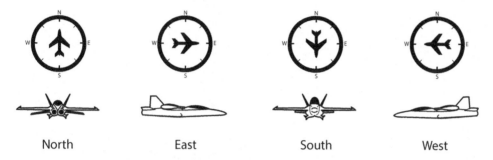

| North | East | South | West |

Figure 10.3. The Compass

In the correct answer choice, the nose of the aircraft will point in the direction indicated by the arrow in the compass. When looking at the aircraft silhouette, candidates are always looking north. Thus a plane heading north will look like it is flying into the page, and a plane heading south will appear to be flying out of the page. An aircraft headed east will have its nose pointed to the right, and an aircraft headed west will have its nose pointed left.

11

BLOCK COUNTING

The Block Counting chapter of the exam tests candidates' ability to quickly analyze spatial relationships. Candidates are asked to examine a stack of blocks and to determine how many blocks are touching certain numbered blocks. Each stack of blocks will include five numbered blocks, and the answer choices for that figure will be presented in table format. Candidates will have four and a half minutes to answer thirty questions, which equates to answering roughly seven questions a minute.

Example

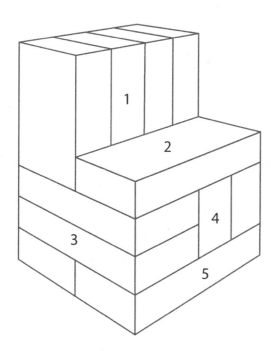

Block	A	B	C	D	E
1	4	2	1	3	9
2	5	3	7	3	4
3	7	2	6	8	4
4	6	5	7	4	8
5	5	4	2	1	7

Practice is the best way to improve on the Block Counting test. Speed is important, so the more comfortable candidates are with the test format, the more questions can be answered. Here are a few strategies for answering questions quickly:

- All blocks are the same size and shape.
- Candidates should focus on the numbered block in question rather than looking at the whole stack of blocks in the graphic.
- The blocks should be counted in the same order for each question: blocks on (1) top, (2) right, (3) left, and (4) bottom of the numbered block.
- Answer choice tables should be read carefully. Candidates may cover unneeded rows if the extra numbers are confusing.
- There is no penalty for wrong answers, so all questions should be answered.

ANSWER KEY

1. (A)

2. (C)

3. (E)

4. (C)

5. (B)

12

AVIATION INFORMATION

This Aviation section tests knowledge of topics related to aircraft operations, including the physics of flight, aircraft performance and structures, airfield and airspace operations, flight controls, and instrument comprehension, as well as a brief history of aviation.

THE PHYSICS OF FLIGHT

A successful aircraft flight is the result of an understanding of the scientific theories and principles involved in moving 300 to 400 tons of machinery through the skies at speeds ranging from 100 to 750 miles per hour (mph). Newton's laws of motion, Newton's law of universal gravitation, and Bernoulli's principle, along with weight, balance, the factors that constitute the flight envelope, and the axes of an aircraft all play a part in aeronautics.

Newton's Laws of Motion

Isaac Newton's three laws of motion detail the fundamental mechanics of motion. The first law focuses on inertia, the second law defines when an accelerated motion is applied to a force, and the third law explains the relationship of motion between any two objects.

NEWTON'S FIRST LAW OF MOTION, also called the LAW OF INERTIA, states that an object at rest will stay at rest, and an object in motion will remain in motion at a constant velocity unless acted upon by an unbalanced force. The unbalanced force may be any force, such as gravity or friction. For example, a ball sitting on the floor will remain still unless a force is exerted upon it—a kick from a foot, a push from a hand, or a strong wind moving it.

There are four types of friction:

- SLIDING, or KINETIC, FRICTION results when the surface of one object slides along the surface of another object. This is commonly seen when pushing a solid object, such as a plate or book along a tabletop.

HELPFUL HINT

Inertia is the tendency of an object to resist changes in velocity whether the object is in motion or motionless.

- **FLUID FRICTION** is the resistance on an object when it is moved through either air (gas) or water (liquid). This is witnessed when a fish moves through water, a bird flies through air, or an airplane creates drag.

- **ROLLING FRICTION** is similar to sliding friction except rolling friction occurs when an object rolls—instead of slides—across a surface. This is observed when a bowling ball rolls down an alley. The ball, once pushed, moves at a particular rate, or velocity, while also resisting that movement due to qualities of the surface on which it is rolling.

- **STATIC FRICTION** is what keeps an object at rest when that object is acted upon by an external force. A trash can initially remains in place due to static friction when an attempt is made to drag it across a floor.

As an example of the four frictions, if a car is traveling at 40 mph, the passengers and contents inside the car are also moving at a rate of 40 mph, until the driver applies the brakes to avoid a collision with a tree. If the passengers are not restrained by seat belts, the full effects of a collision pass from the vehicle to them as well as to the contents of the vehicle. The tires of the vehicle rolling along the road overcome rolling friction. The vehicle counteracts fluid friction from any oncoming wind. When the driver applies the brakes, the wheels may stop rolling but the car skids along the surface of the road, exemplifying sliding friction. At the moment of the car's impact with the tree, objects inside the vehicle overcome static friction as they scatter.

NEWTON'S SECOND LAW OF MOTION states that when a body is acted upon by a constant force, its resulting acceleration is inversely proportional to the mass of the body and directly proportional to the applied force.

The net force of an object is equal to the product of the mass of the object and the acceleration. The equation to determine the amount of force is $F = ma$. One unit of force (F) is defined as Newtons (N). Mass is weighed in kilograms (kg) and acceleration is measured in meters per second per second (m/s/s or m/s^2).

NEWTON'S THIRD LAW OF MOTION states that if two objects interact, the force exerted by the first object on the second object is equal in magnitude and opposite in direction to the force exerted by the second object on the first object.

For example, the force exerted by a tennis racket hitting a tennis ball is equal in magnitude and opposite the force exerted by the ball on the tennis racket. Likewise, during a launch of a rocket into space, the gases expelled under the rocket exert enough force to cause the rocket to lift off the launchpad in the opposite direction.

Example

1. Consider an object acted on by only two forces, as shown below. If the magnitudes of F_1 and F_2 are equal, which of the following statements is true?

    (A) The velocity of the object must be zero.

    (B) The velocity of the object must be constant.

    (C) The velocity of the object must be increasing.

    (D) The velocity of the object must be decreasing.

    (E) The object must remain stationary.

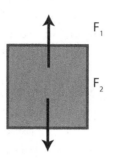

Newton's Law of Universal Gravitation

Isaac Newton's law of universal gravitation states that a particle attracts every other particle in the universe with a force that is directly proportional to the product of their masses and inversely proportional to the square of the distance between them. This law helps scientists understand the effects of gravity on aircraft during flight, because the gravitational force between two objects increases with mass and decreases with distance.

Example

2. Consider two objects a distance d apart. According to Newton's law of universal gravitation, what happens to the force between the two objects if the distance (d) is increased by a factor of 4?

    (A) The force decreases by a factor of 4.

    (B) The force increases by a factor of 4.

    (C) The force increases by a factor of 2.

    (D) The force decreases by a factor of 16.

    (E) The force decreases by a factor of 32.

Bernoulli's Principle

Mathematician and physicist Daniel Bernoulli devised the following principle in relation to hydrodynamics: within a horizontal flow of fluid, points of faster fluid speed will experience less pressure than points of slower fluid speed.

This principle is imperative when analyzing the flow of hydraulic fluids through an aircraft. An accurate pressure flow of fluids is essential to the intricate operation of braking and flight control systems.

Bernoulli's principle also applies to airflow during the basic phases of flight: takeoff, in-flight, and landing. The curvature of an airplane wing causes air to pass faster over the top of the wing (creating a lower pressure area) than under the wing (a higher pressure area). During takeoff, this produces the lift an airplane requires. During flight and when landing, the aircraft must compensate for and utilize all four forces of flight: WEIGHT (the force of gravity pushing the aircraft down), LIFT (the force required to raise the aircraft), THRUST (the force applied in order to move the aircraft forward), and DRAG (the force that slows the aircraft down in preparation for landing).

Example

3. Which statement is true about fluid pressure according to Bernoulli's principle?

    (A) Fluids moving at a point in a horizontal pipe at a higher speed have lower pressure than fluids moving at a point at a slower speed.

    (B) Fluids moving at a point in a horizontal pipe at a higher speed have higher pressure than fluids moving at a point at a slower speed.

    (C) Fluids moving along a vertical pipe at a slower speed have higher pressure than fluids moving along at a higher speed.

    (D) Horizontal and vertical pipe fluid pressure levels do not change.

    (E) The fluid pressure at constricting points along a pipe does not differ from the fluid pressure at free-flowing areas of that pipe.

Aircraft Weight and Balance

The calculation of an aircraft's weight and balance must be identified during preflight. It is important that the combination of passengers, baggage, usable and unusable fuel or fluids, and cargo are within established weight and balance limits. A predetermined *empty weight center of gravity (EWCG)* is provided by the aircraft's manufacturer along with a weight limit, which is specific to each aircraft.

The following are acronyms of other weight specifications:

- **MANUFACTURER'S EMPTY WEIGHT (MEW)** is the total weight of the aircraft as it was built. This includes systems and components required for the aircraft to operate. It does not include the weight of baggage, passengers, or either usable or unusable fuel or fluids.

- **OPERATING EMPTY WEIGHT (OEW)** is the MEW plus the weight of the crew, fluids, unusable fuel, and the equipment required for flight. It does not include baggage, passengers, or usable fuel.

- **ALL-UP WEIGHT (AUW)**, or **AIRCRAFT GROSS WEIGHT (AGW)**, is the total aircraft weight at any given moment during a flight. The AUW decreases as fuel and fluids are consumed during the operation of the flight.

- **MAXIMUM LANDING WEIGHT (MLW)** is an aircraft's weight limit for landing. Exceeding this weight increases stress on the landing gear and may affect the distance required for a safe landing.

- **MAXIMUM ZERO FUEL WEIGHT (MZFW)** is the permissible weight of an aircraft with its contents and includes unusable fuel. The total MZFW excludes the weight of usable fuel on board and any consumable fluids.

- **Maximum takeoff weight (MTOW)** is an aircraft's weight limit for takeoff. Exceeding this limit increases the power required for takeoff, lengthens the runway distance needed for a successful lift off, and places excess stress on the aircraft structure.

- **Maximum ramp weight (MRW)** is the weight limit for an aircraft to taxi or be towed on the ground.

HELPFUL HINT
Takeoff weight is determined by totaling the OEW, the cargo, the passengers, the baggage, and the taxi, flight, and reserve fuel requirements.

Example

4. Why is it important for an airplane not to exceed the MLW limit?

   (A) All-up weight is calculated correctly.

   (B) Most airplanes do not have to consider MLW.

   (C) Undue stress may be placed on the landing gear system while landing.

   (D) The airplane may not have enough fuel for the scheduled flight.

   (E) The airplane can land on any runway length.

The Flight Envelope

The **flight envelope** encompasses the limits of speed, altitude, and angle of attack required by any aircraft to maintain a stable flight. An incorrect combination of these factors may result in a stall, during which the aircraft experiences a decrease in lift and a reduction in airspeed.

The **angle of attack (AOA)** is the angle between the direction of the airflow against the wing and the **chord**, an imaginary reference line that extends from the leading edge to the trailing edge of the wing.

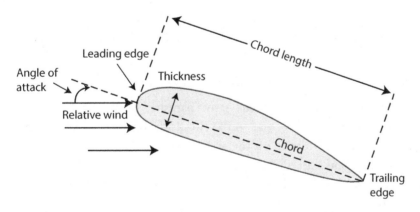

Figure 12.1. Identifying the AOA

An aircraft's airfoil section (wing) is designed for maximum lift and fuel efficiency. An aircraft wing is curved along its front, leading edge, which creates low pressure above and high pressure below as air passes by the wing. As air passes over the end of the wing, or over the end of a helicopter rotor blade, it changes direction, a deflection called **downwash**. This deflection of air downward helps produce lift. This is clearly visible when a helicopter hovers above water.

The air deflected off the rotor blades accelerates downward, causing outward ripples in the water under the helicopter.

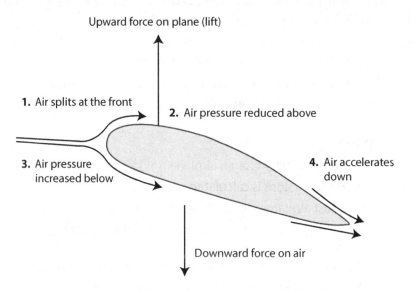

Figure 12.2. Downwash Producing Lift

The trailing edge of a wing has two control parts—ailerons and flaps—which extend outward and in opposite directions to aid the aircraft in rolling. The AILERONS are located from the midpoint of the trailing edge of the wing to the wing's tip. The FLAPS are located from the fuselage (main cabin body) to about the midpoint of the wing. Ailerons and flaps are in a closed position (flush against the wing's surface) during cruising altitude.

To land, the pilot first creates drag to slow the aircraft. SPOILERS are extended upward to help reduce airspeed. As the pilot approaches the runway, the wing flaps are progressively extended too. Once the aircraft is on the ground, raising the spoilers assists in slowing the airplane while the pilot also brakes. The following figure illustrates the positions of the flaps during takeoff, flight, and landing.

Drag is air resistance experienced during flight:

Best efficiency: for climbing, cruising, and descent

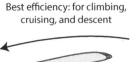

Increased wing area: for takeoff and initial climb

Maximum lift and high drag: approach and landing

Maximum drag and reduced lift: for braking on runway

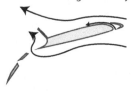

Figure 12.3. Wing Positions during Flight

- **PARASITE DRAG** is just that—any "parasite" on the structure of the aircraft: low air pressure in the tires, skin friction, or anything that increases turbulence on the aircraft. *Skin friction* refers to any rough spot on the skin of the aircraft structure. This, along with rivet heads that may project above the skin, causes resistance to the air current flowing across the wing.

- **PROFILE DRAG** is produced mainly by the shape of the aircraft. A smaller, slimmer aircraft reduces profile drag.

- **INDUCED DRAG** is when, at the back of the wing, air flowing rapidly across the top meets air flowing more slowly underneath, creating a vortex. This type of drag depends on the performance of the aircraft. When lift, airspeed, and AOA increase, induced drag automatically increases too.

Examples

5. What is an example of induced drag?

   (A) a decrease in airspeed

   (B) a decrease in AOA

   (C) a decrease in lift

   (D) an increase in AOA

   (E) the landing gear system set in the UP position

6. When an airplane increases its lift, which statement is true about the air pressure flowing above and below its wings?

   (A) Air pressure is equal above and below the wings since the wings split the air evenly.

   (B) Air pressure is higher above the wings and lower below the wings.

   (C) Air pressure is lower above the wings and higher below the wings.

   (D) Air pressure causes the trailing edges of the wings to extend outward.

   (E) Both B and D are true.

The Axes of an Aircraft

Aircraft fly on a combination of three axes: longitudinal, lateral, and vertical. The **LONGITUDINAL AXIS** (roll) runs lengthwise from the nose (front) of the aircraft to the tail (rear) of the aircraft; the **LATERAL AXIS** (pitch) runs wingtip to wingtip; and the **VERTICAL AXIS** (yaw) runs perpendicular to the wings at the center of the aircraft.

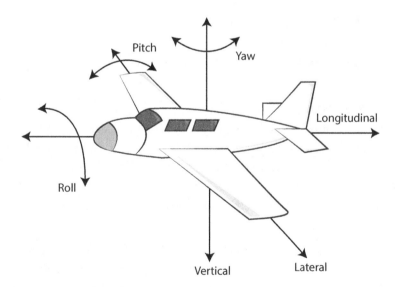

Figure 12.4. Aircraft Axes

Controlling the axes of the aircraft is necessary to keep the aircraft in TRIM, its desired position. **ROLL** along the aircraft's longitudinal axis is controlled by an adjustment of the ailerons, located at the trailing edges of the wings. **PITCH**—

the lateral angle of ascent or descent—is controlled by the elevators, located in the rear portion of the horizontal tail assembly. **YAW** is controlled by the rudder, located in the rear portion of the vertical tail assembly; movement of the rudder causes the nose of the aircraft to move from side to side.

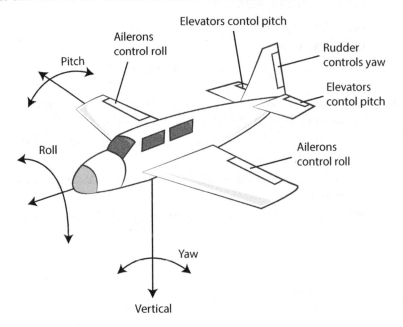

Figure 12.5. Controls for Roll, Pitch, and Yaw

Example

7.   Which components increase the pitch of an airplane?

   (A) the ailerons and elevators along the longitudinal axis

   (B) the ailerons and rudder along the vertical axis

   (C) the elevators along the lateral axis

   (D) the elevators along the longitudinal axis

   (E) the rudder along the longitudinal axis

The Atmosphere

Atmospheric pressure is an extreme concern for a pilot when flying. Air weighs approximately 14.7 pounds per square inch (psi), and flight controls are calibrated for a standard atmosphere. Humidity and low air density levels reduce an aircraft's capability for power, thrust, and lift. When the intake engines receive less air, the propellers are less efficient, and thin air applies less force on the wings, resulting in less than maximum lift.

Altitude, pressure, temperature, and humidity all affect the performance of an aircraft. The **PRESSURE ALTIMETER** in the cockpit is automatically calibrated for 29.92 inches of mercury (Hg). A pilot resets the pressure altitude indicator after departing an airfield to ensure the correct pressure altitude of the aircraft is displayed for the destination airfield (if it is different from the departure airfield). If this is not done, the aircraft may be at a lower altitude than what the altimeter displays.

All aircraft perform more efficiently in colder temperatures because the air is denser than when the air is warm. However, if the temperature drops too low, de-icing of the wings may be required during preflight procedures, extending the time required to complete preflight checks.

Example

8. How does air density affect the performance of an airplane?

    (A) Low air density and humidity increase engine performance.

    (B) High air density decreases engine performance.

    (C) High air density increases engine performance.

    (D) Low temperatures and low air density increase engine performance.

    (E) Temperature and air density have no effect on engine performance.

FIXED-WING AIRCRAFT STRUCTURE

The Fuselage

The **FUSELAGE** of an aircraft is the main section that holds the crew, passengers, and cargo. The wings, tail, engines, and landing gear attach to the fuselage, so this structure must be extremely strong to withstand stresses while minimizing weight. The fuselage also functions in the stabilization of an aircraft during flight.

The two main types of aircraft structures are truss and monocoque. A **TRUSS STRUCTURE** consists of welded steel-tubing longerons separated by diagonal members to endure the loads placed upon the aircraft.

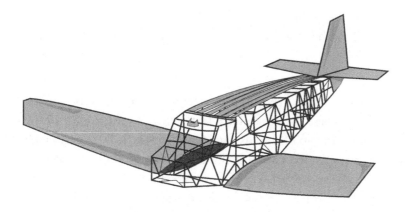

Figure 12.6. Truss Structure

A **MONOCOQUE STRUCTURE** consists of a thin sheet-aluminum alloy curved to fit the shell of the fuselage. This metal skin is designed to withstand the stress of loads and minimize the total weight of the aircraft.

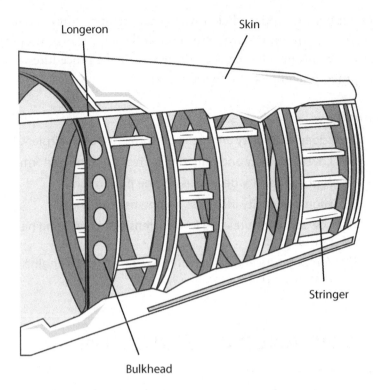

Longeron

Skin

Stringer

Bulkhead

Figure 12.7. Monocoque Structure

Example

9. What considerations do aircraft manufacturers address when selecting materials for a fuselage?

    (A) a large enough area to hold the fuel tanks under the fuselage

    (B) a non-bending material to withstand stress while flying

    (C) a strong plastic framing that does not break easily

    (D) the weight and strength of a material

    (E) both C and D

The Wings

Several designs of wings are in use in aircraft. Wings may be attached to the bottom of the fuselage (what's called a **LOW WING**), to the middle of the fuselage (a **MID WING**), or on top of the fuselage (a **HIGH WING**). If no external braces are required, the wing is of a **CANTILEVER** design. Some smaller fixed-wing aircraft are made with a **SEMI-CANTILEVER** design, meaning external braces are attached to the wings. An aircraft with two levels of wings (one above the other) is called a **BIPLANE**.

Wings also may be **DIHEDRAL** or **ANHEDRAL** to assist with stabilization. Note the angle of the wings in Figure 12.8.

The wings of an aircraft enable lift; the characteristics of the airfoil determine the lift capabilities.

The **CHORD**, touched on earlier, is the imaginary line in an airfoil; it establishes a baseline for the amount of camber and width required of the wing along its wingspan (the distance from one wingtip to the other wingtip). When the measurements of the chord line and the camber line differ greatly, the curvature of the wing will provide more lift.

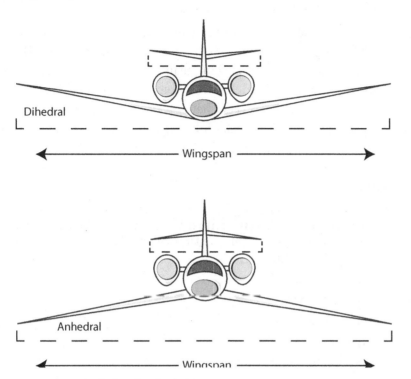

Figure 12.8. Dihedral and Anhedral Wings

THICKNESS is a percentage of the wing chord; it typically ranges from 6.5 to 13.5 percent.

The **CAMBER LINE** is the amount of curvature of the wing. This additional imaginary line runs halfway between the upper and lower surfaces of the wing.

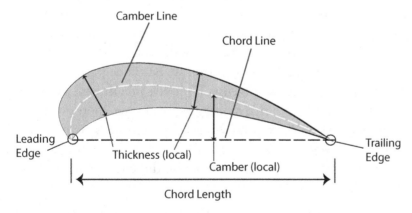

Figure 12.9. Wing Chord Length

There are four types of wing planforms:

- The **RECTANGULAR** is the simplest type, highly inefficient, and typically used for light general aviation.

- The **ELLIPTICAL** is the most efficient style, with the lowest possible induced drag.

- The **TAPERED** is a cross between a rectangular and an elliptical, providing better lift distribution and moderate efficiency. Aircraft with these wings have a wide range of speeds.

- The **SWEPT** is tapered back to reduce drag. This category includes slightly swept, moderately swept, and sharply swept types. The disadvantages of the swept wing planform include its tendency to twist under stress. The delta wing, found on supersonic aircraft, is a highly swept triangular type that is very strong and has the ability to hold a large volume of fuel. Unlike the more standard swept wings, though, the delta has a high incidence of induced drag.

Example

10. Complete the following sentence with the term that establishes the size of the wing and the amount of camber an aircraft requires: *The amount of lift generated is dependent on the difference between the camber line and the _____.*

    (A) anhedral

    (B) wingspan

    (C) chord line

    (D) dihedral

    (E) swept edge

The Powerplant

An aircraft's **POWERPLANT** encompasses the engines and propellers as well as the induction, exhaust, electrical, cooling, lubrication, and fuel systems.

In accordance with Newton's third law of motion, an aircraft must generate enough thrust to create enough lift to overcome the drag produced during flight. Thrust is accomplished by converting an exploding gas-air mixture into mechanical energy in an **ENGINE**. In modern turbofan engines, this mechanical energy turns the fan to produce thrust, much the same as a propeller on a smaller aircraft. The fan or propeller has an airfoil shape which produces "left" in the forward direction, referred to as thrust. Typically, aircraft with a cruising speed not exceeding 250 mph use a *reciprocating engine*. Larger, more powerful aircraft use a *gas turbine engine*. Aircraft traveling at high altitudes (above 30,000 feet) use a *turbo-supercharged reciprocating engine*. Aircraft operating at Mach 1 or higher use a *turbojet engine*; the afterburner on this engine enhances the power to reach such high speeds.

All engines must also meet certain requirements for fuel efficiency. During takeoff, engines operate at maximum performance. The level of power is cut back during the climb and then reduced to a fuel-efficient level when the aircraft levels off at cruising speed.

There are a few types of **PROPELLERS**. The *fixed pitch propeller* is set by the manufacturer. The *variable pitch propeller* allows the pilot to adjust the blade pitch during flight. A *pusher propeller* is installed on the rear of an aircraft and faces to the rear; the thrust created from its rotation pushes instead of pulls the

HELPFUL HINT

Thrust Horsepower equation:

$$thp = \frac{thrust \times aircraft\ speed\ \text{(in mph)}}{375\ pph}$$

thp: thrust horsepower

Aircraft speed: in miles per hour (mph)

pph: pounds per hour

aircraft, contrary to the fixed and variable pitch propellers. The pitch of any style of propeller affects the way it cuts through the air, producing air mass.

Example

11. If an engine produces 3500 pounds of thrust and travels at 500 mph, what is the thp?

(A) 3500 thp

(B) 3550.75 thp

(C) 4000 thp

(D) 4666.67 thp

(E) 7500.25 thp

The Landing Gear

The landing gear must support the weight of an aircraft during takeoff, landing, and ground maneuvering. The styles of landing gear include the following: tail wheel, tandem, and tricycle landing gear.

When an aircraft's main landing gear is positioned forward of its center of gravity, the use of a TAIL WHEEL system is required. This type of landing gear consists of a third wheel assembly, which is beneficial for landing on non-paved runways. Improvements to the assembly allow for steering the tail wheel through the rudder.

TANDEM landing gear has both main and tail portions mounted along the longitudinal axis of the aircraft. This style supports the use of very flexible wings.

TRICYCLE landing gear includes a main gear and a nose gear, which together support increased braking ability, higher landing speeds, and better visibility for ground operations. The nose gear is steered through either mechanical linkage or, in larger aircraft, hydraulic power. Having multiple wheels on each main gear improves safety if one tire fails.

Example

12. Match the type of landing gear (letters A through C) with its design and purpose (numbers 1 through 4). A through C may be attributed to more than one design and purpose.

(A) tail wheel

(B) tandem

(C) tricycle

1. This functional style is helpful when landing on non-paved runways.

2. The main and tail portions of this style are positioned along the longitudinal axis.

3. This style includes nose gear.

4. This style is required when the main landing gear is positioned forward of the aircraft's center of gravity.

The Tail Assembly

The rear portion of an aircraft is the tail assembly (also known as the *empennage*). It provides stability to the aircraft and consists of a rudder, a vertical stabilizer, a horizontal stabilizer, the trim tabs, and two elevators.

The **RUDDER** and the **VERTICAL STABILIZER** are part of the *vertical tail structure*. The rudder is at the rear of the vertical tail structure and is used to keep the aircraft in coordinated flight. The vertical stabilizer, further forward, prevents the aircraft from yawing back and forth.

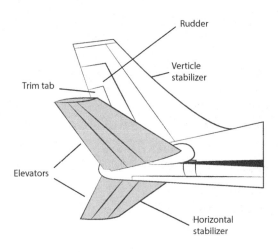

Figure 12.10. Tail Assembly

The **HORIZONTAL STABILIZER** and the **ELEVATORS** are part of the *horizontal tail structure*. The horizontal stabilizer is at the front of the horizontal tail structure; it prevents the aircraft from pitching up and down. The elevators are hinged to the horizontal stabilizer; they direct the up and down motion of the aircraft's nose.

TRIM TABS are on the trailing edges of the wings toward the fuselage, the rudder, and the elevators. Adjusting angles of the trim tabs acts as a secondary flight control system, helping to offset an undesirable attitude of the aircraft and relieving pressure on the controls. Moving trim tabs on the elevators shifts the elevators in the opposite direction: aiming the trim tabs down moves the elevators up, and aiming the trim tabs up moves the elevators down, relieving pressure on the controls. (Trim tabs located on the wings assist with stabilizing the aircraft if a wing dips left or right unnecessarily, maintaining the aircraft's center of gravity.)

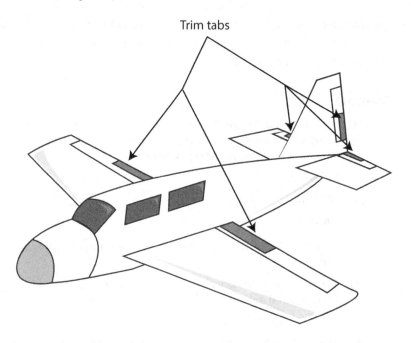

Figure 12.11. Aircraft Trim Tabs

Example

13. What component is designed to relieve pressure on the controls?

    (A) the empennage

    (B) the horizontal stabilizer

    (C) the rudder

    (D) the trim tabs

    (E) the vertical stabilizer

The Flight Controls

Flight control instrumentation devices in the cockpit allow the pilot to manage the performance, attitude, and movement of an aircraft. Every aircraft has both a primary and a secondary flight control system.

The **PRIMARY FLIGHT CONTROL SYSTEM** manages the *ailerons*, *elevators*, and *rudder*. These devices are designed for the safe maneuvering of the aircraft and the elimination of over-controlling measures introduced by the pilot. An input to this system changes the airflow and pressure distribution needed to ensure a smooth flight. As mentioned earlier, all aircraft fly along three axes: longitudinal, vertical, and lateral. A smooth adjustment correcting aircraft movement directly affects roll, pitch, and yaw of the aircraft. The ailerons keep roll in check along the longitudinal axis. The elevators stabilize pitch along the lateral axis. The rudder controls yaw movement along the vertical axis.

The **SECONDARY FLIGHT CONTROL SYSTEM** manages the *wing flaps*, *leading edge devices*, *spoilers*, and *trim tabs*. This system assists the pilot in optimizing aircraft performance during flight. An input to this system increases lift and adjusts drag. During takeoff and landing, a pilot maximizes the airflow needed for lift by adjusting the wing flaps. Devices such as moveable slats are added to the leading edges of the flaps to increase the available AOA and avoid a stall. The trailing edges of the flaps extend from the wings to increase drag and thus slow the aircraft when landing. Spoilers are also used to reduce lift, increase drag, and control speed when descending. Additionally, they assist the aircraft to roll (bank) to the right or left. The trim system, as mentioned earlier, improves the overall attitude of an aircraft by relieving pressure on the controls.

Also inside the cockpit are the throttle, joystick or control wheel, and pedals, which coordinate the movement of the aircraft. The **THROTTLE** increases and decreases power. The **JOYSTICK OR CONTROL WHEEL** directs the aircraft left, right, nose up, and nose down. The **PEDALS** shift the rudder, which moves the aircraft left or right.

Example

14. Which component(s) help optimize the performance of an aircraft as part of the secondary flight control system?

    (A) the elevators

    (B) leading edge devices

    (C) the rudder

    (D) the spoilers

    (E) both B and D

THE FOUR FUNDAMENTAL FLIGHT MANEUVERS

The four fundamentals of flight are STRAIGHT-AND-LEVEL FLIGHT, TURNS, CLIMBS, and DESCENTS.

Straight-and-Level Flight

The key to smooth flight is the handling of the flight controls by the pilot. The controls should be held with a light touch, not gripped strongly. Straight-and-level flight is achieved when the aircraft is in cruising mode and the four forces of flight—weight, lift, thrust, and drag—are in balance. Straight-and-level flight still requires a monitoring of the controls, but it does not necessarily require moving the controls when the aircraft is not set to autopilot. Avoiding rash inputs on the flight controls maintains a smooth flight.

When an aircraft banks, it tends to change attitude while in the turn. After the turn is complete, the altitude indicator (among the flight instruments discussed later) will confirm the aircraft's heading. The pilot must ensure the natural reference point of the horizon and the perpendicular positions of the wings to return to level flight.

Example

15. Which of the following is NOT considered necessary to achieve straight-and-level flight?

    (A) monitoring the controls

    (B) setting the aircraft in cruising mode

    (C) moving the flight controls

    (D) using a light touch

    (E) avoiding rash inputs

Turns

When an aircraft is turned, its ailerons should be banked toward the direction of the turn. The degree of the bank angle determines how much input and adjustment a pilot must make to restore the airplane or helicopter to level flight. The lift force acts at the same angle as the angle of bank to tilt the aircraft away from the vertical. To return to level flight, the vertical lift component must equal the weight of the aircraft. When a pilot pulls back on the stick (or cyclic in helicopters), the total lift is greater than the total aircraft weight, counterbalancing the vertical lift component with the weight to maintain altitude. The horizontal lift component becomes unbalanced and causes the aircraft to accelerate inward to perform the turn.

To perform a turn, the following actions are required.

- The pilot first moves the stick (or cyclic): to the left for left turns or to the right for right turns.

- Enough power or pitching up is also added to counteract the loss of lift.

- The controls are neutralized to stop any increase in the bank angle and to maintain the desired bank angle.
- After the turn is accomplished, the ailerons are leveled to resume flight.

During a turn maneuver, a pilot must maintain visual reference with the horizon and keep alert to the aircraft limits of airspeed and attitude displayed on the flight instruments. Typically, altitude and airspeed decrease in a turn. The elevators are used to hold altitude, and the throttle is used to increase speed. As airspeed and altitude decrease, a stall and loss of lift on the wings may result. In this case, the pilot must lower the AOA by one of several means to apply power.

There are three types of turns: shallow, medium, and steep turns. A SHALLOW TURN consists of a bank of up to 20 degrees; after such a turn, the stability of an aircraft naturally returns it to level flight without pilot interference. The bank of a MEDIUM TURN is between 20 and 45 degrees; the pilot during this turn must input aileron pressure to return the aircraft to level flight. A STEEP TURN includes any bank greater than 45 degrees; after a steep turn the pilot must input opposite pressure on the controls to return the aircraft to level flight.

Example

16. What action must a pilot perform when flying out of a steep turn that is not usually required during a shallow or medium turn?

(A) apply drag by lowering the aileron on the rising wing

(B) decrease airspeed

(C) exceed aircraft limits to finish the turn as soon as possible

(D) ensure a smooth descent

(E) input opposite pressure on the controls

Climbs

A CLIMB is when an aircraft flight path changes from a lower to a higher level in altitude. During this maneuver, a pilot must increase lift to overcome the aircraft's weight. Climbing without increasing thrust results in a decrease in airspeed. The corrective action is to input additional thrust without exceeding the aircraft's maximum power settings.

A NORMAL CLIMB—sometimes referred to as a CRUISE CLIMB—is performed within the aircraft manufacturer's standards; the aircraft increases airspeed, but it may not be operating at its optimum performance. A BEST RATE OF CLIMB (V_y) involves gaining the most altitude in a given amount of time using the most power available to reach cruising altitude. This climb is steeper than a normal climb and results in the greatest altitude gain over a set amount of time. It is used when an aircraft must take off or gain altitude quickly. A BEST ANGLE OF CLIMB (V_x) involves gaining the most altitude over a given distance. This climb is also used during takeoff but especially at airports where there are obstructions in the flight path. Navigating obstacles typically requires this climbing technique.

17. Which statement is correct regarding the best rate of climb?

(A) The least amount of power should be applied.

(B) Obstructions in the flight path require a best rate of climb.

(C) The most altitude in a given amount of time can be obtained.

(D) The best rate of climb accomplishes the best climb angle over a given distance.

(E) A best rate of climb is also referred to as a *cruise climb*.

Descents

The opposite of a climb in aviation is a DESCENT. When lift is decreased, induced drag is minimized, and the aircraft has a tendency to gain airspeed and thrust. Engine power levels must be reduced to maintain airspeed and avoid an excess speed situation.

A PARTIAL POWER DESCENT is the preferred way to decrease altitude. During this type of descent the aircraft should drop at a rate of 500 feet per minute (fpm). A DESCENT AT MINIMUM SAFE AIRSPEED (MSA) is a nose-high controlled descent used to clear obstacles on short approach to a short runway. The aircraft's angle during this descent is steeper than during a partial power descent. An EMERGENCY DESCENT occurs when the aircraft rapidly loses altitude. Emergency procedures dictate the power settings and control positions for all emergency descents.

A fixed-wing aircraft is by design able to GLIDE for a short distance, including during a descent with little or no engine power; gravity naturally takes over. The best glide speed allows for traveling the greatest distance while still airborne.

Example

18. What is the standard rate of descent for a partial power descent?

(A) 100 fpm

(B) 200 fpm

(C) 500 fpm

(D) 1,000 fpm

(E) 1,500 fpm

ROTARY-WING AIRCRAFT

Disclaimer: For the purposes of this section we will be discussing a helicopter with an underslung rotor system and skid-type landing gear. Popular versions of this type of aircraft include the Bell 206B3 (US Army TH-67) and the Bell 205 (US Army UH-1).

Rotary-Wing Aircraft Structure

The major components of a rotary-wing aircraft allow the aircraft to hover and fly directionally. Some of the most vital of these will be detailed in this section.

The **MAST** (also known as the **SHAFT**) is a long cylindrical component that extends vertically from the main rotor transmission up to the **MAIN ROTOR HUB**. The mast is responsible for the rotational drive force that turns the main rotor hub, where all components of the main rotor head are attached. These include the blade grips, the rotor blades, the pitch horn (or yoke), the stabilizer bar and weight (or flybar), and the teeter hinge (or trunnion).

The **BLADE GRIPS** connect the rotor blades to the rotor system. The primary responsibility of the blade grips is to allow the rotor blades to feather. *Feathering* is a term used to describe the change of the blades' angle relative to their rotation plane (also known as *angle of attack*).

ROTOR BLADES are most often made of metal, but as rotorcraft and composite technologies evolve, more rotor blades are being made of composites such as fiberglass or carbon fiber. The rotor blades give a rotary-wing aircraft lift. Shaped much like airplane wings, the airfoils of rotor blades, when spun along a rotational axis, ultimately create lift for the aircraft.

The **PITCH HORN** (or **YOKE**) extends perpendicular to the main rotor blades. It connects directly to the blade grips and stabilizer bar and receives control inputs from the pitch links. Its job is to collect control input from the pilot and translate that input into force, moving the blade grips. This force feathers the blades, or changes their angle of attack.

The **STABILIZER BAR AND WEIGHT** (or **FLYBAR**) help to maintain a constant plane of rotation for the rotor blades. The stabilizer bar is connected to the swashplate (described more fully later in this section) via a series of mechanical linkages, which combine with the stabilizer bar to dampen any over-control by the pilot as well as help the aircraft weather extreme wind gusts, thereby reducing pilot workload.

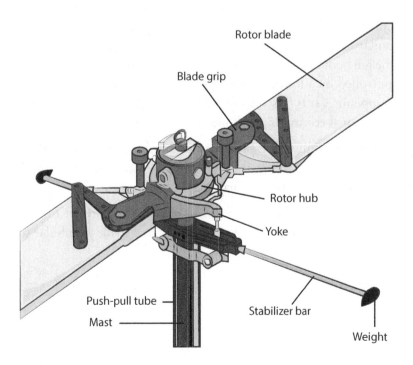

Figure 12.12. Main Rotor System Assembly

The TEETER HINGE (also known as the TRUNNION) connects the mast to the main rotor hub. The teeter hinge allows the rotor hub and blades to flap up or down depending on control input and aerodynamic forces. As one blade rises, the teeter hinge enables the opposite blade to fall in its plane of rotation, much like the up and down of a teeter-totter.

Below the mast and the main rotor hub's components is the main rotor transmission. Mounted to this transmission is the SWASHPLATE, without which directional control of a rotary-wing aircraft would not be possible. Although there are a number of helicopter rotor designs, from the single main rotor to the tandem rotor (like the CH-47 Chinook) to the coaxial rotor (like the Kamov KA-50), all these aircraft have a swashplate. The two primary components of the swashplate—the inner, or non-rotating, swashplate and the outer, or rotating, swashplate—form concentric rings, which rest on a type of bearing. This bearing allows the swashplate to tilt along a horizontal plane as well as move up and down. The mast runs through the center of the swashplate, and as the mast turns, driving the main rotor system, a SCISSORS LINK connected to the mast in turn drives the outer, rotating swashplate. The inner, non-rotating swashplate lifts and tilts, controlling the directional movement of the outer, rotating swashplate, which changes the pitch of the rotor blades.

PITCH LINKS, or PUSH-PULL TUBES, connect to both the rotating swashplate and the stabilizer bar, or directly to the pitch horn. Pitch links are the mechanical linkage that translates pilot input to control the blade's pitch.

The TAIL BOOM is the structural component of the helicopter that supports the tail rotor and in some cases the directional fins.

In a helicopter design known as a NOTAR (no tail rotor), a DUCTED FAN is used in place of a traditional tail rotor to cancel out torque effect or the counter-rotating force applied to the airframe as a main rotor system turns. This ducted fan is usually connected to the engine, and as the fan rotates, it creates thrust similar to that of a rotating propeller. As this thrust is forced through a duct in the tail boom it is vented out the back of the aircraft at a 90-degree angle and is controlled by a louver that allows either more or less air to pass out of the thrust opening. It is this vectored thrust that gives a NOTAR rotary-wing aircraft directional control in the hover and cancels out torque effect.

COWLINGS are removable pieces of an aircraft's outer skin that protect important areas of the aircraft from aerodynamic and environmental forces. They also allow for inspection or maintenance of those areas.

SKIDS, a type of landing gear, allow a rotary-wing aircraft to land safely without damaging its undercarriage. Skids are often made of tubular steel and run parallel to the airframe.

HELPFUL HINT

The tail boom of most light rotary-wing aircraft has almost no internal support structure. On the Bell 206B3 Jet Ranger there is structural reinforcement where the tail boom couples with the fuselage and where the tail rotor gearbox couples with the tail boom, but the rest of the tail boom is hollow.

19. Which rotary-wing aircraft component allows the rotor hub and blades to flap?

(A) the teeter hinge

(B) the rotor hub

(C) the swashplate

(D) the skids

(E) the pitch horn

The Physics of Rotary-Wing Aircraft

Hovering flight is the balance of the four aerodynamic forces—weight, lift, thrust, and drag—at a given period of time. In a rotary-wing aircraft during a hover, these forces are in opposition straight up and straight down. In order for the aircraft to hover, it has to overcome its weight via the generation of lift. If lift is greater than the aircraft's weight, then the helicopter rises from the ground.

A rotary-wing aircraft creates lift via the rotational movement of its airfoils. As its rotor blades turn, the slow-moving high-pressure air below the blades pushes up against the faster-moving low-pressure air above the blades. This upward force is known as the **MAGNUS EFFECT**.

Once the aircraft is airborne, it must produce enough lift and thrust to counteract the weight and drag of the aircraft and keep the aircraft in the air. As long as the helicopter maintains a balance between these forces, it will remain in a stabilized hover, suspended in a column of air created by the rotational movement of the rotor blades. This column of air passing through the rotor blades is known as **INDUCED FLOW**, or downwash.

While the aircraft is in a stabilized hover, it is attempting to counteract another aerodynamic principle of vertical flight: translating tendency. **TRANSLATING TENDENCY** is the tendency of a rotary-wing aircraft to drift laterally due to tail rotor thrust. The tail rotor of a rotary-wing aircraft is used to counteract torque and to provide directional control of the aircraft. As the main rotor blades turn, the airframe wants to rotate opposite to that movement. The tail rotor creates the horizontal thrust necessary to counteract that rotational pull of the airframe, which results in the helicopter drifting laterally—its translating tendency.

GYROSCOPIC PRECESSION is another aerodynamic factor exhibited in rotary-wing aircraft. When a force is applied to a rotating rotor, the force will be felt 90 degrees later in the plane of rotation, just as it would in a gyroscope. For example, if force is applied at the six o'clock position of a counterclockwise spinning component, the force is felt or viewed at the three o'clock position.

HELPFUL HINT

The Magnus effect was first described (though not named) by Isaac Newton in 1672. In fact, in 1742 a British mathematician named Benjamin Robins arguably described the Magnus effect, though only as it relates to the trajectory of a spinning musket ball. However, the force itself would not actually be *called* the Magnus effect until 1852, when German physicist Gustav Magnus officially "discovered" it.

As a rotary-wing aircraft moves forward, the next aerodynamic factor it will encounter is known as **TRANSVERSE FLOW EFFECT**. When the helicopter begins to accelerate, the induced flow created by the lifting action of the rotor blades drops to nearly zero in the front half of the rotor system and increases in the rear half of the rotor system. This drop in induced flow causes the angle of attack in the front half of the rotor system to increase, causing the blades to flap up. In contrast, as the induced flow increases in the rear half of the rotor system, the angle of attack decreases, causing the blades to flap down. Due to gyroscopic precession, the displacement of the flapping blades is not felt until 90 degrees later in the plane of rotation, which causes the rotary-wing aircraft to roll laterally.

TRANSLATIONAL LIFT is another factor that rotary-wing aircraft have to contend with. While a rotary-wing aircraft hovers, the induced flow created is nearly vertical. As this vertical column of air hits the ground, it extends outward in all directions and often is pulled back vertically to be recirculated through the aircraft's rotor system. This movement of air creates vortices at the ends of the rotor blades. It is these vortices that hinder the effectiveness of the rotor system, requiring more power for the aircraft to stay aloft.

To achieve an *effective translational lift (ETL),* the efficiency of the main rotor system must be increased. When an aircraft moves either forward or laterally, it begins to outrun its rotor vortices and thereby creates greater efficiency in the rotor system. The efficiency is not directionally equal, though, since the rotor system does not outrun different vortices at the same time. As the forward half of the rotor system becomes more efficient, the blades flap up, creating more lift and causing the nose of the aircraft to pitch up and, due to gyroscopic precession, to roll laterally. Both transverse flow effect and translational lift can be countered by using the cyclic pitch control (detailed in the upcoming controls section), which can tip the aircraft's plane of rotation.

Lifting forces in the main rotor are not equal at all times either. **DISSYMME-TRY OF LIFT** is an unequal lifting of forces created by the advancing and retreating blades. As a rotary-wing aircraft moves forward through the air, *relative wind* is created, which is the motion of air across an airfoil. As a counterclockwise rotating blade moves an aircraft forward, it encounters fast-moving air along the right-hand side of that aircraft. As it encounters this fast-moving air, more lift is created. Conversely, the leading edge of the airfoil on the left-hand side of the aircraft—the retreating blade—does not run into fast-moving air; therefore lift decreases. Due to this difference in lift between the advancing and retreating halves of the rotor system, the aircraft is inclined to roll toward the left.

One of the things that make a rotary-wing aircraft unique is its ability to autorotate. **AUTOROTATION** is a situation in which the rotor blades are driven by relative wind rather than by the aircraft's powerplant. For example, in the event of an engine failure a pilot can adjust his or her flight controls to allow the induced flow of air through the rotor system to reverse the aircraft's direction. As gravity pulls the aircraft back to the ground, this induced flow can travel vertically through the rotor system and continue to drive the blades in their plane of rotation. As long as the rotor system is turning, the pilot can maintain full directional control of the aircraft and steer it to a suitable landing area. The rotor system stores inertia, giving the pilot an opportunity to cushion the helicopter upon landing. This is a skilled maneuver and if not performed well can cause the rotor system to lose all rotational movement and, in turn, the last remaining vestiges of lift.

Example

20. Which direction will a rotary-wing aircraft roll due to the transverse flow effect?

(A) upside down

(B) vertically

(C) backward

(D) laterally

(E) inverted

Rotary-Wing Aircraft Controls

There are four primary controls of the rotary-wing aircraft. The CYCLIC CONTROL SYSTEM, mounted on the flight deck floor and centered between the pilot's legs, is utilized to adjust the aircraft's pitch and roll axes. A causal effect of the spinning motion of rotor blades is vertical thrust. As the blades spin, a column of air is created that the pilot can manipulate via the use of the helicopter's flight controls. When the cyclic control is pushed forward, the column of air supporting the rotary-wing aircraft is directed aft, creating a forward lift vector that moves the helicopter forward. This cyclic movement is able to change the direction of the lift vector up to 360 degrees around the aircraft, allowing a pilot to hover in one location.

The COLLECTIVE CONTROL, located to the left of the pilot's seat, is used to "collectively" change the pitch of the rotor blades. When the pilot raises the collective, the pitch angle of the blades increases simultaneously. As the pitch angle increases, so does the angle of attack of the blades; this in turn creates more lift. To perform a level climb the pilot simply pulls the collective up; to descend, he or she pushes it down.

Yaw control of the aircraft is adjusted by the use of the TAIL ROTOR PEDALS, or the DIRECTIONAL CONTROLS. Much like the collective control over the main rotor system, the tail rotor pedals change the pitch of the tail rotor blades, causing a larger or smaller horizontal lifting vector.

Many modern rotary-wing aircraft also have a self-governing THROTTLE CONTROL, meaning once the throttle is switched to a flight setting, engine performance is managed by a computer. Smaller as well as some older aircraft have a manual throttle control, which requires the pilot to increase and reduce the throttle to maintain optimal flying parameters. The throttle can be located in a variety of places within the aircraft, but the majority of throttle controls are found on the collective control in the form of an attached twisting grip, very similar to a collar. By twisting this grip, the throttle can be either increased or decreased.

21. Which primary rotary-wing flight control increases the pitch angle of the blades simultaneously?

(A) the cyclic

(B) the directional controls

(C) the ducted fan

(D) the collective

(E) the throttle

FLIGHT INSTRUMENTS

A pilot uses outside visual reference cues against the horizon to maneuver a helicopter. When weather degrades to less than the minimum visual flight rules (VFR), flight instruments must be relied upon for guiding the helicopter along the flight path, providing altitude, heading, and airspeed. The altimeter, the airspeed indicator, and the vertical speed indicator are common pitot-static instruments. A pitot tube and static ports extend outside the aircraft's structure to collect the outside air and static pressure. The air passes through a pitot line to the instruments calibrated to measure the aircraft's altitude and speed.

Altimeter

An altimeter displays the altitude of a helicopter. It computes this by measuring the atmospheric pressure at the aircraft's current altitude and comparing this to a preset value. Air pressure decreases 1 inch of mercury for each 1,000 feet of altitude.

Figure 12.13. Three-Pointer Altimeter

There are three types of altimeters: the three-pointer, the counter drum, and the encoding.

Of the three "hands" on a **THREE-POINTER ALTIMETER**, the longest, thinnest hand displays altitude in tens of thousands of feet; the shortest hand displays thousands of feet; and the medium-length hand displays hundreds of feet. The box on the right side of the altimeter displays the set ground atmospheric pressure. This setting may be adjusted using the knob at the bottom left of the instrument.

The **COUNTER DRUM ALTIMETER** digitally displays the altitude without needing manual figuring. Just as the three-pointer altimeter, it also displays the set ground atmospheric pressure.

Figure 12.14. Counter Drum Altimeter

The **ENCODING ALTIMETER** converts the altitude into a digital code, which is then relayed to ground control radar via a transponder.

Several types of altitudes may be displayed on an altimeter:

- **INDICATED ALTITUDE** is the altitude actually displayed on the altimeter.

- **TRUE ALTITUDE** is the height of the aircraft above mean sea level (MSL).

- **ABSOLUTE ALTITUDE** is the height of the aircraft above ground level (AGL).

- **PRESSURE ALTITUDE** is a pre-calibrated altitude with a standard atmosphere level setting of 29.92 inches of Hg. (This altitude is often used in flight planning calculations.)

- **DENSITY ALTITUDE** is pressure altitude modified for a nonstandard temperature.

Figure 12.15. Encoding Altimeter

Example

22. Air pressure decreases 1 inch of mercury for each _____ feet of altitude.

    (A) 100
    (B) 500
    (C) 1,000
    (D) 1,500
    (E) 2,000

Vertical Speed Indicator

A vertical speed indicator (VSI) displays the vertical speed of an aircraft, in 500-foot increments, measured in thousands of feet per minute, and indicates if the aircraft is climbing, descending, or in level flight, and it shows the rate of climb or descent. The instrument uses a diaphragm to compare the static pressure outside the aircraft to the static pressure surrounding the diaphragm inside the instrument. The difference in the pressures identifies a climb or a descent. When the aircraft is on the ground, the pilot may reset the indicator to zero with a *zeroing screw*.

The VSI does not display in real time; there is typically a six- to nine-second delay, or *lag*, in the reading. *Trend information* (a sudden climb or descent) shows initially, then the feet per minute rate is displayed.

Figure 12.16. Vertical Speed Indicator

Example

23. An increase in the static pressure, as measured around the diaphragm inside the VSI, indicates an aircraft is in which of the following maneuvers?

    (A) a bank
    (B) a climb
    (C) a descent
    (D) a straight-and-level flight
    (E) a yaw

Airspeed Indicator

The airspeed indicator is a differential pressure gauge that determines how fast the aircraft is moving by contrasting the ambient (inside) air pressure with the ram (outside) air pressure using the aircraft's pitot tube and static ports. A diaphragm in the indicator expands and contracts, causing the linkage to the indicator pointer to move. Airspeed is measured in knots, and each level of airspeed is color-coded:

Figure 12.17. Airspeed Indicator

- The **WHITE ARC** displays the flap operating speed. The lower limit of the white arc (V_{SO}) is the stalling speed with the flaps down. The upper limit (V_{FE}), where the white and green arcs meet, indicates the maximum speed at which the flaps can be extended.
    - The **GREEN ARC** displays the aircraft's normal operating range, from the lowest limit (V_{S1}) to the highest limit(V_{NO}), also known as the *maximum structural cruising speed*.
    - The **RED RADIAL LINE** represents the never-exceed speed (V_{NE}).

There are different types of airspeed: **INDICATED AIRSPEED** is what is displayed on the indicator instrument; **CALIBRATED AIRSPEED** is the indicated airspeed corrected for position error; **EQUIVALENT AIRSPEED** is the calibrated airspeed corrected for non-standard pressure; and **TRUE AIRSPEED** is the equivalent airspeed corrected for non-standard density.

Example

24. Which type of airspeed is displayed on the airspeed indicator?
    - **(A)** calibrated airspeed
    - **(B)** equivalent airspeed
    - **(C)** indicated airspeed
    - **(D)** pressure airspeed
    - **(E)** true airspeed

Turn and Slip Indicator

The turn and slip indicator combines a turn indicator pointer and a slip indicator ball (inclinometer) in the same housing to measure the yaw rotation of the aircraft. This instrument indicates if the pilot is making a coordinated left or right standard turn. The turn and slip indicator operates on a gyro in a vertical plane aligned with the longitudinal axis, and displays the bank of the aircraft along its vertical axis as well as the rate at which the aircraft turns. A 360-degree turn completed in 2 minutes, at 3 degrees per second, would be considered a standard turn.

The indicator also displays the direction of the turn the aircraft takes.

- In a **SLIPPING TURN**, there is more bank than needed and gravity is greater than the centrifugal force reaction on the slip indicator ball, thus the ball moves toward the inside of the turn.

- In a **SKIDDING TURN**, the centrifugal force reaction is greater than gravity on the slip indicator ball, and the ball moves toward the outside of the turn.

- In a **COORDINATED TURN**, centrifugal force and gravity react equally on the slip indicator ball, and the ball remains in the lowest part of the glass.

Attitude Indicator

The attitude indicator provides real-time and direct attitude information during changes in an aircraft's pitch (along the lateral axis) and when banking (along the longitudinal axis). It displays the relationship of the aircraft's orientation to an artificial horizon. Modern aircraft may have additional features included in the attitude indicator to assist with flight navigation.

The indicator's **BANK SCALE** represents the sky in blue and the ground/horizon in brown or black. The numbers are in degrees of attitude. The top hashes are degrees of bank, displayed in 30-degree increments. The **POINTER** at the 12 o'clock position of the indicator (an upside down triangle) is used to check the aircraft's position; it turns toward the direction the aircraft banks.

Figure 12.18 displays a straight-and-level flight in progress. If the aircraft is performing, for example, a *level left bank*, the indicator would show the miniature aircraft tilting to the left with the center of the aircraft wings remaining at the horizontal bar. A *climbing right bank* would be displayed with the aircraft's wings above the horizontal bar and the artificial horizon dipping to the left and rising on the right (thus the right wing would be closer to the ground). In a *level climb* or *dive* the wings would be displayed parallel along the horizontal bar, and the aircraft would

Figure 12.18. Attitude Indicator

be moving toward the blue portion of the indicator for a climb or the brown or black portion for a dive.

Magnetic Compass

The magnetic compass is a navigational instrument that displays the cardinal headings (north, south, east, and west) in 30-degree increments. Long vertical hash marks identify 10-degree increments, and short vertical hashes identify 5-degree increments. Due to nearby electromagnetic interference from metal structures and electrical components in an aircraft, COMPASS MAGNETIC DEVIATION exists. This deviation is allowable up to 10 degrees.

When the compass card is not level, the magnets dip downward toward Earth. This process, called MAGNETIC DIP, happens when the aircraft is in a bank toward the west or east or when it is accelerating or decelerating while on a west or east heading. Also, when on a west or east heading, any increase in airspeed during a turn causes the compass to reflect a false turn toward the north. A decrease in airspeed during the turn causes the compass to reflect a false turn toward the south.

Also, it is common for the direction on magnetic compasses to lag when an aircraft makes a turn. For example, when turning left from a north heading, the compass turns right to 30 degrees and will reset itself once 270 degrees is reached. When turning from a south heading, the compass leads at the same rate of location at degrees latitude. If the aircraft was at 40 degrees latitude, the pilot would have to roll back approximately 40 degrees past the south reading.

A number of other variations and errors can occur with a compass. A compass dial aligns itself with the north and south MAGNETIC POLES, not with geographic true north and south. Pilots fly with the aid of sectional charts that use the geographic poles instead. The difference between true north or south and magnetic north or south is called MAGNETIC VARIATION.

To identify the variation (in degrees) between magnetic and geographic north, say, a pilot must convert true north (from the sectional charts) to magnetic north (from the aircraft's magnetic compass). If the magnetic variation is east of true north, the degree of variation is subtracted from the map's true heading. If the magnetic variation is west of true north, that degree of variation is added to the map's true heading. The line where the true north and magnetic north variation is zero degrees is called an AGONIC LINE. Lines where the variation is greater or less than zero degrees are called ISOGONIC LINES.

Compass deviations may be corrected by using an airfield's compass rose. These indications are recorded on a compass compensation card placed near the compass in the cockpit.

Example

27. If the variation between the magnetic north pole and the true north pole is greater than +12 degrees west, how does a pilot adjust for the compass heading?

(A) by adding 6 degrees to the compass heading displayed

(B) by adding 12 degrees to the compass heading displayed

(C) No adjustment is needed; the magnetic compass automatically adjusts for the degree of variation.

(D) by subtracting 6 degrees to the compass heading displayed

(E) by subtracting 12 degrees to the compass heading displayed

---

HELPFUL HINT

Compass deviations are caused by electromagnetic influences on the magnets in the compass.

HELPFUL HINT

East is least, west is best. Subtract the degree of variation if the variation is east of true north; add the degree of variation if the variation is west of true north.

Heading Indicator

The heading indicator is similar to a magnetic compass but functions with a gyroscope and is not subject to the magnetic deviations inherent in magnetic compasses. Direction in this indicator is defined by the aircraft's horizontal plane. When this plane does not match Earth's horizon, a gimbal error exists, called a DRIFT. This drift needs to be corrected every ten to fifteen minutes by confirming the heading using the magnetic compass.

Figure 12.19. Heading Indicator

Example

28. Using Figure 12.19, what is the closest degree heading of this aircraft?
    (A) 0 degrees
    (B) 26 degrees
    (C) 60 degrees
    (D) 120 degrees
    (E) 240 degrees

Vertical Card Compass

A vertical card compass is a dry compass, not a float-type compass. As seen in Figure 12.20, it is etched out in 30-degree increments with 3 representing 30, 6 representing 60, etc., and there is no overshoot with delayed readings. The heading is read from the 12 o'clock position and the nose of the miniature aircraft on the instrument.

Figure 12.20. Vertical Card Compass

Example

29. Using Figure 12.20, what is the degree heading of this aircraft?
    (A) 10 degrees
    (B) 20 degrees
    (C) 100 degrees
    (D) 190 degrees
    (E) 290 degrees

AIRPORTS AND FLIGHT PROTOCOLS

Runway Design and Function

The Federal Aviation Administration (FAA) oversees airport designs and improvements for federal airports, and has established a twenty-year structural design life expectancy for runway pavements. Runway materials must hold up to the stresses placed on them from the weight and impact of aircraft, and foreign object damage (FOD). Runways must also avoid causing undue wear on aircraft tires and provide water runoff and protection from harsh weather conditions.

Currently runways must be 9 to 12 inches deep at regional airfields capable of servicing smaller aircraft. Hub airports frequented by jumbo jets require a

15- to 18-inch depth of pavement. Of the different runway designs, a FLEXIBLE PAVEMENT consists of hot-mix asphalt installed on a base course and subbase, if required. This type of pavement resists cracking (versus rigid pavements). A FULL-DEPTH ASPHALT PAVEMENT contains asphaltic cement as its main material. A RIGID PAVEMENT may use rubberized Portland cement as a subbase. All pavement styles consist of layers: a base course (stabilized), a subbase, and a subgrade, and it is important that loose, gritty material does not exist between the layers.

Runway lengths are dependent on several factors, including the type of aircraft expected to use the runway, the expected maximum takeoff weight (MTOW), the elevation of the airfield, and the maximum local air temperature.

The movement area of an airfield includes the aprons and areas for takeoff, landing, and taxiing. Runway markings are designed to guide an aircraft through a safe landing and takeoff. Runways are defined by their markings, and there are three types.

VISUAL RUNWAY MARKINGS are visible so a pilot can view them as the aircraft approaches the runway. These runways are commonly small airstrips.

A NONPRECISION INSTRUMENT RUNWAY is generally found in small- to medium-size airports and displays a centerline, a threshold mark, and designators, as well as a visual cue called an *aiming point*—a wide strip located on both sides of the runway and approximately 1,000 feet from the landing threshold. This signifies the runway contains navigation facilities for an instrument approach with only horizontal guidance.

A PRECISION INSTRUMENT RUNWAY, found in larger airports, displays all the same markings of a nonprecision instrument runway as well as a touchdown zone and side stripes. This type of runway also contains an *instrument landing system (ILS)* or *precision approach radar (PAR)*. An ILS approach receives radio responses that provide both vertical and horizontal guidance (if a pilot is too low or too high, or too far left or right, as the aircraft approaches). Additionally, a runway number identifies the approach direction as read from a magnetic azimuth and left, center, and right designations identify parallel runways.

Along with physical design, features such as approach lighting and instrumentation requirements limit the type of aircraft a runway may service. RUNWAY END IDENTIFICATION LIGHTS (REILs) are synchronized illuminated lights placed on each side of the runway threshold to help a pilot identify the approach end of a runway. Additionally, the lights at the end of the runway are red, and outward from the runway end they are green, to indicate the threshold. RUNWAY EDGE LIGHTS identify the edges of the runway. These are of variable intensity and white in color, although instrument runways have yellow edge lighting along the last 2,000 feet, or half the length of runway, whichever is less.

An APPROACH LIGHT SYSTEM (ALS) assists a pilot in transitioning from instrument flight to visual flight for landing. Some airports have the flashing lights blink sequentially to guide a pilot to the end of the runway under instrument landings. A VISUAL APPROACH SLOPE INDICATOR (VASI) will assist with descents during visual landings. Each indicator has a white light on the upper portion and a red light on the lower portion to identify to the pilot his or her position along the glide path to the runway.

Example

30. Which answer lists different types of marked runways?

(A) approach, instrument, and visual

(B) FOD, REIL, and VASI

(C) precision instrument, non-precision instrument, and visual

(D) REIL and visual

(E) VASI, precision non-instrumentation, and visual

Airspace

Controlled airspace is the area controlled and maintained by the FAA-regulated air traffic control (ATC) service. This service controls the movement of all aviation assets within its designated area.

Airspace is divided into six classes by the FAA. (Note that aircraft must have operable equipment and meet certain certification to operate in certain classes. Student and recreational pilots must also be certified to conduct flight operations in certain classes of airspace. Pilots are required to contact the ATC controller to obtain clearance, when necessary, prior to inadvertently entering any controlled airspace.)

- **CLASS A**—Airspace from 18,000 feet MSL to pressure altitude of 60,000 feet, 12 nautical miles (NM) off the coast of the United States, and international airspace beyond 12 NM that is within the navigational signal of ATC radar. All aircraft must operate under instrument flight rules (IFR) at this level.

- **CLASS B**—Airspace from ground level to 10,000 feet MSL surrounding the busiest airports capable of IFR operations and commercial passenger traffic. ATC clearance is required to enter and leave this airspace. Aircraft and pilots must be certified to operate in this airspace.

- **CLASS C**—Airspace from ground level to 4,000 feet above the airport elevation surrounding airports with an operational control tower and serviced by radar approach control, IFR operations, and commercial passenger traffic. Airspace extends from 5 NM radius (surface to 4,000 feet above airport elevation) to 10 NM radius from 1,200 to 4,000 feet. No pilot certification is required to operate in this airspace; however, clearance is required to enter and exit this airspace. A two-way radio and an operable radar beacon transponder with automatic altitude reporting equipment are required.

- **CLASS D**—Airspace from ground level to 2,500 feet above the airport elevation surrounding airports with an operational control tower. Notices to Airmen (NOTAM) identify any specific requirements for pilots to operate in this controlled airspace. A two-way radio is required to operate in this airspace.

- **CLASS E**—Any controlled airspace not included in class A through class D. Special VFR operations are permitted with prior clearance obtained by the controlling facility. Class E airspace is distinguished on sectional charts in blue or magenta, and white on low altitude en route charts. No specific pilot or equipment requirement exists.

- **CLASS G**—Uncontrolled airspace with visibility requirements of 1 mile during the day and 3 miles at night. This airspace is valid for altitudes 1,200 feet AGL to 10,000 feet MSL. Above 10,000 feet, 5 miles of visibility is required day or night. Class G airspace is identified on sectional maps by a faded, thick blue line.

For any airspace, required flight visibility is 3 statute miles, except in Class A and Class E. There are established elevations where aircraft must remain clear of clouds in the controlled airspace. These restrictions are typically 1,000 feet above the clouds, 500 feet below the clouds, and anywhere from 1,000 feet to 1 statute mile when horizontal with the clouds. Obstacles and urban development may preclude the ability to abide by these set restrictions, but a pilot must display good judgment in this case.

Requirements to establish radio communications with a pilot are different among the classes of airspace.

- **CLASSES A AND B**—The ATC controller must verbally grant clearance. Acknowledgment of the aircraft call sign is not considered an established communication.

- **CLASSES C AND D**—If the ATC controller acknowledges with the aircraft call sign, communication is considered established. This is true even if the ATC controller responds with the aircraft call sign and instructs the pilot to "standby."

Example

31. Which of the following statements is true about controlled airspace?

    (A) An operable two-way radio is all that is required for communications in any airspace.

    (B) ATC controllers must verbally grant clearance for entry and exit of Class A and Class B airspaces.

    (C) Controllers of Class A through Class D airspaces may establish communications by acknowledging the pilot with the aircraft call sign.

    (D) Flight visibility required for Class B airspace is 5 NM.

    (E) Pilots must operate under IFR when passing through Class B airspace.

Right-of-Way

All aircraft have an inherent duty to steer clear of other aircraft and hot-air balloons. Steering clear means that an aircraft may not pass over, under, or ahead of another aircraft unless it is well clear. The following six rules establish the right-of-way for certain situations:

1. An aircraft in distress always has the right-of-way over all other air traffic.

2. When two aircraft of the same category approach each other (except head-on) at generally the same altitude, the aircraft on the right has the right-of-way.

3. When approaching aircraft are of different categories, refer to the following list, presented in order of right-of-way:
   - ☐ Hot-air balloons
   - ☐ Gliders
   - ☐ Airships
   - ☐ Powered parachutes
   - ☐ Powered hang gliders and ultra-light aircraft
   - ☐ Airplanes
   - ☐ Rotorcraft

   An exception to this list is an aircraft towing or refueling another aircraft, which has the right-of-way over all other engine-driven aircraft.

4. When two aircraft approach head-on, the pilot of each aircraft should change course to the right.

5. An overtaking aircraft has the right-of-way, and the pilot of the aircraft being overtaken must shift course to the right to stay clear.

6. When landing, an aircraft on final approach or beginning to land has the right-of-way, as long as it does not force an already landed aircraft off the runway. When two aircraft are landing at the same time, the aircraft at a lower altitude has the right-of-way but cannot cut in front of the other aircraft to become the lower level aircraft.

Example

32. Which right-of-way statement is true?
    (A) An aircraft being towed must yield to a rotorcraft when the two aircraft approach each other.
    (B) Aircraft in distress have the right-of-way despite their category.
    (C) A landing aircraft on short final approach may force a landed aircraft to move off the runway.
    (D) Rotorcraft has the right-of-way over a glider when both are approaching at the same time.
    (E) When two aircraft approach head-on, both descend to the left until they are clear of each other.

AVIATION HISTORY

Since 1900, the year of the first flight of a Zeppelin, aircraft technology and capabilities have evolved beyond expectations. The following timeline includes some of the milestones in aviation history.

July 2, 1900: The Zeppelin makes its first flight.

October 22, 1900: The Wright brothers make their first glider flight.

December 17, 1903: The Wright brothers complete the first powered, manned, heavier-than-air controlled flight (it lasted twelve seconds).

February 22, 1920: The first transcontinental mail service is established, from San Francisco to New York.

May 3, 1923: The first nonstop coast-to-coast airplane flight travels from New York to San Diego.

May 21, 1927: Charles A. Lindbergh accomplishes the first nonstop solo flight across the Atlantic Ocean.

June 29, 1927: The first trans-Pacific flight travels from California to Hawaii.

June 1, 1937: Amelia Earhart is lost en route to Howland Island from New Guinea.

June 28, 1939: Pan American Airways flies the first trans-Atlantic passenger service.

October 14, 1947: Captain Charles E. Yeager exceeds the sound barrier in a rocket.

May 5, 1961: Alan Shepard pilots the first US manned space flight.

February 20, 1962: John Glenn becomes the first American to orbit Earth.

December 27, 1968: Apollo 8 is the first human flight to orbit the moon.

September 3, 1971: The Concorde makes its first transatlantic crossing.

1978: The US Airline Deregulation Act ends government regulation of airline routes and rates.

October 24, 2003: The Concorde supersonic jet makes its last flight.

ANSWER KEY

1. (A) is incorrect. An object experiencing a net force of zero can be in motion.

   (B) is correct. The velocity of an object experiencing a net force of zero will remain constant (meaning its acceleration is zero).

   (C) is incorrect. The velocity of an object experiencing a net force of zero cannot change.

   (D) is incorrect. The velocity of an object experiencing a net force of zero cannot change.

   (E) is incorrect. An object experiencing a net force of zero can be in motion.

2. **(D) is correct.** In the equation for Newton's law of universal gravitation, , increasing d by a factor of 4 decreases the value of F_g by a factor of d^2, or 16.

3. **(A) is correct.** This statement is congruent with Bernoulli's principle.

   (B) is incorrect. This statement is the opposite of Bernoulli's principle.

   (C) is incorrect. Bernoulli's principle applies to the horizontal flow of fluid.

   (D) is incorrect. Bernoulli's principle applies to the horizontal flow of fluid.

   (E) is incorrect. This statement contradicts Bernoulli's principle.

4. (A) is incorrect. The all-up weight is the total weight of the airplane during all phases of flight, not just landing.

   (B) is incorrect. Every pilot must consider MLW when assessing whether an aircraft's landing gear can support its weight and the runway is long enough for the aircraft's safe landing.

   (C) is correct. By not exceeding the MLW, the pilot ensures that the landing gear will be able to support the weight of the aircraft and a longer than normal runway will not be required to land the plane.

   (D) is incorrect. Although the MLW includes fuel on board, a pilot must ensure enough fuel is on board to reach his or her destination, or an alternate airfield if required.

   (E) is incorrect. The MLW does not allow an airplane to land on any runway.

5. (A) is incorrect. A decrease in airspeed does not result in a form of induced drag.

   (B) is incorrect. A decrease in the AOA also does not result in a form of induced drag.

   (C) is incorrect. A decrease in lift does not result in induced drag either.

   (D) is correct. An increase in AOA, lift, or airspeed will result in induced drag on an airplane.

   (E) is incorrect. A landing gear system in the UP position will not create induced drag.

6. (A) is incorrect. Air pressure is not equal above and below the wings.

(B) is incorrect. Air pressure is not higher above the wings, which would defeat the purpose of lift.

(C) is correct. Air pressure is lower above the wings and higher below the wings, producing lift.

(D) is incorrect. A pilot's input at the controls causes the wings to extend outward.

(E) is incorrect. Both statements are incorrect.

7. (A) is incorrect. The ailerons control roll along the longitudinal axis.

(B) is incorrect. Neither component nor the vertical axis affects the pitch of an airplane.

(C) is correct. The elevators may increase or decrease the pitch of an airplane along the lateral axis.

(D) is incorrect. The elevators affect the lateral axis, not the longitudinal axis.

(E) is incorrect. The rudder affects the yaw along the vertical axis.

8. (A) is incorrect. Low air density and humidity decrease engine performance.

(B) is incorrect. High air density does not decrease engine performance.

(C) is correct. High air density increases engine performance.

(D) is incorrect. Low temperatures and low air density levels decrease engine performance.

(E) is incorrect. All aspects of the atmosphere affect the performance of airplane engines.

9. (A) is incorrect. Fuel tanks are typically placed inside the wings.

(B) is incorrect. The material must be able to curve around the frame of a fuselage.

(C) is incorrect. Plastic is not used.

(D) is correct. Both weight and strength are considered when selecting materials for fuselages.

(E) is incorrect. Although answer D is correct, answer C is not.

10. (A) is incorrect. Anhedral is a type of wing.

(B) is incorrect. Though the total surface area of a wing indeed influences lift, that area is not considered in relation to the camber line.

(C) is correct. When the measurements of the chord line and the camber line differ greatly, the curvature of the wing will provide more lift.

(D) is incorrect. The dihedral is another type of wing.

(E) is incorrect. Swept is a type of wing planform.

11. (A) is incorrect. Thrust is not the answer.

(B) is incorrect.

(C) is incorrect. Do not just add the thrust and the airspeed.

(D) is correct. Multiply the thrust by the aircraft speed and then divide that amount by 375.

(E) is incorrect.

12. **1. (A)** Tail wheel gear is preferred when landing on non-paved runways.

2. (B) Tandem landing gear is positioned along the longitudinal axis of an aircraft.

3. (C) Tricycle landing gear includes nose and main portions.

4. (A) The tail wheel helps support the aircraft's weight since the center of gravity is forward of the main landing gear.

13. (A) is incorrect. The empennage, or tail assembly, includes the rudder, the vertical stabilizer, the horizontal stabilizer, and two elevators. The empennage controls the stability of the aircraft.

(B) is incorrect. The horizontal stabilizer helps to control the pitch of an aircraft.

(C) is incorrect. The rudder is used to turn an aircraft left or right.

(D) is correct. The trim tabs relieve pressure on the controls.

(E) is incorrect. The vertical stabilizer prevents yawing of an aircraft.

14. (A) is incorrect. The elevators are part of the primary flight control system.

(B) is incorrect. Leading edge devices are indeed part of the secondary flight control system, but so are the spoilers, so the best answer is E.

(C) is incorrect. The rudder is part of the primary flight control system.

(D) is incorrect. The spoilers are indeed part of the secondary flight control system, but so are leading edge devices, so the best answer is E.

(E) is correct. Leading edge devices and the spoilers are part of the secondary flight control system, and they optimize the performance of that system.

15. (A) is incorrect. Monitoring the controls assures a successful straight-and-level flight.

(B) is incorrect. A straight-and-level flight is achieved when the aircraft is in cruising mode.

(C) is correct. Moving the controls is not always necessary to maintain a straight-and-level flight.

(D) is incorrect. A light touch is essential to a straight-and-level flight.

(E) is incorrect. Rash inputs on the flight controls will not achieve a smooth flight.

16. (A) is incorrect. Additional drag during turns should not be applied. Airspeed and altitude decrease naturally due to the airflow around the wings.

(B) is incorrect. Aircraft airspeed decreases naturally. An additional loss of airspeed may result in a stall.

(C) is incorrect. An aircraft's limitations should never be exceeded.

(D) is incorrect. Altitude should be maintained during turns.

(E) is correct. An input of opposite pressure on the controls will return the aircraft to level flight.

17. (A) is incorrect. The best rate of climb requires the most amount of available power.

(B) is incorrect. Obstructions in the flight path require a best angle of climb.

(C) is correct. The best rate of climb results in the most altitude gain over a given amount of time.

(D) is incorrect. The best rate of climb is not the best angle of climb.

(E) is incorrect. A normal climb is referred to as a *cruise climb*.

18. (A) is incorrect. This is not the preferred rate of descent.

(B) is incorrect. This is not the preferred rate of descent.

(C) is correct. This is indeed the preferred rate of descent for a partial power descent.

(D) is incorrect. This is not the preferred rate of descent.

(E) is incorrect. This is not the preferred rate of descent.

19. **(A) is correct.** The teeter hinge allows the blades to flap up and down.

(B) is incorrect. The rotor hub is the center attachment point for the rotor head components.

(C) is incorrect. The swashplate is the component that allows for directional movement of the aircraft.

(D) is incorrect. The skids are used as landing gear on a rotary-wing aircraft.

(E) is incorrect. The pitch horn's job is to collect control input from the pilot and translate that input into movement of the blade grips.

20. (A) is incorrect. The aircraft will not roll upside down.

(B) is incorrect. The aircraft will not roll vertically.

(C) is incorrect. The aircraft will not roll backward.

(D) is correct. The aircraft will roll laterally due to the transverse flow effect.

(E) is incorrect. The aircraft will not roll inverted.

21. (A) is incorrect. The cyclic controls the pitch and roll axes of the aircraft.

(B) is incorrect. The directional controls manage the aircraft's yaw.

(C) is incorrect. The ducted fan is a component of the NOTAR aircraft design.

(D) is correct. The collective control changes the pitch of the blades simultaneously.

(E) is incorrect. The throttle manages the engine performance.

22. (A) is incorrect. Changes in air pressure are not measured at 1 inch of mercury for each 100 feet of altitude.

(B) is incorrect. Changes in air pressure are not measured at 1 inch of mercury for each 500 feet of altitude.

(C) is correct. Air pressure indeed decreases 1 inch of mercury for each 1,000 feet of altitude.

(D) is incorrect. Changes in air pressure are not measured at 1 inch of mercury for each 1,500 feet of altitude.

(E) is incorrect. Changes in air pressure are not measured at 1 inch of mercury for each 2,000 feet of altitude.

23. (A) is incorrect. A level bank would not cause a difference between the static pressure of the aircraft and the static pressure surrounding the diaphragm of the flight instrument.

(B) is correct. An increase in static pressure surrounding the diaphragm indicates the aircraft is in a climb.

(C) is incorrect. A descent would cause a decrease in the static pressure surrounding the diaphragm versus the static pressure of the aircraft.

(D) is incorrect. Straight-and-level flight does not cause a decrease in the static pressure surrounding the diaphragm versus the static pressure of the aircraft.

(E) is incorrect. A yaw also would not cause a decrease in the static pressure surrounding the diaphragm versus the static pressure of the aircraft.

24. (A) is incorrect. Calibrated is the airspeed on the indicator corrected for position error.

(B) is incorrect. Equivalent airspeed is the calibrated airspeed measurement corrected for non-standard pressure.

(C) is correct. Indicated airspeed is indeed what is displayed on the airspeed indicator instrument.

(D) is incorrect. This is not a type of airspeed.

(E) is incorrect. True airspeed is the equivalent airspeed corrected for non-standard density.

25. (A) is incorrect. This indicator does not identify the angle of an aircraft's descent.

(B) is incorrect. This indicator does not identify the actual degree of a turn.

(C) is incorrect. This indicator does not display any need for an increase of altitude.

(D) is correct. The turn and slip indicator allows the pilot to confirm whether he or she is making a coordinated turn and if any adjustments are needed.

(E) is incorrect. This indicator does not identify the rate of a climb.

26.   (A) is incorrect. The longitudinal axis controls banking.

(B) is incorrect. The longitudinal axis controls all banks.

(C) is correct. The lateral axis controls the pitch of the aircraft.

(D) is incorrect. The longitudinal axis controls turns.

(E) is incorrect. The vertical axis controls yaw.

27.   (A) is incorrect. The entire degree variation, not half, is added.

(B) is correct. Convert to magnetic north by adding the 12-degree variation.

(C) is incorrect. The magnetic compass does not automatically adjust for variation.

(D) is incorrect. The magnetic variation is west of true north, so add the degree of variation.

(E) is incorrect. The magnetic variation is west of true north, so add the degree of variation.

28.   **(E) is correct.** The heading indicator reads 240 degrees. Read the compass needle at the nose of the miniature aircraft and add a zero after the numeral increment.

29.   **(A) is correct.** Add a zero after the numeral increment. The heading is 10 degrees.

(B) is incorrect. The heading is closer to 10 degrees than 20 degrees.

(C) is incorrect. A 100-degree heading would be an easterly heading.

(D) is incorrect. Do not read the compass from the tail of the miniature aircraft.

(E) is incorrect. A 290-degree heading would be a westerly heading.

30.   (A) is incorrect. Approach is not a type of marked runway.

(B) is incorrect. FOD is not a marked runway and REIL and VASI are lighting systems.

(C) is correct. These are the three types of marked runways.

(D) is incorrect. Visual is a type of marked runway; however, REIL is not.

(E) is incorrect. Visual is a type of marked runway; however, VASI and precision non-instrumentation are not.

31.   (A) is incorrect. Class D is the only airspace that requires only an operable two-way radio.

(B) is correct. Clearance is required to enter and exit Class A and Class B airspaces.

(C) is incorrect. Airspace Classes A and B require the ATC controller to grant clearance—not merely by acknowledging with the aircraft call sign.

(D) is incorrect. Flight visibility for Class B is 3 statute miles.

(E) is incorrect. Pilots must operate under IFR when passing through Class A airspace.

32. (A) is incorrect. An aircraft in tow has the right-of-way over the rotorcraft (an engine-driven aircraft).

(B) is correct. Any aircraft in distress always has the right-of-way.

(C) is incorrect. An aircraft on short final approach may not force an already landed aircraft off the runway.

(D) is incorrect. A glider has the right-of-way over a rotorcraft when they approach at the same time.

(E) is incorrect. When two aircraft approach head-on, both descend to their right until they are clear of each other.

PRACTICE TEST

VERBAL ANALOGIES

This part of the test measures your ability to reason and see relationships among words. You are to choose the option that best completes the analogy developed at the beginning of each statement.

1. TIDY is to FASTIDIOUS as MESSY is to
   (A) ORGANIZED
   (B) MALICIOUS
   (C) SILENT
   (D) NEAT
   (E) CHAOTIC

2. JARGON is to TERMINOLOGY as NONCHALANCE is to
   (A) CONCERN
   (B) FEAR
   (C) CASUALNESS
   (D) JOY
   (E) IRRITATION

3. 100 is to 20 as
   (A) 1,000 is to 10
   (B) 1 is to 0.5
   (C) 5 is to 15
   (D) DOLLAR is to PENNY
   (E) 10 is to 2

4. GENEROSITY is to GRATITUDE as
   (A) SYMPATHY is to COMPASSION
   (B) DERISION is to HUMILIATION
   (C) NEGLIGENCE is to CAUTIOUSNESS
   (D) THOUGHTFULNESS is to CONSIDERATION
   (E) MALICE is to CRUELTY

5. FACILITATE is to ASSIST as OBLITERATE is to
   (A) CONSTRUCT
   (B) CREATE
   (C) QUESTION
   (D) BOTHER
   (E) DESTROY

6. DECADE is to 10 as
   (A) FINGERS are to 10
   (B) 50 is to 500
   (C) 13 is to 26
   (D) CENTURY is to 100
   (E) FIFTY is to 50

7. ANTELOPE is to HERD as LION is to
    (A) PRIDE
    (B) TROOP
    (C) FLOCK
    (D) ZEBRA
    (E) PACK

8. MARRED is to REPAIRED as EFFACED is to
    (A) OBLITERATED
    (B) HIGHLIGHTED
    (C) STEADIED
    (D) BACKED
    (E) DISRESPECTED

9. IRRITATED is to FURIOUS as
    (A) SATISFIED is to CONTENTED
    (B) GLAD is to JUBILANT
    (C) UNHAPPY is to DISPLEASED
    (D) HOPELESS is to OPTIMISTIC
    (E) CALM is to TRANQUIL

10. CAREFUL is to PAINSTAKING as GOOD is to
    (A) OUTSTANDING
    (B) DECENT
    (C) PASSABLE
    (D) CRUEL
    (E) UNSATISFACTORY

11. OBSCURE is to HIDDEN as MALICIOUS is to
    (A) WICKED
    (B) LONELY
    (C) SHY
    (D) KIND
    (E) GREEDY

12. DIMINUTIVE is to COLOSSAL as PENNILESS is to
    (A) PETITE
    (B) DOLLARS
    (C) AFFLUENT
    (D) BROKE
    (E) CURRENCY

13. MASON is to BRICKS as CARPENTER is to
    (A) CONSTRUCTION
    (B) HAMMERS
    (C) STRUCTURES
    (D) WOOD
    (E) MEASURES

14. DOWNPOUR is to FLOODING as
    (A) EARTHQUAKE is to DESTRUCTION
    (B) DROUGHT is to ABUNDANCE
    (C) TORNADO is to HURRICANE
    (D) EXPLOSION is to BLAST
    (E) SOIL is to MUDDY

15. PEDAL is to BICYCLE as ZIPPER is to
    (A) CLOSURE
    (B) METAL
    (C) BUTTON
    (D) INVENTION
    (E) JACKET

16. 5 is to 5,000 as
    (A) 10 is to 100
    (B) 20 is to 20,000
    (C) 30 is to 90
    (D) 40 is to 45
    (E) 50 is to 501

17. STUDENT is to CLASS as TEACHER is to
    (A) KINDERGARTEN
    (B) INSTRUCTOR
    (C) FACULTY
    (D) CLASSROOM
    (E) PRINCIPAL

18. ODD is to BIZARRE as SILLY is to
    (A) VIVACIOUS
    (B) COMPOSED
    (C) RIDICULOUS
    (D) INCOMPREHENSIBLE
    (E) EDGY

19. CALORIES are to ENERGY as LITERS are to
    (A) CONTAINERS
    (B) LENGTH
    (C) VOLUME
    (D) HEIGHT
    (E) MILILITERS

20. ERG is to WORK as DECIBEL is to
    (A) VOLUME
    (B) WIDTH
    (C) DISTANCE
    (D) WEIGHT
    (E) SOUND

21. ELEPHANT is to LUMBERS as HUMMINGBIRD is to
    (A) FLITS
    (B) SLINKS
    (C) TROTS
    (D) CLUMPS
    (E) SQUIRMS

22. HUNGRY is to RAVENOUS as SAD is to
    (A) EMOTION
    (B) ECSTATIC
    (C) UNCONCERNED
    (D) VORACIOUS
    (E) MISERABLE

23. BORING is to MIND-NUMBING as
    (A) CURIOUS is to INDIFFERENT
    (B) OBEDIENT is to REBELLIOUS
    (C) FAMISHED is to STARVING
    (D) PARSIMONIOUS is to MISERLY
    (E) DISPLEASED is to LIVID

24. SNAKE is to SLITHERS as KANGAROO is to
    (A) AMPHIBIANS
    (B) BOUNDS
    (C) MARSUPIALS
    (D) POUCHES
    (E) SCALES

25. BEQUEATH is to INHERIT as DONATE is to
    (A) PROVIDE
    (B) RENEW
    (C) LINGER
    (D) REQUIRE
    (E) RECEIVE

ARITHMETIC REASONING

This part of the test measures your ability to use arithmetic to solve problems. Each problem is followed by five possible answers. You are to decide which one of the five choices is correct.

1. A high school cross country team sent 25 percent of its runners to a regional competition. Of these, 10 percent won medals. If 2 runners earned medals, how many members does the cross country team have?

   (A) 8

   (B) 10

   (C) 80

   (D) 125

   (E) 1250

2. Convert 55 meters to feet (round to the nearest tenth of a foot).

   (A) 16.8 feet

   (B) 21.7 feet

   (C) 139.7 feet

   (D) 165.0 feet

   (E) 180.4 feet

3. If a person reads 40 pages in 45 minutes, approximately how many minutes will it take her to read 265 pages?

   (A) 202

   (B) 236

   (C) 265

   (D) 298

   (E) 300

4. The average speed of cars on a highway (s) is inversely proportional to the number of cars on the road (n). If a car drives at 65 mph when there are 250 cars on the road, how fast will a car drive when there are 325 cars on the road?

   (A) 50 mph

   (B) 55 mph

   (C) 60 mph

   (D) 85 mph

   (E) 87 mph

5. If three burgers and two orders of fries costs $26.50 and a burger costs $6.50, how much does one order of fries cost?

   (A) $1.75

   (B) $3.50

   (C) $6.75

   (D) $7.00

   (E) $10.00

6. A worker was paid $15,036 for 7 months of work. If he received the same amount each month, how much was he paid for the first 2 months?

   (A) $2,148

   (B) $4,296

   (C) $5,137

   (D) $6,444

   (E) $8,592

7. The probability of drawing a blue marble from a bag of marbles is $\frac{1}{20}$ and the probability of drawing a red marble from the same bag is $\frac{7}{20}$ What is the probability of drawing a blue marble or a red marble?

   (A) $\frac{1}{10}$

   (B) $\frac{3}{10}$

   (C) $\frac{7}{20}$

   (D) $\frac{2}{5}$

   (E) $\frac{1}{2}$

8. The population of a town was 7,250 in 2014 and 7,375 in 2015. What was the percent increase from 2014 to 2015 to the nearest tenth of a percent?

   (A) 1.5%

   (B) 1.6%

   (C) 1.7%

   (D) 1.8%

   (E) 2.0%

9. Lynn has 4 test scores in science class. Each test is worth 100 points, and Lynn has an 85% average. If Lynn scored 100% on each of the first 3 tests, what did she score on her 4th test?

(A) 40%

(B) 55%

(C) 60%

(D) 85%

(E) 100%

10. Allison used $2\frac{1}{2}$ cups of flour to make a cake, and $\frac{3}{4}$ of a cup of flour to make a pie. If she started with 4 cups of flour, how many cups of flour does she have left?

(A) $\frac{3}{4}$

(B) 1

(C) $\frac{5}{4}$

(D) $\frac{5}{2}$

(E) $\frac{13}{4}$

11. Alex cleans houses and charges $25 per bedroom, $35 per bathroom, and $40 per kitchen. If he cleans a house with 4 bedrooms, 2 bathrooms, and 1 kitchen, how much will he be paid?

(A) $205

(B) $210

(C) $215

(D) $230

(E) $245

12. Valerie receives a base salary of $740 a week for working 40 hours. For every extra hour she works, she is paid at a rate of $27.75 per hour. If Valerie works t hours in a week, which of the following equations represents the amount of money, A, she will receive?

(A) $A = 740 + 27.75(t - 40)$

(B) $A = 740 + 27.75(40 - t)$

(C) $A = 740 - 27.75(40 - t)$

(D) $A = 27.75t - 740$

(E) $A = 27.75t + 740$

13. Juan plans to spend 25% of his workday writing a report. If he is at work for 9 hours, how many hours will he spend writing the report?

(A) 2.25

(B) 2.50

(C) 2.75

(D) 3.25

(E) 4.00

14. If $\triangle ABD \sim \triangle DEF$ and the similarity ratio is 3:4, what is the measure of DE if $AB = 12$?

(A) 6

(B) 9

(C) 12

(D) 16

(E) 96

15. Justin has a summer lawn care business and earns $40 for each lawn he mows. He also pays $35 per week in business expenses. Which of the following expressions represents Justin's profit after x weeks if he mows m number of lawns?

(A) $40m - 35x$

(B) $40m + 35x$

(C) $35x(40 + m)$

(D) $35(40m + x)$

(E) $40x(35 + m)$

16. Micah has invited 23 friends to his house and is having pizza for dinner. If each pizza feeds 4 people, how many pizzas should he order?

(A) 4

(B) 5

(C) 6

(D) 7

(E) 8

17. If a plane travels 2775 miles in 3 hours, how far will it travel in 5 hours?

(A) 1665 miles

(B) 3475 miles

(C) 4625 miles

(D) 5550 miles

(E) 13,875 miles

18. In the fall, 425 students pass the math benchmark. In the spring, 680 students pass the same benchmark. What is the percentage increase in passing scores from fall to spring?

   (A) 37.5%
   (B) 55%
   (C) 60%
   (D) 62.5%
   (E) 80%

19. Maria paid $24.65 for her meal at a restaurant. If that price included a tax of 8.25 percent, what was the price of the meal before tax?

   (A) $22.61
   (B) $22.68
   (C) $22.77
   (D) $22.82
   (E) $22.93

20. A high school football team played 12 games in a season. If they won 75 percent of their games, how many games did they lose?

   (A) 3
   (B) 4
   (C) 6
   (D) 9
   (E) 10

21. Aprille has $50 to buy the items on her shopping list. Assuming there is no sales tax, about how much change will Aprille receive after buying all the items on her list?

   Aprille's List

ITEM	PRICE
Hammer	$13.24
Screwdriver	$11.99
Nails	$4.27
Wrench	$5.60

   (A) $12
   (B) $13
   (C) $14
   (D) $15
   (E) $16

22. A fruit stand sells apples, bananas, and oranges at a ratio of 3:2:1. If the fruit stand sells 20 bananas, how many total pieces of fruit does the fruit stand sell?

   (A) 10
   (B) 30
   (C) 40
   (D) 50
   (E) 60

23. A company interviewed 21 applicants for a recent opening. Of these applicants, 7 wore blue and 6 wore white, while 5 applicants wore both blue and white. What is the number of applicants who wore neither blue nor white?

   (A) 1
   (B) 6
   (C) 8
   (D) 12
   (E) 13

24. In the sequence below, each term is found by finding the difference between the previous two numbers and mulitplying the result by −3. What is the 6th term of the sequence?

   {3, 0, −9, −36, ... }

   (A) −81
   (B) −135
   (C) 45
   (D) 81
   (E) 135

25. If the length of a rectangle is increased by 40% and its width is decreased by 40%, what is the effect on the rectangle's area?

   (A) The area is the same.
   (B) It increases by 16%.
   (C) It increases by 20%.
   (D) It decreases by 16%.
   (E) It decreases by 20%.

WORD KNOWLEDGE

This part of the test measures your knowledge of words and their meanings. For each question, you are to choose the word below that is closest in meaning to the capitalized word above.

1. PACIFY
   (A) soothe
   (B) transport
   (C) bathe
   (D) motivate
   (E) nurture

2. INDOLENCE
   (A) serenity
   (B) bliss
   (C) laziness
   (D) tolerance
   (E) sympathy

3. ARDENT
   (A) silvery
   (B) stubborn
   (C) metallic
   (D) passionate
   (E) vicious

4. COUNTENANCE
   (A) strict law
   (B) total amount
   (C) fancy clothing
   (D) body language
   (E) facial expression

5. CHARISMA
   (A) love
   (B) motion
   (C) character
   (D) sneakiness
   (E) attractiveness

6. DAUNT
   (A) thrill
   (B) shove
   (C) intimidate
   (D) encourage
   (E) silence

7. CREDULOUS
   (A) naïve
   (B) amazing
   (C) tedious
   (D) optimistic
   (E) genuine

8. LABYRINTH
   (A) maze
   (B) dungeon
   (C) workshop
   (D) basement
   (E) laboratory

9. SACROSANCT
   (A) handy
   (B) quiet
   (C) dim
   (D) secure
   (E) holy

10. RUDIMENTARY
    (A) impolite
    (B) basic
    (C) juvenile
    (D) innovative
    (E) additional

11. IMPARTIAL
   (A) fond
   (B) incomplete
   (C) objective
   (D) mathematical
   (E) heartless

12. REITERATE
   (A) recite
   (B) repeat
   (C) reunite
   (D) reread
   (E) return

13. PRECEDENT
   (A) event
   (B) birth
   (C) idea
   (D) model
   (E) leader

14. PRUDENT
   (A) sensible
   (B) inquisitive
   (C) terrified
   (D) squeamish
   (E) modest

15. FIGURATIVE
   (A) lofty
   (B) lengthy
   (C) nonliteral
   (D) uncooperative
   (E) hypocritical

16. INNOCUOUS
   (A) susceptible
   (B) sickly
   (C) bland
   (D) cautious
   (E) senseless

17. NEGLIGENCE
   (A) malice
   (B) immorality
   (C) inattention
   (D) nothingness
   (E) magnetism

18. LAX
   (A) salty
   (B) decorative
   (C) malicious
   (D) meddlesome
   (E) permissive

19. EQUIVOCATE
   (A) be evasive
   (B) be dishonest
   (C) devise plots
   (D) trap others
   (E) add numbers

20. PONDEROUS
   (A) thoughtful
   (B) marshy
   (C) boisterous
   (D) rotting
   (E) weighty

21. CIRCUMSPECT
   (A) round
   (B) viewed
   (C) guarded
   (D) dominant
   (E) winding

22. ASSIDUOUS
   (A) complicated
   (B) critical
   (C) generous
   (D) bitter
   (E) industrious

23. SOLICITOUS
    (A) attentive
    (B) persuasive
    (C) cheerful
    (D) serene
    (E) fiery

24. APTITUDE
    (A) talent for socializing
    (B) constant hunger
    (C) capacity to learn
    (D) love of pleasure
    (E) lofty height

25. JEOPARDY
    (A) prediction
    (B) danger
    (C) choice
    (D) destiny
    (E) nature

Math Knowledge

This part of the test measures your knowledge of mathematical terms and principles. Each problem is followed by five possible answers. You are to decide which one of the five choices is correct.

1. Which of the following is equivalent to $z^3(z+2)^2 - 4z^3 + 2$?

   (A) 2

   (B) $z^5 + 4z^4 + 4z^3 + 2$

   (C) $z^6 + 4z^3 + 2$

   (D) $z^5 + 4z^4 + 2$

   (E) $z^5 + 4z^3 + 6$

2. Simplify: $\frac{(3x^2y^2)^2}{3^3x^{-2}y^3}$

   (A) $3x^6y$

   (B) $\frac{x^6y}{3}$

   (C) $\frac{x^4}{3y}$

   (D) $\frac{3x^4}{y}$

   (E) $\frac{3x^6}{y^7}$

3. What is the value of $(\frac{1}{2})^3$?

   (A) $\frac{1}{8}$

   (B) $\frac{1}{6}$

   (C) $\frac{1}{4}$

   (D) $\frac{3}{8}$

   (E) $\frac{3}{2}$

4. The line of best fit is calculated for a data set that tracks the number of miles that passenger cars traveled annually in the US from 1960 to 2010. In the model, $x = 0$ represents the year 1960, and y is the number of miles traveled in billions. If the line of best fit is $y = 0.0293x + 0.563$, approximately how many additional miles were traveled for every 5 years that passed?

   (A) 0.0293 billion

   (B) 0.1465 billion

   (C) 0.5630 billion

   (D) 0.7100 billion

   (E) 2.9615 billion

5. How many cubic feet of soil would be required to cover a circular garden with a diameter of 8 feet if the soil needs to be 0.5 feet deep (use $\pi = 3.14$)?

   (A) 6.28 ft^3

   (B) 12.56 ft^3

   (C) 25.12 ft^3

   (D) 100.48 ft^3

   (E) 200.96 ft^3

6. Which of the following sets of shapes are NOT all similar to each other?

   (A) right triangles

   (B) spheres

   (C) 30–60–90 triangles

   (D) squares

   (E) cubes

7. Simplify: $\sqrt[3]{64} + \sqrt[3]{729}$

   (A) 13

   (B) 15

   (C) 17

   (D) 31

   (E) 35

8. What is the remainder when 397 is divided by 4?

   (A) 0

   (B) 1

   (C) 2

   (D) 3

   (E) 4

9. If the surface area of a cylinder with radius of 4 feet is 48π square feet, what is its volume?

   (A) $1\pi \text{ ft.}^3$

   (B) $16\pi \text{ ft.}^3$

   (C) $32\pi \text{ ft.}^3$

   (D) $48\pi \text{ ft.}^3$

   (E) $64\pi \text{ ft.}^3$

10. Which expression is equivalent to $(x + 3)(x - 2)(x + 4)$?

    (A) $x^3 - 2x + 24$

    (B) $x^3 + 5x - 24$

    (C) $x^3 + 9x^2 - 24$

    (D) $x^3 + 5x^2 - 2x - 24$

    (E) $x^3 + 9x^2 + 6x + 24$

11. Which of the following is a solution of the given equation?

    $4(m + 4)^2 - 4m^2 + 20 = 276$

    (A) 3

    (B) 4

    (C) 6

    (D) 12

    (E) 24

12. What is the x-intercept of the given equation?

    $10x + 10y = 10$

    (A) $(1, 0)$

    (B) $(0, 1)$

    (C) $(0, 0)$

    (D) $(1, 1)$

    (E) $(10, 10)$

13. Which of the following is closest in value to $129,113 + 34,602$?

    (A) 162,000

    (B) 163,000

    (C) 164,000

    (D) 165,000

    (E) 166,000

14. The coordinates of point A are $(7, 12)$ and the coordinates of point C are $(-3, 10)$. If C is the midpoint of $\overline{AB}$, what are the coordinates of point B?

    (A) $(-13, 8)$

    (B) $(-13, 11)$

    (C) $(2, 11)$

    (D) $(2, 14)$

    (E) $(17, 14)$

15. Solve for x: $x^2 - 3x - 18 = 0$

    (A) $x = -3$

    (B) $x = 2$

    (C) $x = -3$ and $x = 6$

    (D) $x = 2$ and $x = 3$

    (E) $x = 3$ and $x = -6$

16. Which of the following could be the perimeter of a triangle with two sides that measure 13 and 5?

    (A) 24.5

    (B) 26.5

    (C) 36

    (D) 37

    (E) 37.5

17. What is $\frac{5}{8}$ as a percent?

    (A) 1.6%

    (B) 16%

    (C) 0.625%

    (D) 6.25%

    (E) 62.5%

18. What is the value of z in the following system?

    $z - 2x = 14$

    $2z - 6x = 18$

    (A) -7

    (B) -2

    (C) 3

    (D) 5

    (E) 24

19. What is the value of the expression $15m + 2n^2 - 7$ if $m = 3$ and $n = -4$?

    (A) -49

    (B) -31

    (C) 6

    (D) 70

    (E) 102

20. Which number has the greatest value?

    (A) 9299 ones

    (B) 903 tens

    (C) 93 hundreds

    (D) 9 thousands

    (E) 9 thousandths

21. Which of the following is an equation of the line that passes through the points $(4, -3)$ and $(-2, 9)$ in the xy-plane?

    (A) $y = -2x + 5$

    (B) $y = -\frac{1}{2}x - 1$

    (C) $y = \frac{1}{2}x - 5$

    (D) $y = 2x - 11$

    (E) $y = 4x + 1$

22. $W, X, Y,$ and Z lie on a circle with center A. If the diameter of the circle is 75, what is the sum of $\overline{AW}, \overline{AX}, \overline{AY},$ and $\overline{AZ}$?

    (A) 75

    (B) 100

    (C) 125

    (D) 300

    (E) 150

23. Which inequality is equivalent to $10 \le k - 5$?

    (A) $k \le 15$

    (B) $k \ge 15$

    (C) $k \le 5$

    (D) $k \ge 5$

    (E) $k \le 10$

24. Rectangular water tank A is 5 feet long, 10 feet wide, and 4 feet tall. Rectangular tank B is 5 feet long, 5 feet wide, and 4 feet tall. If the same amount of water is poured into both tanks and the height of the water in Tank A is 1 foot, how high will the water be in Tank B?

    (A) 1 foot

    (B) 2 feet

    (C) 3 feet

    (D) 4 feet

    (E) 5 feet

25. The inequality $2a - 5b > 12$ is true for which values of a and b?

    (A) $a = 2$ and $b = 6$

    (B) $a = 1$ and $b = -3$

    (C) $a = -1$ and $b = 3$

    (D) $a = 7$ and $b = 2$

    (E) $a = 2$ and $b = -1$

READING COMPREHENSION

This part of the test measures your ability to read and understand written material. Each passage is followed by a series of multiple-choice questions. You are to choose the option that best answers the question based on the passage. No additional information or specific knowledge is needed.

Much of the complexity of the Korean War derives from the very different perspectives of the participants. In reality, the conflict was actually three wars in one, with each faction believing itself to be protecting Korea from an oppressive, invasive force. The participants can be visualized as three concentric circles of increasingly indirect interest in the war.

In the outermost circle were the United States and the Soviet Union. For these two countries, Korea was simply the next stage in their ongoing battle for global power. In 1945, the Soviets invaded Manchuria in their campaign against Japan and seized control of Korea. When the war ended, the United States—in agreement with the Soviet Union—sent an expeditionary force to southern Korea to disarm and repatriate the hundreds of thousands of Japanese soldiers and citizens there. With Soviet troops in the north and American troops in the south, neither side wanted to relinquish control. The Soviets, excluded from the occupation of Japan, feared an American attempt to control Asia; the United States feared the same from the Soviets as the USSR became increasingly supportive of the Chinese communists.

As a compromise, the two powers decided to temporarily divide Korea on the thirty-eighth parallel, keeping their respective troops in place. Each installed a pliable government, but tensions grew within each part of Korea. Internal resistance to foreign occupation as well as aggressive moves from the north and the Soviet Union to reunite the country ultimately resulted in war in 1950.

In the middle ring of participants were the nations of Asia. Suffering from the aftermath of World War II, few Asian countries were able to actively participate in the Korean War, although all watched events closely. The exception was China, which was undergoing its own political transformation.

With the support of the Soviet Union, Mao Zedong seized control of China and established the People's Republic of China in 1949. The United States perceived Zedong's success to be a serious blow to both American political ideas and American global power. But Zedong's dominance was not complete: a second Chinese government persisted, exiled to Taiwan but politically sanctioned by the United States. Korea's fate, then, was dependent on the future security of each of these two Chinas. In addition, all of Asia was concerned about containing Japan, which had pursued aggressive imperialism on the mainland since the end of the nineteenth century, conquering Korea, the Philippines, Thailand, and parts of China. The question of the Korean War became a question of which government could best keep Japan at bay.

Finally, in the innermost circle were North Korea and South Korea, the two supposedly temporary states created by the World War II allies and controlled by opposing governments. For these two factions, the war was a civil war. Before 1945, Korea did not view itself as two different countries but as one unified nation. However, that nation had been occupied by Japan for much of its history, making it automatically resistant to the interference of both Soviet and American troops. The division of the country, while militarily reasonable for the United States and the Soviet Union, was incredibly damaging to Korea itself. The country's most valuable resources—its gold and coal mines, fertilizer and concrete plants, and hydroelectric power system—were all concentrated in the northern zone. However, the scarce arable land and two-thirds of the people were in the southern zone. Economically crippled and resentful of another long occupation, communist leaders in the South revolted against American troops, attempting to seize control from the UN-approved government.

Kim Il-sung, the communist leader of North Korea, enjoying enthusiastic support from the Soviet Union and reluctantly backed by China, capitalized on the unrest to attempt to reunite the country under his rule. The resulting war brought all these various actors, motivations, and agendas into a conflict in which no clear winner would emerge. The only guarantee who was a loser: the Korean nation.

1. The main idea of the passage is that
   (A) the Korean War was unwinnable because different countries viewed the conflict differently.
   (B) the Korean War involved many actors from both within and outside of Asia.
   (C) the Korean people had little involvement in the issues that ultimately resulted in the war.
   (D) the United States and the Soviet Union both feared that the other wanted to control Asia.
   (E) the division of Korea on the thirty-eighth parallel was economically devastating for the country.

2. According to the passage, why was Japan viewed as a threat?
   (A) Japan actively opposed the spread of communism throughout Asia.
   (B) Japan's rise to power weakened the influence of American ideals in Asia.
   (C) Hundreds of thousands of Japanese soldiers remained stationed in Korea and throughout Asia.
   (D) Japan had previously used its military to extend control over much of mainland Asia.
   (E) Japanese support helped to maintain the exiled Chinese government in opposition to Mao Zedong.

3. It can be inferred from the passage that in the period leading up to the Korean War,
   (A) both North and South Koreans actually wanted a communist government.
   (B) tensions between the United States and the Soviet Union increased.
   (C) Mao Zedong strongly influenced Kim Il-Sung's aggression against the south.
   (D) most Koreans resented the American occupation of Japan.
   (E) the Soviet Union greatly profited from the industrial resources in North Korea.

4. The primary purpose of the passage is to
   (A) describe the Asian perspective on the Korean War.
   (B) discuss the Korean War's impact on the United States and the Soviet Union.
   (C) provide a history of the lead-up to the Korean War.
   (D) inform the reader about the different leaders involved in the Korean War.
   (E) explain the reasons why the Korean War was so complicated.

5. Which of the following is NOT a fact stated in the passage?
   (A) The Soviet Union had troops in Korea first, followed by the United States.
   (B) The majority of Korea's population was concentrated in the south of the country.
   (C) The United States and the Soviet Union agreed to permanently divide Korea into two countries.
   (D) Koreans were fed up with occupying forces and resistant to more foreign troops.
   (E) In 1949, two competing governments claimed to rule China.

6. With which of the following claims about the Korean War would the author most likely agree?

   (A) If the United States had pursued a different policy in Japan, China would not have supported North Korea.

   (B) The Soviet Union was hesitant to risk a conflict with the United States in the postwar era.

   (C) Japanese occupation left Korea unable to govern itself or to thrive economically.

   (D) The actions of the United States and the Soviet Union increased conflict in Korea and ultimately led to war.

   (E) Kim Il-sung would not have attempted an invasion of the south if he had the economic means to support his citizens.

By 1993, US troops were deeply involved in trying to end Somalia's complicated and violent civil war involving competing warlords and clans. Because of the deeply fractured nature of the country at the time, the US mission was a daunting task without a clear goal. American strategy involved deploying American Special Forces, or Army Rangers, on raids to capture key members of the various factions that were causing the most strife and conflict, with particular focus on the Somali National Alliance (SNA), a group organized under the warlord Mohamed Aidid. Due to American technological superiority, many of these raids were very successful, increasing US confidence.

In October of 1993, US forces received intelligence that some of Aidid's top officials would be gathering at a hotel in the heart of the capital city of Mogadishu, which was also deep in Aidid's territory. Military leaders planned a raid to seize the officials, thereby delivering a severe blow to the SNA. The mission, known as the Battle of Mogadishu, or—more popularly—as Black Hawk Down, did not go as planned. Rather than quickly extract their targets, the Rangers were bogged down by gunfire on the streets, and the two Black Hawk helicopters providing support were shot down, turning the mission into an unplanned search and rescue as the Rangers attempted to save the crew of the helicopters. While the mission was ultimately successful in obtaining its targets, it was a strategic failure that resulted in significant Somali and American loss of life and a swell of opposition to the overall mission in Somalia at home.

The disintegration of the mission shocked military leaders at the time and highlighted a significantly flawed approach to urban warfare. Previous American raids had been successful for three primary reasons: (1) they occurred in more remote locations, (2) they occurred under the cover of night, and (3) they utilized the element of surprise by maximizing American technological superiority. The first two factors were altered in the Battle of Mogadishu simply by circumstance: the leaders were meeting in the center of a densely populated area in the middle of the day. While that could not be avoided, neither the mission planners nor the Rangers adequately planned for these changes. The Rangers assumed the mission would be quick, like others had been, and lightened their equipment loads, leaving behind water and night-vision goggles. The mission planners did not realize that a daylight mission in the heart of Aidid's territory would be significantly more complicated, and so they did not allow sufficient flexibility for the commander, nor did they provide sufficient contingencies.

Most significantly, though, US officials overestimated the advantage their technology provided. First, American overconfidence resulted in little attempt at secrecy in planning. American forces were based out of the airport, giving many Somali contractors regular access to American plans, which were then leaked to the SNA. They were prepared for the American raid before it ever began. Also, while American helicopters provided stealth and speed, they also became the Rangers' downfall.

The SNA studied American tactical patterns and adjusted their own strategies accordingly. For example, they knew that the US would use the helicopters for air support during the raid, so Aidid stationed surface-to-air missiles. They also knew that American policy was to rescue the helicopter crew once it was downed, which gave the SNA the tactical advantage. Because of the fluid and unofficial nature of factions in Somalia, friends and foes were not clearly labeled, allowing SNA fighters to easily blend in and out of the densely packed city. The SNA had the objective of crippling US forces with little regard to collateral loss of life, whereas they knew American policy would be to minimize civilian deaths. This became increasingly difficult as plain-clothed SNA fighters made it hard to tell combatant from civilian.

When the images of the dead were broadcast back home, public outrage ultimately led to American withdrawal from Somalia altogether and to the country's descent into deeper chaos. American officials were very reluctant to commit US troops to future humanitarian missions, resulting in a reorientation of American foreign policy. Tactically, the Battle of Mogadishu awoke military officials to the deep complexities of urban warfare and led to increased focus on improving information gathering, developing ways of observing targets from a safe distance, and creating more flexible and thorough plans for urban missions. It also was a significant motivation for the development of the US military drone program. However, the true lasting message is that there is no surefire way to be successful in urban warfare, and the tools that make the United States so powerful can sometimes lead to its downfall.

7. The primary purpose of the passage is to
   (A) explain the reasons for American involvement in the Somalian civil war.
   (B) inform the reader about the role Army Rangers played in Somalia.
   (C) describe American domestic response to the Battle of Mogadishu.
   (D) analyze the mistakes made by Army Rangers during the Battle of Mogadishu.
   (E) identify military lessons learned from the Battle of Mogadishu.

8. According to the passage, why were helicopters a problem for US forces during the battle?
   (A) They were unable to determine who was a combatant and so were responsible for the majority of civilian deaths.
   (B) The SNA intentionally targeted them in order to shift the mission to a rescue mission.
   (C) They were unable to land in the densely populated section of Mogadishu.
   (D) The SNA had weapons designed specifically to target and destroy helicopters.
   (E) Their loud noise drew attention to the incoming Rangers and eliminated the element of surprise.

9. It can be inferred from the passage that Mohamed Aidid
   (A) primarily dominated in the rural, low-population areas of Somalia.
   (B) had little understanding of military tactics and strategy.
   (C) was the warlord believed to be most responsible for the violence in Somalia.
   (D) wanted to capture and study American military technology.
   (E) was the sole impediment to brokering a peace to end the civil war.

10. Which of the following is NOT a fact stated in the passage?
    (A) A degree of stability returned to Somalia shortly after the withdrawal of American troops.
    (B) Most US raids in Somalia occurred at night rather than during daylight hours.
    (C) The Rangers did succeed in obtaining the officials the mission targeted.
    (D) The United States did not have a clear endgame in Somalia.
    (E) The Rangers were pinned down by gunfire before the helicopters were brought down.

11. With which of the following claims about urban warfare would the author most likely agree?

    (A) Once its particular challenges are understood, urban environments are the best for American military missions.

    (B) Looking back through history, the majority of US wars have been fought in urban settings.

    (C) Thanks to advancements in military technology, battles fought in cities incur the fewest civilian deaths.

    (D) Because of the unpredictability of urban missions, the US military should develop more effective strategies.

    (E) Based on past experiences, military experts have learned that surprise and stealth missions are more successful in cities.

12. In the third paragraph, the world *collateral* most nearly means

    (A) additional.

    (B) native.

    (C) intentional.

    (D) unimportant.

    (E) unpopular.

Adapted from George Washington's farewell address given in 1796.

The great rule of conduct for us, in regard to foreign nations, is, in extending our commercial relations, to have with them as little political connection as possible. So far as we have already formed engagements, let them be fulfilled with perfect good faith. Here let us stop.

Europe has a set of primary interests, which to us have none, or a very remote relation. Hence she must be engaged in frequent controversies, the causes of which are essentially foreign to our concerns. Hence, therefore, it must be unwise in us to implicate ourselves, by artificial ties, in the ordinary vicissitudes of her politics, or the ordinary combinations and collisions of her friendships or enmities.

Our detached and distant situation invites and enables us to pursue a different course. If we remain one people, under an efficient government, the period is not far off, when we may defy material injury from external annoyance; when we may take such an attitude as will cause the neutrality, we may at any time resolve upon, to be scrupulously respected; when belligerent nations, under the impossibility of making acquisitions upon us, will not lightly hazard the giving us provocation; when we may choose peace or war, as our interest, guided by justice, shall counsel.

Why forego the advantages of so peculiar a situation? Why quit our own to stand upon foreign ground? Why, by interweaving our destiny with that of any part of Europe, entangle our peace and prosperity in the toils of European ambition, rivalship, interest, humor, or caprice?

It is our true policy to steer clear of permanent alliances with any portion of the foreign world; so far, I mean, as we are now at liberty to do it; for let me not be understood as capable of patronizing infidelity to existing engagements. I hold the maxim no less applicable to public than to private affairs, that honesty is always the best policy. I repeat it, therefore, let those engagements be observed in their genuine sense. But, in my opinion, it is unnecessary and would be unwise to extend them.

13. The main idea of the passage is that
    (A) America should back out of the alliances it has made with other countries.
    (B) America should increase its involvement with foreign nations.
    (C) America should attempt to intervene in European conflicts whenever international safety is a concern.
    (D) America should avoid foreign entanglements whenever it is able to do so.
    (E) America should weigh its options carefully before making decisions in the international sphere.

14. In the second paragraph, *vicissitudes* most nearly means
    (A) fluctuations
    (B) ideals
    (C) mutations
    (D) stagnation
    (E) rules

Skin coloration and markings have an important role to play in the world of snakes. Those intricate diamonds, stripes, and swirls help the animals hide from predators, but perhaps most importantly (for us humans, anyway), the markings can also indicate whether the snake is venomous. While it might seem counterintuitive for a venomous snake to stand out in bright red or blue, that fancy costume tells any nearby predator that approaching him would be a bad idea.

If you see a flashy-looking snake in the woods, though, those markings don't necessarily mean it's venomous: some snakes have found a way to ward off predators without the actual venom. The scarlet kingsnake, for example, has very similar markings to the venomous coral snake with whom it frequently shares a habitat. However, the kingsnake is actually nonvenomous; it's merely pretending to be dangerous to eat. A predatory hawk or eagle, usually hunting from high in the sky, can't tell the difference between the two species, and so the kingsnake gets passed over and lives another day.

15. The primary purpose of the passage is to
    (A) explain how the markings on a snake are related to whether it's venomous.
    (B) teach readers the difference between coral snakes and kingsnakes.
    (C) illustrate why snakes are dangerous.
    (D) demonstrate how animals survive in difficult environments.
    (E) disprove popular notions of the snake species.

16. In can be inferred from the passage that
    (A) the kingsnake is dangerous to humans.
    (B) the coral snake and the kingsnake are both hunted by the same predators.
    (C) it's safe to handle snakes in the woods because you can easily tell whether they're poisonous.
    (D) the kingsnake changes its markings when hawks or eagles are close by.
    (E) the coral snake and the kingsnake are equally dangerous to humans.

17. Which statement is NOT a detail from the passage?
   (A) Predators will avoid eating kingsnakes because their markings are similar to those on coral snakes.
   (B) Kingsnakes and coral snakes live in the same habitats.
   (C) The coral snake uses its coloration to hide from predators.
   (D) The kingsnake is not venomous.
   (E) Snakes' markings allow them to hide from predators.

18. In the first paragraph, the word *intricate* most nearly means
   (A) complex
   (B) colorful
   (C) purposeful
   (D) changeable
   (E) delicate

19. According to the passage, what is the difference between kingsnakes and coral snakes?
   (A) Both kingsnakes and coral snakes are nonvenomous, but coral snakes have colorful markings.
   (B) Both kingsnakes and coral snakes are venomous, but kingsnakes have colorful markings.
   (C) Kingsnakes are nonvenomous while coral snakes are venomous.
   (D) Coral snakes are nonvenomous while kingsnakes are venomous.
   (E) Coral snakes and kingsnakes have differently colored markings.

Hand washing is one of our simplest and most powerful weapons against infection. The idea behind hand washing is deceptively simple. Many illnesses are spread when people touch infected surfaces, such as door handles or other people's hands, and then touch their own eyes, mouths, or noses. So, if pathogens can be removed from the hands before they spread, infections can be prevented. When done correctly, hand washing can prevent the spread of many dangerous bacteria and viruses, including those that cause the flu, the common cold, diarrhea, and many acute respiratory illnesses.

The most basic method of hand washing involves only soap and water. Just twenty seconds of scrubbing with soap and a complete rinsing with water is enough to kill and/or wash away many pathogens. The process doesn't even require warm water—studies have shown that cold water is just as effective at reducing the number of microbes on the hands. Antibacterial soaps are also available, although several studies have shown that simple soap and cold water are just as effective.

In recent years, hand sanitizers have become popular as an alternative to hand washing. These gels, liquids, and foams contain a high concentration of alcohol (usually at least 60 percent) that kills most bacteria and fungi; they can also be effective against some, but not all, viruses. There is a downside to hand sanitizer, however. Because the sanitizer isn't rinsed from hands, it only kills pathogens and does nothing to remove organic matter. So, hands "cleaned" with hand sanitizer may still harbor pathogens. Thus, while hand sanitizer can be helpful in situations where soap and clean water aren't available, a simple hand washing is still the best option.

20. In the third paragraph, the word *harbor* most nearly means
    (A) to disguise
    (B) to hide
    (C) to wash away
    (D) to give a home
    (E) to breed

21. Which of the following is NOT a fact stated in the passage?
    (A) Many infections occur because people get pathogens on their hands and then touch their own eyes, mouths, or noses.
    (B) Antibacterial soaps and warm water are the best way to remove pathogens from hands.
    (C) Most hand sanitizers have a concentration of at least 60 percent alcohol.
    (D) Hand sanitizer can be an acceptable alternative to hand washing when soap and water aren't available.
    (E) While hand sanitizer kills most bacteria, it does nothing to remove them from the users' hands.

22. Knowing that the temperature of the water does not affect the efficacy of hand washing, it can be inferred from the passage that water plays an important role in hand washing because it
    (A) has antibacterial properties.
    (B) physically removes pathogens from hands.
    (C) cools hands to make them inhospitable to dangerous bacteria.
    (D) is hot enough to kill bacteria.
    (E) hydrates the skin.

23. Which of the following is the best summary of this passage?
    (A) Many diseases are spread by pathogens that can live on the hands. Hand washing is the best way to remove these pathogens and prevent disease.
    (B) Simple hand washing can prevent the spread of many common illnesses, including the flu, the common cold, diarrhea, and many acute respiratory illnesses. Hand sanitizer can also kill the pathogens that cause these diseases.
    (C) Simple hand washing with soap and cold water is an effective way to reduce the spread of disease. Antibacterial soaps and hand sanitizers may also be used but are not significantly more effective.
    (D) Using hand sanitizer will kill many pathogens but will not remove organic matter. Hand washing with soap and water is a better option when available.
    (E) Many people become pick up infectious diseases during their regular interactions with other people and the world around them.

24. The primary purpose of the passage is to

(A) persuade readers of the importance and effectiveness of hand washing with soap and cold water.

(B) dissuade readers from using hand sanitizer.

(C) explain how many common diseases are spread through daily interaction.

(D) describe the many ways hand washing and hand sanitizer provide health benefits.

(E) encourage readers to save money by not purchasing antibacterial soaps.

25. It can be inferred from the passage that

(A) hand washing would do little to limit infections that spread through particles in the air.

(B) hand washing is not necessary for people who do not touch their eyes, mouths, or noses with their hands.

(C) hand sanitizer serves no purpose and should not be used as an alternative to hand washing.

(D) hand sanitizer will likely soon replace hand washing as the preferred method of removing pathogens from hands.

(E) hand washing is unnecessary unless one is ill.

PHYSICAL SCIENCE

This part of the test measures your knowledge in the area of science. Each of the questions or incomplete statements is followed by five choices. You are to decide which one of the choices best answers the question or completes the statement.

1. The rate at which velocity changes is
   (A) power.
   (B) force.
   (C) displacement.
   (D) acceleration.
   (E) energy.

2. The magnitude of an earthquake refers to its
   (A) power.
   (B) energy release.
   (C) destructive ability.
   (D) depth.
   (E) location.

3. When Earth moves between the moon and the sun, it is called a(n)
   (A) solar eclipse.
   (B) lunar eclipse.
   (C) black hole.
   (D) supernova.
   (E) aurora.

4. $2C_6H_{14} + 19O_2 \rightarrow 12CO_2 + 14H_2O$
   What type of reaction is shown above?
   (A) substitution reaction
   (B) acid-base reaction
   (C) decomposition reaction
   (D) combustion reaction
   (E) synthesis reaction

5. Friction is defined as a force that always
   (A) opposes motion.
   (B) pushes down onto a surface.
   (C) rotates an object.
   (D) increases the force of gravity.
   (E) opposes the normal force.

6. A microscope makes use of which property of waves to make objects appear larger?
   (A) wavelength
   (B) diffraction
   (C) amplitude
   (D) reflection
   (E) refraction

7. Isotopes of an element will have the same number of _____ and different numbers of _____.
   (A) electrons; neutrons
   (B) neutrons; electrons
   (C) protons; neutrons
   (D) protons; electrons
   (E) electrons; protons

8. A box sliding down a ramp experiences all of the following forces EXCEPT
   (A) tension.
   (B) friction.
   (C) gravitational.
   (D) normal.
   (E) buoyant.

9. The state of matter at which particles are most loosely packed is
   (A) liquid.
   (B) gas.
   (C) solid.
   (D) plasma.
   (E) crystal.

10. Which planet orbits closest to Earth?
    (A) Mercury
    (B) Venus
    (C) Jupiter
    (D) Saturn
    (E) Neptune

11. Which layer of the earth, primarily made up of iron and nickel, is composed of a very hot liquid that flows around the center?

(A) lithosphere

(B) asthenosphere

(C) mesosphere

(D) inner core

(E) outer core

12. An atom has 5 electrons and 12 protons. What is the total charge of the atom?

(A) $-17e$

(B) $-7e$

(C) $+7e$

(D) $+17e$

(E) The atom is neutral.

13. Which is NOT a characteristic of a mineral?

(A) They are naturally occurring.

(B) They are organic.

(C) They are solids.

(D) They have a crystalline structure.

(E) They have a single chemical compound.

14. Which of the following describes a physical change?

(A) Water becomes ice.

(B) Batter is baked into a cake.

(C) An iron fence rusts.

(D) A firecracker explodes.

(E) Neutralizing an acid with a base.

15. Which statement about the solar system is true?

(A) Earth is much closer to the sun than it is to other stars.

(B) The moon is closer to Venus than it is to Earth.

(C) At certain times of the year, Jupiter is closer to the sun than Earth is.

(D) Mercury is the closest planet to Earth.

(E) Uranus is closer to the sun than Jupiter.

16. Which layer of the atmosphere absorbs harmful ultraviolet radiation from the sun?

(A) the mesosphere

(B) the stratosphere

(C) the troposphere

(D) the thermosphere

(E) the exosphere

17. Which trait defines a saturated solution?

(A) The solute and solvent are not chemically bonded.

(B) Both the solute and solvent are liquid.

(C) The solute is distributed evenly throughout the solution.

(D) The solute is unevenly distributed throughout the solution.

(E) No more solute can be dissolved in the solution.

18. Which of the following is caused by geothermal heat?

(A) geysers

(B) glaciers

(C) tsunamis

(D) tornadoes

(E) hurricanes

19. Energy is stored in a compressed spring in the form of

(A) chemical potential energy.

(B) elastic potential energy.

(C) gravitational potential energy.

(D) electric potential energy.

(E) kinetic energy.

20. How long does it take the earth to rotate on its axis?

(A) one hour

(B) one day

(C) one month

(D) one year

(E) one century

TABLE READING

This part of the test measures your ability to read a table quickly and accurately. Your task will be to find the block where the column and row intersect, note the number that appears there, and then find this number among the five answer options.

Y-VALUE	X-VALUE	1,000	1,200	1,300	1,500	1,750	1,800
	65	0.42	0.51	0.55	0.64	0.74	0.76
	70	0.46	0.55	0.59	0.69	0.80	0.82
	72	0.47	0.56	0.61	0.71	0.82	0.85
	75	0.49	0.59	0.64	0.74	0.86	0.88
	78	0.51	0.61	0.66	0.76	0.89	0.92

	x	y	(A)	(B)	(C)	(D)	(E)
1.	1,300	72	0.61	0.59	0.71	0.64	0.55
2.	1,500	75	0.69	0.64	0.71	0.74	0.86
3.	1,800	65	0.82	0.76	0.74	0.80	0.92
4.	1,200	78	0.51	0.66	0.61	0.59	0.56
5.	1,750	70	0.86	0.82	0.74	0.69	0.80

Comparison of Measurements

LITERS	US CUPS	IMPERIAL CUPS
1.5	6.25	5.28
2	8.33	7.04
2.5	10.42	8.80
3	12.50	10.56
3.5	14.58	12.32
4	16.67	14.08
4.5	18.75	15.84
5	20.83	17.60

6. How many US cups equal 4 liters?
   (A) 12.50
   (B) 10.42
   (C) 18.75
   (D) 10.56
   (E) 16.67

7. How many liters equal 14.08 Imperial cups?
   (A) 4.5
   (B) 5
   (C) 2.5
   (D) 4
   (E) 3

8. How many Imperial cups equal 12.50 US cups?

    (A) 3

    (B) 10.56

    (C) 12.52

    (D) 14.58

    (E) 20.83

10. How many US cups equal 15.84 Imperial cups?

    (A) 4

    (B) 10.42

    (C) 14.58

    (D) 16.67

    (E) 18.75

9. How many liters equal 8.80 Imperial cups?

    (A) 1.5

    (B) 2

    (C) 2.5

    (D) 3.5

    (E) 4

Reciprocal Runway Numbering

IF THE NORTH/EAST END OF THE RUNWAY IS NUMBERED	THEN THE SOUTH/WEST END OF THE RUNWAY IS NUMBERED	IF THE NORTH/EAST END OF THE RUNWAY IS NUMBERED	THEN THE SOUTH/WEST END OF THE RUNWAY IS NUMBERED	IF THE NORTH/EAST END OF THE RUNWAY IS NUMBERED	THEN THE SOUTH/WEST END OF THE RUNWAY IS NUMBERED
01	19	07	25	13	31
02	20	08	26	14	32
03	21	09	27	15	33
04	22	10	28	16	34
05	23	11	29	17	35
06	24	12	30	18	36

11. If the North/East end of the runway is numbered 13, what is the South/West end of that runway numbered?

    (A) 17

    (B) 19

    (C) 28

    (D) 31

    (E) 33

13. If the North/East end of the runway is numbered 11, what is the South/West end of that runway numbered?

    (A) 15

    (B) 20

    (C) 23

    (D) 25

    (E) 29

12. If the South/West end of the runway is numbered 23, what is the North/East end of that runway numbered?

    (A) 02

    (B) 03

    (C) 05

    (D) 08

    (E) 23

14. If the South/West end of the runway is numbered 35, what is the North/East end of that runway numbered?

    (A) 15

    (B) 17

    (C) 20

    (D) 24

    (E) 35

15. If the North/East end of the runway is numbered 02, what is the South/West end of that runway numbered?

    (A) 20
    (B) 25
    (C) 27
    (D) 28
    (E) 33

Basic Pay of Air Force Officer

		YEARS OF SERVICE			
		0 – 2	3	4	5
RANK	O-1	35,668	37,126	44,881	44,881
	O-2	41,094	46,803	53,903	55,724
	O-3	47,563	53,913	58,190	63,446
	O-4	54,093	62,618	66,798	67,726
	O-5	62,694	70,628	75,513	76,435
	O-6	75,204	82,623	88,045	88,045

	Years of Service	Rank	(A)	(B)	(C)	(D)	(E)
16.	4	O-2	53,903	58,190	46,803	41,904	55,724
17.	2	O-3	54,093	41,094	63,446	47,563	53,913
18.	5	O-4	66,798	67,726	75,513	62,618	63,446
19.	0	O-2	35,668	47,563	41,094	37,126	46,803
20.	3	O-4	54,093	62,618	66,798	70,628	62,694

Speed Comparison (Statute mph converted to Knots and Nautical mph)

STATUTE MILES PER HOUR (MPH)	KNOTS (KTS)	NAUTICAL MILES PER HOUR (MPH)
6.25	5.28	5.43
70	60.8	60.83
90	78.2	78.21
115	100	99.93
138	120	119.92
172.6	150	149.99
200	173.8	173.79
350	304.14	304.14

21. If traveling at 150 kts, what does that equate to in statute mph?
    (A) 119.92
    (B) 149.99
    (C) 150
    (D) 172.6
    (E) 200

22. How many nautical mph equates to 115 statute mph?
    (A) 78.21
    (B) 99.93
    (C) 100
    (D) 120
    (E) 138

23. How many knots equate to 200 statute mph?
    (A) 60.83
    (B) 115
    (C) 173.8
    (D) 200
    (E) 304.14

24. How many knots equate to 60.83 nautical mph?
    (A) 60.8
    (B) 70
    (C) 78.2
    (D) 100
    (E) 115

25. An airplane traveling at 350 mph equates to how many knots?
    (A) 150
    (B) 172.6
    (C) 173.8
    (D) 200
    (E) 304.14

US Currency Exchange (approximate)

US ($)	EUROPEAN UNION (EUROS)	BRITISH (POUNDS)
1	0.93	0.80
150	139.55	120.31
200	186.08	160.41
300	279.14	240.62
400	372.19	320.84
500	465.23	401.05

26. How many British pounds would $400 buy?
    (A) 186.08
    (B) 160.41
    (C) 320.84
    (D) 372.19
    (E) 401.05u

27. How many euros would $200 buy?
    (A) 0.93
    (B) 186.08
    (C) 160.41
    (D) 200.00
    (E) 240.62

28. How many British pounds would $150 buy?

(A) 0.80

(B) 120.31

(C) 139.55

(D) 150.00

(E) 240.62

30. How many euros would $500 buy?

(A) 373.12

(B) 418.69

(C) 465.23

(D) 481.25

(E) 558.27

29. When converting $300 into pounds, how much would be received?

(A) 120.31

(B) 139.55

(C) 240.62

(D) 279.14

(E) 372.19

Y-VALUE		X-VALUE 5	10	30	35	40	50
	A	125	164	324	425	846	1,215
	B	274	464	512	784	623	856
	C	613	444	754	825	1,012	873
	D	303	586	715	289	684	691
	E	124	714	386	255	784	634
	F	379	180	730	426	741	909

	x	y	(A)	(B)	(C)	(D)	(E)
31.	35	B	164	425	754	784	846
32.	5	E	124	125	379	586	634
33.	30	A	164	324	444	512	715
34.	10	C	274	303	444	464	586
35.	40	D	180	289	623	684	909

Celsius (°C) and Fahrenheit (°F) Temperature Comparison

LOCATION	TEMP (°C)	TEMP (°F)
Boston	5	41
Chicago	13	55
Florida Keys	26	78
Harvard	6	43
Los Angeles	13	56
Macon	29	84
Minneapolis	22	72
Orlando	37	98

36. What does 56 °F equate to in °C?
   (A) 6°
   (B) 13°
   (C) 22°
   (D) 29°
   (E) 84°

37. When it is 84 °F in Macon, what is it in oC?
   (A) 5°
   (B) 6°
   (C) 13°
   (D) 22°
   (E) 29°

38. What does 6 °C equate in °F?
   (A) 43°
   (B) 55°
   (C) 56°
   (D) 72°
   (E) 78°

39. Which location is listed with a temperature of 72 °F?
   (A) Harvard
   (B) Los Angeles
   (C) Macon
   (D) Minneapolis
   (E) Orlando

40. What is the difference in °C temperature listed between the Florida Keys and Chicago?
   (A) 11
   (B) 12
   (C) 13
   (D) 14
   (E) 26

INSTRUMENT COMPREHENSION

This part of the test measures your ability to determine the position of an airplane in flight from reading instruments showing its compass direction heading, amount of climb or dive, and degree of bank to right or left.

Each problem consists of two dials and four airplanes in flight. Your task is to determine which one of the four airplanes is most nearly in the position indicated by the two dials. You are always looking north at the same altitude as the four airplanes. East is always to your right as you look at the page.

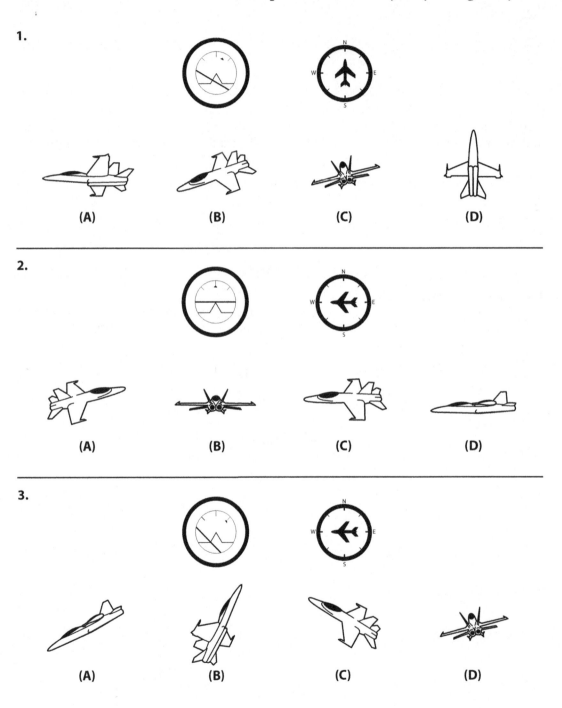

1.

(A)   (B)   (C)   (D)

2.

(A)   (B)   (C)   (D)

3.

(A)   (B)   (C)   (D)

4.

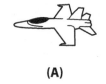

(A)   (B)   (C)   (D)

5.

(A)   (B)   (C)   (D)

6.

(A)   (B)   (C)   (D)

7.

 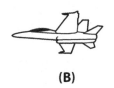 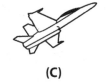

(A)   (B)   (C)   (D)

8.

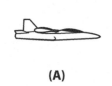  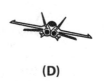

(A)   (B)   (C)   (D)

9.

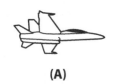

(A)   (B)   (C)   (D)

10.

   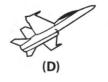

(A)   (B)   (C)   (D)

11.

(A)   (B)   (C)   (D)

12.

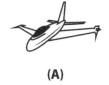 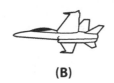 

(A)   (B)   (C)   (D)

13.

 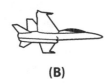 

(A)   (B)   (C)   (D)

14.

(A)   (B)   (C)   (D)

15.

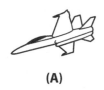  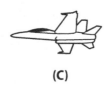

(A)   (B)   (C)   (D)

16.

   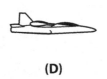

(A)   (B)   (C)   (D)

17.

  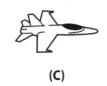

(A)   (B)   (C)   (D)

18.

 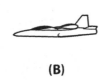 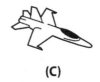 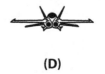

(A)   (B)   (C)   (D)

19.

   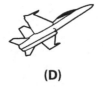

(A)   (B)   (C)   (D)

20.

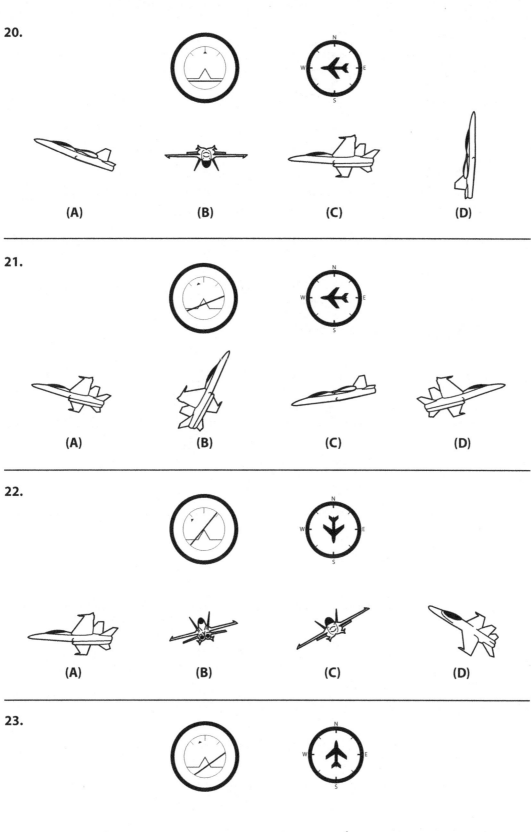

(A)   (B)   (C)   (D)

21.

(A)   (B)   (C)   (D)

22.

(A)   (B)   (C)   (D)

23.

(A)   (B)   (C)   (D)

24.

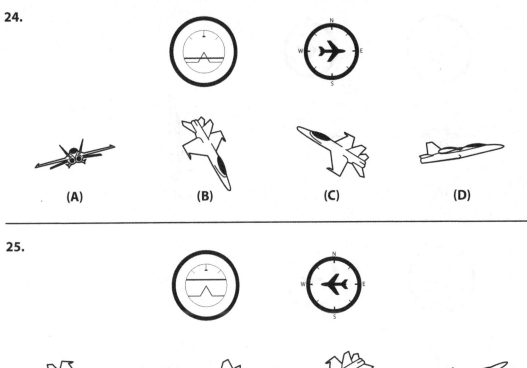

(A)   (B)   (C)   (D)

25.

(A)   (B)   (C)   (D)

BLOCK COUNTING

Given a certain numbered block, your task is to determine how many other blocks the numbered block touches. Blocks are considered touching only if all or part of their faces touch. Blocks that only touch corners do not count. All of the blocks in each pile are the same size and shape.

Shape One

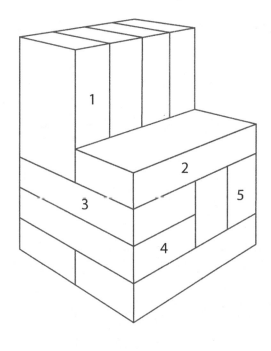

Shape Two

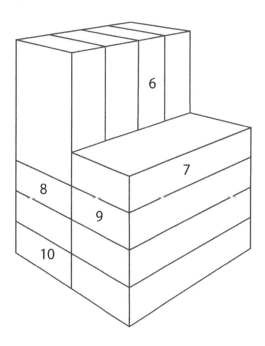

BLOCK	A	B	C	D	E
1	5	2	7	3	1
2	3	8	7	10	9
3	5	6	4	2	1
4	3	2	4	7	1
5	6	5	9	3	7

BLOCK	A	B	C	D	E
6	5	2	4	3	7
7	3	5	6	9	4
8	4	6	1	8	5
9	3	4	6	2	1
10	3	9	1	4	2

Shape Three

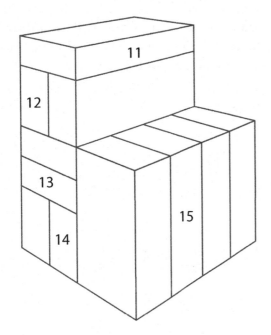

Shape Four

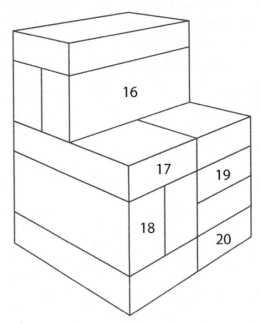

BLOCK	A	B	C	D	E
11	4	2	1	3	9
12	5	2	7	3	4
13	7	2	6	8	9
14	7	5	6	4	8
15	5	6	2	1	7

BLOCK	A	B	C	D	E
16	4	5	2	1	6
17	3	8	5	4	7
18	5	4	6	2	3
19	8	3	2	5	4
20	3	1	4	2	7

Shape Five

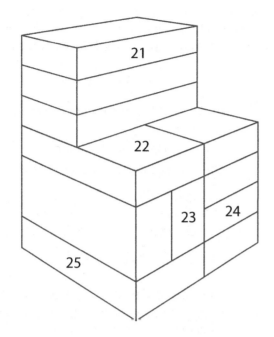

Shape Six

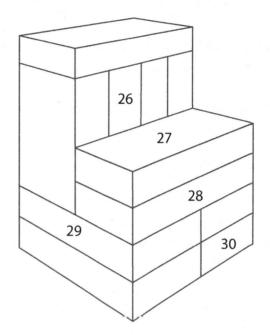

BLOCK	A	B	C	D	E
21	2	1	7	3	4
22	4	8	3	5	9
23	7	4	5	1	2
24	6	4	2	5	3
25	1	2	4	3	5

BLOCK	A	B	C	D	E
26	5	3	7	6	4
27	4	5	7	3	6
28	6	3	5	8	7
29	4	5	6	7	3
30	2	3	4	1	5

Aviation Information

This part of the test measures your knowledge of aviation. Each of the questions or incomplete statements is followed by five choices. You are to decide which one of the choices best answers the question or completes the statement.

1. When raised elevators push down on the tail of an aircraft, what effect does that have on the aircraft?

   (A) The ailerons automatically extend simultaneously.

   (B) The nose of the aircraft lowers.

   (C) The nose of the aircraft rises.

   (D) The aircraft veers left.

   (E) The aircraft veers right.

2. Which aircraft component(s) affect yaw?

   (A) the ailerons

   (B) the elevators

   (C) the rudder

   (D) the spoilers

   (E) the wings

3. What part of a rotary-wing aircraft makes directional control possible?

   (A) the teeter hinge

   (B) the swashplate

   (C) the ducted fan

   (D) the tail boom

   (E) the skids

4. Which type of climb produces the most altitude in a given distance?

   (A) a best angle of climb

   (B) a best rate of climb

   (C) a normal climb

   (D) a shallow climb

   (E) a steep climb

5. What causes a rotary-wing aircraft to drift laterally due to tail rotor thrust?

   (A) a coaxial rotor system

   (B) translating tendency

   (C) gyroscopic precession

   (D) the tail rotor

   (E) translational lift

6. If the cyclic or control wheel in a helicopter is moved forward

   (A) the aircraft pitch changes.

   (B) the airspeed decreases.

   (C) the airspeed increases.

   (D) the airspeed increases and the pitch changes.

   (E) the aircraft tends to yaw.

7. If the airspeed indicator needle is in the yellow and approaching the red line during a maneuver, what would be the correct response?

   (A) change attitude by 90 degrees

   (B) decrease altitude

   (C) decrease airspeed

   (D) increase airspeed

   (E) increase thrust

8. In aviation terminology, rate of climb is expressed as

   (A) AGL

   (B) degrees

   (C) fpm

   (D) knots

   (E) MSL

9. Which statement is true about lag and trend information?

   (A) Lag is the same as trend information.

   (B) Lag displays real-time movement of the aircraft.

   (C) Both lag and trend information display real-time movement of the aircraft.

   (D) Trend information displays real-time movement of the aircraft.

   (E) Trend information does not display real-time movement of the aircraft.

10. The lateral axis of an aircraft controls which of the following?

(A) adverse yaw
(B) banks
(C) pitch
(D) roll
(E) yaw

11. Which component allows the rotor blades to feather?

(A) the teeter hinge
(B) the rotor hub
(C) the blade grips
(D) the skids
(E) the pitch horn

12. Which of the following is expressed in degrees that include the area between the direction of the wind and the chord of the aircraft wing?

(A) AOA
(B) the artificial horizon
(C) the lower limits of the vertical speed indicator
(D) the pressure altitude
(E) a stall

13. When entering and exiting Class C controlled airspace, which statement is true regarding airspace clearance?

(A) The ATC must acknowledge the pilot by responding with the aircraft's call sign for communication to be considered established.
(B) An ATC response of only "Standby" is enough to establish approval for entry to the controlled airspace.
(C) No approval for clearance is needed.
(D) Only jets flying faster than 200 mph need to request or receive approval for clearance.
(E) A pilot does not need approval to exit Class C airspace.

14. If there is no increase in thrust, which action would result in an ultimate stall?

(A) descending to a lower altitude
(B) decreasing pitch
(C) extending the ailerons and flaps
(D) increasing pitch
(E) turning the rudder to the left or right

15. What one of the acronyms below for all-up weight defined as the total aircraft weight at any given moment during flight?

(A) AGW
(B) MLW
(C) MRW
(D) MTOW
(E) OEW

16. What types of turns require the pilot to input aileron pressure to return the aircraft to level flight?

(A) all turns
(B) medium and shallow turns
(C) a shallow turn
(D) medium and steep turns
(E) a trimmed turn

17. What aerodynamic principle describes the unequal lifting forces of the rotor system due to the advancing and retreating blades?

(A) weight, lift, thrust, and drag
(B) translational lift
(C) dissymmetry of lift
(D) gyroscopic precession
(E) autorotation

18. What flight control maintains the engine within optimal flight parameters?

(A) the cyclic
(B) the collective
(C) the tail rotor pedals
(D) translating tendency
(E) the throttle

19. Which statement describes absolute altitude?

   (A) This is the altitude displayed on the altimeter.

   (B) The altimeter displays this altitude when the setting window reads 29.92 Hg.

   (C) This is the pressure altitude corrected for variations from standard temperature.

   (D) This is the vertical distance above MSL.

   (E) This is the vertical distance AGL.

20. What is the unit of measure for airspeed?

   (A) AOA

   (B) degrees

   (C) knots

   (D) MSL

   (E) rate of climb

ANSWER KEY

VERBAL ANALOGIES

1. **(E)**

Someone who is *extremely* TIDY is FASTIDIOUS; a room that is *extremely* MESSY is CHAOTIC.

2. **(C)**

JARGON is a synonym for TERMINOLOGY; NONCHALANCE is a synonym for CASUALNESS.

3. **(E)**

100 divided by 5 equals 20; 10 divided by 5 equals 2.

4. **(B)**

If A treats B with GENEROSITY, B is likely to feel GRATITUDE; if A treats B with DERISION, B is likely to experience HUMILIATION.

5. **(E)**

FACILITATE is a synonym for ASSIST; OBLITERATE is a synonym for DESTROY.

6. **(D)**

A DECADE is 10 years long; a CENTURY is 100 years long.

7. **(A)**

An ANTELOPE is one member of a HERD; a LION is one member of a PRIDE.

8. **(B)**

MARRED is an antonym for REPAIRED; EFFACED is an antonym for HIGHLIGHTED.

9. **(B)**

Someone who feels *extremely* IRRITATED feels FURIOUS; someone who feels *extremely* GLAD feels JUBILANT.

10. **(A)**

Someone who is *extremely* CAREFUL works in a PAINSTAKING manner; something that is *extremely* GOOD is OUTSTANDING.

11. **(A)**

OBSCURE is a synonym for HIDDEN; MALICIOUS is a synonym for WICKED.

12. **(C)**

DIMINUTIVE is an antonym for COLOSSAL; PENNILESS is an antonym for AFFLUENT. All of these adjectives have to do with size, amount, or degree.

13. **(D)**

A MASON uses BRICKS to build structures; a CARPENTER uses WOOD to build them.

14. **(A)**

    A DOWNPOUR may cause FLOODING; an EARTHQUAKE may cause DESTRUCTION.

15. **(E)**

    A PEDAL is one part of a BICYCLE; a ZIPPER is one part of a JACKET.

16. **(B)**

    5 times 1,000 equals 5,000; 20 times 1,000 equals 20,000.

17. **(C)**

    A STUDENT is one member of a CLASS; a TEACHER is one member of a FACULTY.

18. **(C)**

    Something that is *extremely* ODD is BIZARRE; something that is *extremely* SILLY is RIDICULOUS.

19. **(C)**

    CALORIES measure ENERGY; LITERS measure liquid VOLUME.

20. **(E)**

    An ERG is a unit of measurement that measures WORK; a DECIBEL is a unit of measurement that measures SOUND.

21. **(A)**

    An ELEPHANT LUMBERS through the jungle; a HUMMINGBIRD FLITS through the air.

22. **(E)**

    Someone who is *extremely* HUNGRY is RAVENOUS; someone who is *extremely* SAD is MISERABLE.

23. **(E)**

    Something that is *extremely* BORING is MIND-NUMBING; someone who feels *extremely* DISPLEASED feels LIVID.

24. **(B)**

    A SNAKE SLITHERS along the ground; a KANGAROO BOUNDS across the land.

25. **(E)**

    BEQUEATH is an antonym for INHERIT; DONATE is an antonym for RECEIVE.

ARITHMETIC REASONING

1. **(C)**

   Work backwards to find the number of runners in the competition (c) and then the number of runners on the team (r).

   $\frac{2}{c} = \frac{10}{100}$

   $c = 20$

   $\frac{20}{r} = \frac{25}{100}$

   $r = \mathbf{80}$

2. **(E)**

   Multiply by the converstion factor to get from meters to feet.

   $55 \text{ m} \left(\frac{3.28 \text{ ft.}}{1 \text{ m}}\right) = \mathbf{180.4 \text{ feet}}$

3. **(D)**

   Write a proportion and then solve for x.

   $\frac{40}{45} = \frac{265}{x}$

   $40x = 11{,}925$

   $x = 298.125 \approx \mathbf{298}$

4. **(A)**

   Use the formula for inversely proportional relationships to find k and then solve for s.

   $sn = k$

   $(65)(250) = k$

   $k = 16{,}250$

   $s(325) = 16{,}250$

   $s = \mathbf{50}$

5. **(B)**

   Find the cost of three burgers.
   Cost of 3 burgers = $3(6.50) = 19.50$
   Subtract this value from the total costs of the meal to find the cost of the fries.
   $26.50 - 19.50 = 7$
   Divide by 2 to find the cost of one order of fries.
   $7 \div 2 = \mathbf{\$3.50}$

6. **(B)**

   Write a proportion and then solve for x.

   $\frac{15{,}036}{7} = \frac{x}{2}$

   $7x = 30{,}072$

   $x = \mathbf{4{,}296}$

7. **(D)**

   Add the probability of drawing a blue marble and the probability of drawing a red marble to find the probability of drawing either a blue or red marble.

   $\frac{1}{20} + \frac{7}{20} = \frac{8}{20} = \mathbf{\frac{2}{5}}$

8. **(C)**

   Use the formula for percent change.

   $percent \ change = \frac{amount \ of \ change}{original \ amount}$

   $= \frac{(7{,}375 - 7{,}250)}{7{,}250} = 0.017 = \mathbf{1.7\%}$

9. **(A)**

   To calculate the average, add all of the scores and divide by the total number of scores. Use the variable x in place of the missing score.

   $\frac{(100 + 100 + 100 + x)}{4} = 85$

   $\frac{(300 + x)}{4} = 85$

   $(300 + x) = 340$

   $x = \mathbf{40\%}$

10. **(A)**

    Add the fractions and subtract the result from the amount of flour Allison started with.

    $2\frac{1}{2} + \frac{3}{4} = \frac{5}{2} + \frac{3}{4} = \frac{10}{4} + \frac{3}{4} = \frac{13}{4}$

    $4 - \frac{13}{4} = \frac{16}{4} - \frac{13}{4} = \mathbf{\frac{3}{4}}$

11. **(B)**

    Multiply the number of rooms by the cost of each room to find the total.

    $25(4) + 35(2) + 40(1) = \mathbf{\$210}$

12. **(A)**

    Valerie will receive her base pay plus 27.75 for every hour she worked in addition to her 40 hours.

    $A = base \ pay + 27.75 \times extra \ hours$

    $A = \mathbf{740 + 27.75(t - 40)}$

13. **(A)**

    Use the equation for percentages.

    $part = whole \times percentage =$
    $9 \times 0.25 = \mathbf{2.25}$

14. (D)

Set up a proportion and solve.

$\frac{AB}{DE} = \frac{3}{4}$

$\frac{12}{DE} = \frac{3}{4}$

$3(DE) = 48$

$DE = 16$

15. (A)

His profit will be his income minus his expenses. He will earn $40 for each lawn, or 40$m$. He pays $35 is expenses each week, or 35x.

profit = 40m − 35x

16. (C)

$23 \div 4 = 5.75$ pizzas

Round up to **6 pizzas**.

17. (C)

Set up a proportion and solve.

$\frac{2775 \text{ miles}}{3 \text{ hr}} = \frac{x \text{ miles}}{5 \text{ hr}}$

$2775(5) = 3x$

$x = 4625$ miles

18. (C)

Use the formula for percent change.

$percent\ change = \frac{amount\ of\ change}{original\ amount}$

$= \frac{680 - 425}{425}$

$= \frac{255}{425} = 0.60 = $ **60%**

19. (C)

Use the formula for percentages.

$whole = \frac{part}{percent} = \frac{meal + tax}{1 + 0.0825}$

$= \frac{24.65}{1.0825} = $ **$22.77**

20. (A)

Use the formula for percentages to find the number of games the team won.

$part = whole \times percent =$

$12 \times 0.75 = 9$

Subtract the number of games won from the games played to find the number of games the team lost.

$12 - 9 = $ **3**

21. (D)

To estimate the amount of the change, round the price of each item to the nearest dollar amount and subtract from the total.

$50 − ($13 + $12 + $4 + $6)

$= $50 − $35 = $ **$15**

22. (E)

Assign variables and write the ratios as fractions. Then, cross-multiply to solve for the number of apples and oranges sold.

$x = $ apples

$\frac{apples}{bananas} = \frac{3}{2} = \frac{x}{20}$

$60 = 2x$

$x = 30$ apples

$y = $ oranges

$\frac{oranges}{bananas} = \frac{1}{2} = \frac{y}{20}$

$2y = 20$

$y = 10$ oranges

To find the total, add the number of apples, oranges, and bananas together. $30 + 20 + 10 = $ **60 pieces of fruit**

23. (E)

Set up an equation to find the number of people wearing neither white nor blue. Subtract the number of people wearing both colors so they are not counted twice.

$21 = 7 + 6 + neither − 5$

$neither = $ **13**

24. (B)

Find the 5th term.

$−9 − (−36) = 27$

$27 \times −3 = −81$

Find the 6th term.

$−36 − (−81) = 45$

$45 \times −3 = $ **−135**

25. (D)

Use the formula for the area of a rectangle to find the increase in its size.

$A = lw$

$A = (1.4l)(0.6w)$

$A = 0.84lw$

The new area will be 84% of the original area, a decrease of **16%**.

WORD KNOWLEDGE

1. **(A)**

   The word root *pax* means "peace," and the suffix *–ify* means "to cause to become more," and so, to pacify someone means to cause that person to become more peaceful, or to soothe him.

2. **(C)**

   An indolent person is lazy and avoids activity or exertion.

3. **(D)**

   The word root in the nouns *arson* and *ardor* means "to burn," and the suffix *–ent* means "doing a certain action," and so an ardent person burns with passion.

4. **(E)**

   Someone with a smiling countenance has a smile on her face.

5. **(E)**

   Someone with charisma, or charm, is attractive to others.

6. **(C)**

   To daunt means to intimidate or make someone apprehensive. For example, difficult tests are daunting to most people.

7. **(A)**

   The word root *crēdere* means "to believe," and the suffix *–ous* means "possessing or full of," so a credulous person is naïve enough to believe almost everything he hears or reads.

8. **(A)**

   A labyrinth is a maze or intricate pathway. Once someone enters a labyrinth, she can find it very difficult to find the way out.

9. **(E)**

   The word root *sacrō sānctus* means "made holy by sacred rites." Related words include *sacred*, *sacrifice*, *sanction*, and *sanctuary*.

10. **(B)**

    Rudimentary means "basic or elementary." For example, familiarity with the alphabet is a rudimentary reading skill that children learn at a young age.

11. **(C)**

    The prefix *im–* means "not," and the word root *parcial* means "biased," so an impartial jury is one whose members are not biased and are therefore able to evaluate evidence in an objective, unprejudiced manner.

12. **(B)**

    Reiterate means "to do something over again." For example, when someone reiterates a piece of information, she restates it.

13. **(D)**

    The prefix *pre–* means "before," the word root *cede* means "to go," and the suffix *–ent* means "something that," so a precedent is an event or action that comes before another event or action. A model comes first and is used as a plan to make something else.

14. **(A)**

    Prudent means "wise or judicious." For example, a prudent decision is a wise, practical one.

15. **(C)**

    The word root *figūrāre* means "to shape," and the suffix *–ive* means "indicating a tendency," so a figurative expression, or figure of speech, is shaped or invented rather than based on literal truth.

16. **(C)**

    Innocuous means "harmless or inoffensive." For example, an innocuous substance is not harmful.

17. (C)

The word root *neglegere* means "to neglect," and the suffix root *–ence* means "the act of," so negligence is the act of neglecting—not paying proper attention to—someone or something.

18. (E)

Lax means "loose or open." For example, a lax set of rules would be permissive.

19. (A)

The word root *equi* means "equal," the word root *vōx* means "voice," and the suffix *–ate* means "perform the action of." Thus, to equivocate means to avoid privileging one explanation over another or giving a direct answer.

20. (E)

Ponderous means "very heavy or unwieldy." For example, a huge land animal such as an elephant has a lumbering, ponderous gait.

21. (C)

The word root *circum* means "around," and the word root *specere* means "to look," so a circumspect person looks cautiously around herself—considers her next step—in a self-protective way.

22. (E)

Assiduous means "to show great care or effort." For example, an assiduous person works hard.

23. (A)

Solicitous means "full of concern." For example, good waiters and waitresses are solicitous: they care about keeping their customers happy.

24. (C)

Aptitude means "natural ability or tendency." For example, someone with an aptitude for math can learn mathematical concepts quickly and easily.

25. (B)

The word root *jeu* or *jocus* means "play, game, or joke" and the word root *partir* means "to divide." A divided game is a game of chance that involves great risk, so to be in jeopardy means to be in danger (of losing).

MATH KNOWLEDGE

1. (D)

Simplify using PEMDAS.

$z^3(z + 2)^2 - 4z^3 + 2$

$z^3(z^2 + 4z + 4) - 4z^3 + 2$

$z^5 + 4z^4 + 4z^3 - 4z^3 + 2$

$z^5 + 4z^4 + 2$

2. (B)

Use the rules of exponents to simplify the expression.

$$\frac{(3x^2y^2)^2}{3^3x^{-2}y^3} = \frac{3^2x^4y^4}{3^3x^{-2}y^3} = \frac{x^6y}{3}$$

3. (A)

$$\left(\frac{1}{2}\right)^3 = \frac{1}{2} \times \frac{1}{2} \times \frac{1}{2} = \frac{1}{8}$$

4. (B)

The slope 0.0293 gives the increase in passenger car miles (in billions) for each year that passes. Muliply this value by 5 to find the increase that occurs over 5 years: $5(0.0293) =$ **0.1465 billion miles**.

5. (C)

Use the formula for the area of a cylinder.

$V = \pi r^2 h$

$= \pi(4^2)(0.5) = $ **25.12 ft³**

6. (A)

(A) Corresponding angles in right triangles are not necessarily the same, so they do not have to be similar.

(B) All spheres are similar.

(C) Corresponding angles in 30–60–90 triangles are the same, so all 30–60–90 triangles are similar.

(D) Corresponding angles in a square are all the same (90°), so all squares are similar.

(E) All corresponding angles in cubes are congruent, so they are all similar.

7. (A)

Simplify each root and add.

$\sqrt[3]{64} = 4$

$\sqrt[3]{729} = 9$

$4 + 9 = $ **13**

8. (B)

Find the highest possible multiple of 4 that is less than or equal to 397, and then subtract to find the remainder.

$99 \times 4 = 396$

$397 - 396 = $ **1**

9. (C)

Find the height of the cylinder using the equation for surface area.

$SA = 2\pi rh + 2\pi r^2$

$48\pi = 2\pi(4)h + 2\pi(4)^2$

$h = 2$

Find the volume using the volume equation.

$V = \pi r^2 h$

$V = \pi(4)^2(2) = $ **32π ft.³**

10. (D)

Use FOIL to multiply the first two terms.

$(x + 3)(x - 2) = x^2 + 3x - 2x - 6$

$= x^2 + x - 6$

Multiply the resulting trinomial by $(x + 4)$.

$(x^2 + x - 6)(x + 4) =$

$x^3 + 4x^2 + x^2 + 4x - 6x - 24$

$= x^3 + 5x^2 - 2x - 24$

11. (C)

Plug each value into the equation.

$4(3 + 4)^2 - 4(3)^2 + 20 = 180 \neq 276$

$4(4 + 4)^2 - 4(3)^2 + 20 = 240 \neq 276$

$4(6 + 4)^2 - 4(6)^2 + 20 = $ **276**

$4(12 + 4)^2 - 4(12)^2 + 20 = 468 \neq 276$

$4(24 + 4)^2 - 4(24)^2 + 20 = 852 \neq 276$

12. (A)

Plug 0 in for y and solve for x.

$10x + 10y = 10$

$10x + 10(0) = 10$

$x = 1$

The x-intercept is at **(1, 0)**.

13. (C)

Round each value and add.

$129{,}113 \approx 129{,}000$

$34{,}602 \approx 35{,}000$

$129{,}000 + 35{,}000 = \textbf{164{,}000}$

14. (A)

Use the midpoint formula to find point B.

$M_x: \dfrac{(7 + x)}{2} = -3$

$x = -13$

$M_y: \dfrac{(12 + y)}{2} = 10$

$y = 8$

$B = \textbf{(-13, 8)}$

15. (C)

Factor the trinomial and set each factor equal to 0.

$x^2 - 3x - 18 = 0$

$(x + 3)(x - 6) = 0$

$(x + 3) = 0$

$\boldsymbol{x = -3}$

$(x - 6) = 0$

$\boldsymbol{x = 6}$

16. (B)

Use the triangle inequality theorem to find the possible values for the third side, then calculate the possible perimeters.

$13 - 5 < s < 13 + 5$

$8 < s < 18$

$13 + 5 + 8 < P < 13 + 5 + 18$

$26 < P < 36$

26.5 is the only answer choice in this range

17. (E)

$5 \div 8 = 0.625$

$0.625 \times 100 = \textbf{62.5\%}$

18. (E)

Solve the system using substitution.

$z - 2x = 14 \rightarrow z = 2x + 14$

$2z - 6x = 18$

$2(2x + 14) - 6x = 18$

$4x + 28 - 6x = 18$

$-2x = -10$

$x = 5$

$z - 2(5) = 14$

$\boldsymbol{z = 24}$

19. (D)

Plug $m = 3$ and $n = -4$ into the expression and simplify.

$15m + 2n^2 - 7 =$

$15(3) + 2(-4)^2 - 7 = \textbf{70}$

20. (C)

Write out each number to find the largest.

A. 9299 ones = 9299

B. 903 tens = 9030

C. 93 hundreds = **9300**

D. 9 thousands = 9000

E. 9 thousandths = 0.009

21. (A)

Use the points to find the slope.

$m = \dfrac{y_2 - y_1}{x_2 - x_1} = \dfrac{-3 - 9}{4 - (-2)} = -2$

Use the point-slope equation to find the equation of the line.

$(y - y_1) = m(x - x_1)$

$y - (-3) = -2(x - 4)$

$\boldsymbol{y = -2x + 5}$

22. (E)

All the points lie on the circle, so each line segment is a radius. The sum of the 4 lines will be 4 times the radius.

$r = \dfrac{75}{2} = 37.5$

$4r = \textbf{150}$

23. (B)

Add 5 to each side to isolate the variable k.

$10 \leq k - 5$

$15 \leq k$

$\boldsymbol{k \geq 15}$

24. (B)

Calculate the volume of water in tank A.

$V = l \times w \times h$

$5 \times 10 \times 1 = 50 \text{ ft}^3$

Find the height this volume would reach in tank B.

$V = l \times w \times h$

$50 = 5 \times 5 \times h$

$h = \textbf{2 ft}$

25. (B)

Plug each set of values into the inequality $2a - 5b > 12$ and simplify.

(A) $2(2) - 5(6) = -26 \not> 12$

(B) $2(1) - 5(-3) = \mathbf{17 > 12}$

(C) $2(-1) - 5(3) = -17 \not> 12$

(D) $2(7) - 5(2) = 4 \not> 12$

(E) $2(2) - 5(-1) = 9 \not> 12$

READING COMPREHENSION

1. **(A)**

   (A) is correct. The author writes that "the resulting war brought all these various actors, motivations, and agendas into a conflict in which no clear winner would emerge."

   (B) is incorrect. While the author does discuss the different actors, this is not the main idea of the passage.

   (C) is incorrect. The author describes the many other actors involved in the war but does not indicate that any actor was more involved than the Koreans themselves.

   (D) is incorrect. Though this is stated in the passage, it is not the main idea.

   (E) is incorrect. Though this is discussed in the last paragraph, it is not the main idea.

2. **(D)**

   (A) is incorrect. The text does not describe Japan's views on the spread of communism.

   (B) is incorrect. The text states that it was the rise of Mao Zedong to power in China that threatened America's global influence and power.

   (C) is incorrect. The text discusses American efforts to remove hundreds of thousands of Japanese soldiers and citizens but does not identify them as a threat.

   (D) is correct. The text describes Japan's "aggressive imperialism" as well as its colonization of Korea.

   (E) is incorrect. The text states that the exiled government was supported by the United States, not by Japan.

3. **(B)**

   (A) is incorrect. While the text references a communist government in the north and a communist group in the south, it does not discuss the preference of most Koreans.

   (B) is correct. Although the Soviet Union and the United States were willing to compromise over Korea in 1945, the text later states that by 1950 the two countries were at war due to each other's aggression.

   (C) is incorrect. The text states that Kim Il-sung was "reluctantly backed by China" but does not mention Mao Zedong's influence on the leader.

   (D) is incorrect. The text does not address Koreans' feelings about the US occupation of Japan.

   (E) is incorrect. The text does state that the Soviet Union controlled the area containing most of Korea's industrial resources; however, it does not explain what the Soviet Union did with those resources.

4. **(E)**

   (A) is incorrect. While the text does address this, it is not the primary purpose.

   (B) is incorrect. The text examines the causes of the war rather than its impact.

   (C) is incorrect. The text does not explain the events leading up to the war.

   (D) is incorrect. The text names only two leaders involved in the war, and they are not the primary purpose of the passage.

   (E) is correct. The first sentence states "Much of the complexity of the Korean War derives from the very different perspectives of the participants."

5. **(C)**

   (A) is incorrect. In the second paragraph, the author writes, "In 1945, the Soviets…seized control of Korea. When the war ended, the United States . . . sent an expeditionary force to southern Korea."

   (B) is incorrect. In the sixth paragraph, the author writes, "However, the scarce arable land and two-thirds of the people were in the southern zone."

   (C) is correct. The United States and the Soviet Union agreed to *temporarily* divide Korea.

   (D) is incorrect. In the sixth paragraph, the author writes that Korea "had been occupied by Japan for much of its history, making it automatically resistant to the interference of both Soviet and American troops."

   (E) is incorrect. In the fifth paragraph, the author writes that a "second Chinese government persisted, exiled to Taiwan but politically sanctioned by the United States."

6. **(D)**

(A) is incorrect. While the author explains that Japan was a concern for Asian countries, there is no connection between US policy in Japan and Chinese actions.

(B) is incorrect. The text describes the Soviet Union encouraging aggression by North Korea, which would lead to a conflict with the United States.

(C) is incorrect. The text does not indicate that Japanese occupation created political or economic problems for Korea.

(D) is correct. The author describes several actions taken by the United States and the Soviet Union—namely the division of Korea—which created the internal conflict that resulted in war.

(E) is incorrect. The text describes Kim Il-sung's motivation as reuniting the country, rather than pursuing economic growth.

7. **(E)**

(A) is incorrect. The passage does not explain why the United States became involved in Somalia.

(B) is incorrect. While the passage does address this, it is not the primary purpose.

(C) is incorrect. The passage mentions this in the last paragraph, but it is not the primary purpose of the passage.

(D) is incorrect. The passage does mention the Rangers leaving behind supplies, but this is not the primary purpose of the passage.

(E) is correct. The passage identifies the reasons why the mission went awry and then explains how it led to changes in military operations and planning.

8. **(B)**

(A) is incorrect. The passage does not describe which parts of the US forces were most responsible for civilian deaths.

(B) is correct. The passage states that "they knew that the US would use the helicopters for air support during the raid... They also knew that American policy was to rescue the helicopter crew once it was downed, which gave the SNA the tactical advantage."

(C) is incorrect. While the passage does describe the densely populated city, it does not discuss any failed attempts at landing.

(D) is incorrect. The passage does state that the SNA targeted the helicopters but not that the weapons were specifically designed for that purpose.

(E) is incorrect. The passage does not discuss the noise of the helicopters.

9. **(C)**

(A) is incorrect. The passage states that the center of Aidid's territory was the capital of Mogadishu.

(B) is incorrect. The passage describes how Aidid and his people studied US tactical patterns and developed strategies in response.

(C) is correct. The passage states, "raids [were planned] to capture key members of the various factions that were causing the most strife and conflict, with particular focus on the Somali National Alliance."

(D) is incorrect. There is no evidence in the passage that Aidid wanted to preserve any US military technology.

(E) is incorrect. The passage describes the civil war as the result of multiple competing warlords, and it does not ever state that any others were interested in peace.

10. **(A)**

(A) is correct. The passage states that "public outrage ultimately led to American withdrawal from Somalia altogether and to the country's descent into deeper chaos."

(B) is incorrect. The passage states, "(2) they occurred under the cover of night."

(C) is incorrect. The passage states that "the mission was ultimately successful in obtaining its targets" despite its outcome.

(D) is incorrect. The passage states, "Because of the deeply fractured nature of the country at the time, the US mission was a daunting task without a clear goal."

(E) is incorrect. The passage states that "the Rangers were bogged down by gunfire on the streets, and the two Black Hawk helicopters providing support were shot down."

11. **(D)**

(A) is incorrect. The author argues that "there is no surefire way to be successful in urban warfare."

(B) is incorrect. The passage does not discuss past wars in urban settings, only US raid tactics.

(C) is incorrect. The author states that civilian deaths were high because combatants were able to move in and out of the general population easily because of the density. Advanced technology is not mentioned as an issue.

(D) is correct. The passage states that "deep complexities of urban warfare . . . led to increased focus on improving information gathering, developing ways of observing targets from a safe distance, and creating more flexible and thorough plans for urban missions."

(E) is incorrect. The passage describes the difficulty of keeping military secrets in Mogadishu because of the base of operations at the airport.

12. **(A)**

(A) is correct. The "collateral" refers to civilians, who were killed in addition to the soldiers.

(B) is incorrect. There is no context that implies that the deaths were only about native-born people.

(C) is incorrect. There is no context that implies whether the deaths were intended or not intended.

(D) is incorrect. There is no context that implies the word is about the value of the deaths.

(E) is incorrect. There is no context related to how the deaths were perceived by others.

13. **(D)**

(A) is incorrect. Washington emphasizes that his argument is "not be understood as capable of patronizing infidelity to existing engagements... [L]et those engagements be observed in their genuine sense." He argues that America should avoid future entanglements but indicates that the country should not break from its existing relationships.

(B) is incorrect. Washington states, "It is our true policy to steer clear of permanent alliances with any portion of the foreign world; so far, I mean, as we are now at liberty to do it[...]"

(C) is incorrect. Washington states, "Hence, therefore, it must be unwise in us to implicate

ourselves, by artificial ties, in the ordinary vicissitudes of her [Europe's] politics, or the ordinary combinations and collisions of her friendships or enmities."

(D) is correct. The author writes, "It is our true policy to steer clear of permanent alliances with any portion of the foreign world; so far, I mean, as we are now at liberty to do it[...]"

(E) Incorrect. Washington advocates specifically for a policy of isolationism.

14. **(A)**

(A) is correct. Washington states that Europe is "engaged in frequent controversies" and that it would be "unwise to implicate ourselves...in the ordinary vicissitudes of her politics, or the ordinary combinations and collisions of her friendships and enmities."

(B) is incorrect. This answer choice does not fit in the context of the sentence.

(C) is incorrect. Washington's use of the description "the ordinary combinations and collisions of her friendships and enmities" suggests that European politics are regularly fluctuating, not just mutating in the current moment.

(D) is incorrect. Washington's description of European politics indicates that they are fluctuating, not remaining stagnant.

(E) is incorrect. Washington does not allude to rules or laws in European politics.

15. **(A)**

(A) is correct. The passage indicates that snakes' "intricate diamonds, stripes, and swirls help the animals hide from predators, but perhaps most importantly (for us humans, anyway), the markings can also indicate whether the snake is venomous."

(B) is incorrect. Though the author does mention one difference between the kingsnake and the coral snake, this is not the primary purpose of the passage.

(C) is incorrect. The author does not indicate why snakes are dangerous, only that some of them are.

(D) is incorrect. Though the author does provide some examples of this, this answer choice is more general, while the passage focused on snakes in particular.

(E) is incorrect. While the author may be contradicting readers' understanding of the species, this is not the primary purpose of the passage.

16. **(B)**

(A) is incorrect. The author mentions that "the kingsnake is actually nonvenomous" but provides no more information about whether the kingsnake poses a danger to humans.

(B) is correct. The final paragraph of the passage states that the two species "frequently [share] a habitat" and that "[a] predatory hawk or eagle, usually hunting from high in the sky, can't tell the difference between the two species, and so the kingsnake gets passed over and lives another day."

(C) is incorrect. The author does not imply that it is easy to tell the difference between venomous and nonvenomous snakes, only that it is possible.

(D) is incorrect. The final paragraph states that the kingsnake "has very similar marking to the venomous coral snake" and does not indicate that these markings change with circumstances.

(E) is incorrect. The author mentions that "the kingsnake is actually nonvenomous" but provides no more information about whether the kingsnake poses a danger to humans.

17. **(C)**

(A) is incorrect. The second paragraph states that "[a] predatory hawk or eagle, usually hunting from high in the sky, can't tell the difference between the two species, and so the kingsnake gets passed over and lives another day."

(B) is incorrect. The second paragraph states that "[t]he scarlet kingsnake, for example, has very similar markings to the venomous coral snake with whom it frequently shares a habitat."

(C) is correct. The first paragraph states that "[w]hile it might seem counterintuitive for a venomous snake to stand out in bright red or blue, that fancy costume tells any nearby predator that approaching him would be a bad idea." The coral snake's markings do not allow it to hide from predators but rather to "ward [them] off[.]"

(D) is incorrect. The second paragraph states that "the kingsnake is actually nonvenomous; it's merely pretending to be dangerous to eat."

(E) is incorrect. The first paragraph states that snakes' "intricate diamonds, stripes, and swirls help the animals hide from predators[.]"

18. **(A)**

(A) is correct. The passage states that "intricate diamonds, stripes, and swirls help the animals hide from predators[,]" implying that these markings are complex enough to allow the animals to blend in with their surroundings.

(B) is incorrect. The passage indicates that colorful markings do not allow the animals to hide but rather to ward off predators, so the word *colorful* does not apply in the context of the sentence.

(C) is incorrect. This answer choice does not fit in the context of the sentence, as the animals do not choose their markings.

(D) is incorrect. The author does not suggest that animals' markings are changeable.

(E) is incorrect. This answer choice does not fit in the context of the sentence.

19. **(C)**

(A) is incorrect. The second paragraph states that "[t]he scarlet kingsnake, for example, has very similar markings to the venomous coral snake with whom it frequently shares a habitat. However, the kingsnake is actually nonvenomous[.]"

(B) is incorrect. The second paragraph states that "[t]he scarlet kingsnake, for example, has very similar markings to the venomous coral snake with whom it frequently shares a habitat. However, the kingsnake is actually nonvenomous[.]"

(C) is correct. The second paragraph states that "[t]he scarlet kingsnake, for example, has very similar markings to the venomous coral snake with whom it frequently shares a habitat. However, the kingsnake is actually nonvenomous[.]"

(D) is incorrect. The second paragraph states that "[t]he scarlet kingsnake, for example, has very similar markings to the venomous coral snake with whom it frequently shares a habitat. However, the kingsnake is actually nonvenomous[.]"

(E) is incorrect. The second paragraph states that "[t]he scarlet kingsnake, for example, has very similar markings to the venomous coral snake with whom it frequently shares a habitat. However, the kingsnake is actually nonvenomous[.]"

20. **(D)**

(A) is incorrect. The author includes nothing to suggest that hand sanitizer disguises pathogens.

(B) is incorrect. The author includes nothing to suggest that hand sanitizer hides pathogens.

(C) is incorrect. The author notes that while hand sanitizer kills most of the bacteria on the surface of the hands, it "does nothing to remove organic matter" from them.

(D) is correct. The author writes that "hands 'cleaned' with hand sanitizer may still harbor pathogens" because sanitizer "does nothing to remove organic matter" from the hands. The bacteria are not completely washed off, and therefore some are able to continue living on the surface of the hands.

(E) is incorrect. The author includes nothing to suggest that hand sanitizer breeds pathogens.

21. **(B)**

(A) is incorrect. In the first paragraph, the author writes, "Many illnesses are spread when people touch infected surfaces, such as door handles or other people's hands, and then touch their own eyes, mouths, or noses."

(B) is correct. In the second paragraph, the author writes, "The [hand washing] process doesn't even require warm water—studies have shown that cold water is just as effective at reducing the number of microbes on the hands. Antibacterial soaps are also available, although several studies have shown that simple soap and cold water is just as effective."

(C) is incorrect. In the third paragraph, the author writes, "These gels, liquids, and foams contain a high concentration of alcohol (usually at least 60 percent) that kills most bacteria and fungi; they can also be effective against some, but not all, viruses."

(D) is incorrect. In the final paragraph, the author writes, "Thus, while hand sanitizer can be helpful in situations where soap and clean water aren't available, a simple hand washing is still the best option."

(E) is incorrect. In the third paragraph, the author writes, "There is a downside to hand sanitizer, however. Because the sanitizer isn't rinsed from hands, it only kills pathogens and does nothing to remove organic matter. So,

hands 'cleaned' with hand sanitizer may still harbor pathogens."

22. **(B)**

(A) is incorrect. The author includes nothing to suggest that water has antibacterial properties.

(B) is correct. The author writes that because hand sanitizer "isn't rinsed from hands [as is water], it only kills pathogens and does nothing to remove organic matter."

(C) is incorrect. The author writes, "The [hand washing] process doesn't even require warm water—studies have shown that cold water is just as effective at reducing the number of microbes on the hands. Antibacterial soaps are also available, although several studies have shown that simple soap and cold water are just as effective." This implies that the temperature of the water is unrelated to its effectiveness.

(D) is incorrect. The author indicates that the temperature of the water is unrelated to its effectiveness (see C above).

(E) is incorrect. The passage does not discuss hydrating the skin.

23. **(C)**

(A) is incorrect. While both of these details are included in the passage, they do not provide an adequate summary of the passage overall.

(B) is incorrect. While both of these details are included in the passage, they do not provide an adequate summary of the passage overall.

(C) is correct. Together, these sentences provide an adequate summary of the passage overall.

(D) is incorrect. While both of these details are included in the passage, they do not provide an adequate summary of the passage overall.

(E) is incorrect. While both of these details are included in the passage, they do not provide an adequate summary of the passage overall.

24. **(A)**

(A) is correct. Each paragraph examines hand washing from a different angle.

(B) is incorrect. In the final paragraph, the author writes, "Thus, while hand sanitizer can be helpful in situations where soap and clean water aren't available, a simple hand washing is still the best option." The author acknowledges that hand sanitizer is a viable option when soap and water are unavailable.

(C) is incorrect. Though the author lists a few of the diseases that are spread through daily interaction "including ... the flu, the common cold, diarrhea, and many acute respiratory illnesses[,]" she does not explain any further.

(D) is incorrect. While the author does explain how hand washing and hand sanitizer are effective, her goal is not just to describe hand washing, but rather to convince readers of its importance.

(E) is incorrect. The author writes, "Antibacterial soaps are also available, although several studies have shown that simple soap and cold water are just as effective[,]" but this is the extent of her comment on antibacterial soaps; she does not take a particular stance against them or tell readers not to purchase them.

25. (A)

(A) is correct. In the first paragraph, the author writes, "Many illnesses are spread when people touch infected surfaces, such as door handles or other people's hands, and then touch their own eyes, mouths, or noses." The reader can infer from this sentence that hand washing prevents the spread of surface-borne illnesses.

(B) is incorrect. The author says that "[m]any illnesses are spread" when people touch their "eyes, mouths, and noses[,]" but not all illnesses; thus the reader can infer that hand washing is not solely for people who touch their faces.

(C) is incorrect. The author says that "while hand sanitizer can be helpful in situations where soap and clean water aren't available, a simple hand washing is still the best option." Thus, hand sanitizer should be not used instead of hand washing altogether, but it does effectively serve its purpose as an alternative when soap and water are not available.

(D) is incorrect. The author indicates that hand sanitizer will not replace hand washing altogether because it "does nothing to remove organic matter" from hands after use. Thus, "hands 'cleaned' with hand sanitizer may still harbor pathogens."

(E) is incorrect. The author writes that "if pathogens can be removed from the hands before they spread, infections can be prevented." This implies that healthy people should wash their hands as well to prevent the spread of disease from surfaces they have touched.

PHYSICAL SCIENCE

1. **(D)**

    (A) is incorrect. Power is a measure of the rate at which work is done.

    (B) is incorrect. A force is a push or pull that changes an object's velocity.

    (C) is incorrect. Displacement is the distance between an object's start and end positions.

    (D) is correct. Acceleration is the rate at which velocity changes.

    (E) is incorrect. Energy is the measure of an object's capacity to do work.

2. **(B)**

    (A) is incorrect. The magnitude of an earthquake does not directly refer to its power; rather, it refers to the energy released during the earthquake.

    (B) is correct. The magnitude of an earthquake refers to the energy released during the earthquake.

    (C) is incorrect. The magnitude of an earthquake does not directly refer to its destructive ability; however this is indirectly related due to the impact of the energy released during the earthquake.

    (D) is incorrect. The magnitude of an earthquake does not directly refer to its depth, though the depth of an earthquake can affect its magnitude.

    (E) is incorrect. The magnitude of an earthquake does not describe the location of an earthquake.

3. **(B)**

    (A) is incorrect. A solar eclipse is when the moon moves between the sun and Earth.

    (B) is correct. A lunar eclipse is when Earth moves between the moon and the sun.

    (C) is incorrect. A black hole is a collapsed star with tremendous gravitational pull.

    (D) is incorrect. A supernova is an explosion of the core of a star.

    (E) is incorrect. An aurora occurs when solar winds interact with the Earth's magnetic field.

4. **(D)**

    (A) is incorrect. In a substitution reaction, a single atom or ion swaps places with another atom or ion.

    (B) is incorrect. In an acid-base reaction, an acid and a base react to neutralize each other. This reaction does not include an acid or base.

    (C) is incorrect. In a decomposition reaction, a compound breaks down into smaller molecules or compounds.

    (D) is correct. Combustion is defined as a reaction in which a hydrocarbon reacts with O_2 to produce CO_2 and H_2O.

    (E) is incorrect. In a synthesis reaction, two or more reactants combine to form a single product.

5. **(A)**

    (A) is correct. Friction is a force that opposes motion.

    (B) is incorrect. Friction works in the direction opposite an object's motion, so it will not push down on a surface.

    (C) is incorrect. Torque is the force that creates rotational motion.

    (D) is incorrect. Friction generally works against the force of gravity.

    (E) is incorrect. Friction may work with or against the normal force.

6. **(E)**

    (A) is incorrect. Wavelength is the distance between cycles of a wave. It does not affect how large an object appears to be.

    (B) is incorrect. Diffraction occurs when waves pass through a narrow opening and then spread out.

    (C) is incorrect. Amplitude is the height of a wave; it affects how loud a sound is perceived to be.

    (D) is incorrect. Reflection occurs when waves bounce off an object. When light waves are reflected, it does not change the apparent size of an object being viewed.

    (E) is correct. Lenses refract, or bend, light waves to make objects appear larger.

7. **(C)**

    (A) is incorrect. Isotopes must have the same number of protons, not electrons.

    (B) is incorrect. Isotopes are defined as having different numbers of neutrons, not the same number.

(C) is correct. Isotopes are atoms of the same element with the same number of protons but different numbers of neutrons.

(D) is incorrect. Isotopes have the same number of protons but can also have the same number of electrons.

(E) is incorrect. Atoms with different numbers of protons would not be the same element.

8. **(A)**

    (A) is correct. Tension is the force that results from objects being pulled or hung.

    (B) is incorrect. The box experiences friction as it slides against the ramp.

    (C) is incorrect. Gravity is the force pulling the box down the ramp.

    (D) is incorrect. The normal force is the upward force of the ramp on the box.

    (E) is incorrect. The buoyant force is the upward force experienced by floating objects.

9. **(B)**

    (A) is incorrect. Particles in a liquid are more tightly packed than particles in a gas, but there is more space among particles in a liquid than among them in a solid.

    (B) is correct. Gas is the state of matter in which atomic particles are most loosely packed, and the greatest amount of space exists among atoms.

    (C) is incorrect. Particles are most tightly packed in a solid.

    (D) is incorrect. The nuclei within a plasma are electrically charged, and electrons move about freely.

    (E) is incorrect. A crystal is a type of solid in which atoms are arranged in a rigid structure.

10. **(B)**

    (A) is incorrect. Mercury is the planet closest to the sun. Venus orbits between Mercury and Earth.

    (B) is correct. Venus's orbit is closest to Earth. Venus is the second planet from the sun, and Earth is the third planet from the sun.

    (C) is incorrect. Jupiter is the fifth planet from the sun.

    (D) is incorrect. Saturn is the sixth planet from the sun.

    (E) is incorrect. Neptune is the farthest planet from the sun.

11. **(E)**

    (A) is incorrect. The lithosphere is the rigid outermost layer of the earth.

    (B) is incorrect. The asthenosphere lies beneath the lithosphere and is mostly solid.

    (C) is incorrect. The mesosphere lies beneath the asthenosphere and is mostly solid.

    (D) is incorrect. The inner core is solid and composed primarily of iron.

    (E) is correct. The outer core is composed of a liquid, iron-nickel alloy and flows around the inner core.

12. **(C)**

    (A) is incorrect. An atom with a charge of −17e would have seventeen more electrons than protons.

    (B) is incorrect. An atom with a charge of −7e would have seven more electrons than protons.

    (C) is correct. This atom has a total charge of $-5e + 12e = +7e$.

    (D) is incorrect. An atom with a charge of +17 would have seventeen more protons than electrons.

    (E) is incorrect. Neutral atoms have an equal number of electrons and protons.

13. **(B)**

    (A) is incorrect. A mineral is a naturally occurring substance.

    (B) is correct. A mineral is inorganic; only a rock may be composed of organic material.

    (C) is incorrect. A mineral is a solid.

    (D) is incorrect. A mineral has a crystalline structure.

    (E) is incorrect. A mineral is composed of a single chemical compound.

14. **(A)**

    (A) is correct. When water changes form, it does not change the chemical composition of the substance. Once water becomes ice, the ice can easily turn back into water.

    (B) is incorrect. During a chemical change, the chemical composition of the substance changes and cannot be reversed. Baking a cake is an example of a chemical change.

    (C) is incorrect. Rusting is an example of a chemical change.

(D) is incorrect. Setting off fireworks causes a chemical change.

(E) is incorrect. Neutralizing an acid with a base is a chemical change.

15. **(A)**

(A) is correct. The sun is about ninety-three million miles from Earth; the next closest star is about twenty-five trillion miles away.

(B) is incorrect. The moon orbits Earth.

(C) is incorrect. Earth is always closer to the sun than Jupiter is.

(D) is incorrect. Mercury is the closest planet to the sun, but Venus is closer to Earth.

(E) is incorrect. Uranus is farther from the sun than Jupiter.

16. **(B)**

(A) is incorrect. The mesosphere is the layer where the air becomes thin and has some of the coldest temperatures on Earth.

(B) is correct. The stratosphere contains a sublayer called the ozone layer, which absorbs harmful ultraviolet radiation from the sun.

(C) is incorrect. The troposphere is the layer closest to Earth's surface and is where most of Earth's weather occurs.

(D) is incorrect. The thermosphere contains molecules that are spread far apart and become super-heated.

(E) is incorrect. The exosphere is the outermost layer of the atmosphere and does not absorb ultraviolet radiation.

17. **(E)**

(A) is incorrect. All mixtures, whether saturated or unsaturated, have a solute and solvent that are not chemically bonded.

(B) is incorrect. The state of the solute and solvent has no effect on whether the solution is saturated.

(C) is incorrect. A solution with an evenly distributed solute is homogeneous, and it may be saturated or unsaturated.

(D) is incorrect. A solute is always evenly distributed in a solution. This does not affect whether the solution is saturated.

(E) is correct. No more solute can be dissolved into a saturated solution.

18. **(A)**

(A) is correct. Geysers are caused by geothermal heating of water underground.

(B) is incorrect. Glaciers are formed when snow and ice do not melt before new layers of snow and ice are added.

(C) is incorrect. Tsunamis are caused by earthquakes on the ocean floor.

(D) is incorrect. Tornadoes are caused by instability of warm, humid air in the lower atmosphere mixing with cool air in the upper atmosphere.

(E) is incorrect. Hurricanes are powered by water evaporating from the ocean.

19. **(B)**

(A) is incorrect. Chemical potential energy is stored in the bonds between atoms.

(B) is correct. Elastic potential energy is stored by compressing or expanding an object.

(C) is incorrect. Gravitational potential energy is stored in objects that have been moved away from a gravitational mass.

(D) is incorrect. Electric potential energy is stored in charged objects.

(E) is incorrect. Kinetic energy is the energy of objects in motion.

20. **(B)**

(A) is incorrect. One hour is $\frac{1}{24}$ of the time it takes for the earth to rotate on its axis.

(B) is correct. Earth takes approximately twenty-four hours to rotate on its axis.

(C) is incorrect. The moon takes approximately one month to revolve around the Earth.

(D) is incorrect. The Earth takes approximately one year to revolve around the sun.

(E) is incorrect. A century is one hundred years.

TABLE READING

1.	(A)	21.	(D)
2.	(D)	22.	(B)
3.	(B)	23.	(C)
4.	(C)	24.	(A)
5.	(E)	25.	(E)
6.	(E)	26.	(C)
7.	(D)	27.	(B)
8.	(B)	28.	(B)
9.	(C)	29.	(C)
10.	(E)	30.	(C)
11.	(D)	31.	(D)
12.	(C)	32.	(A)
13.	(E)	33.	(B)
14.	(B)	34.	(C)
15.	(A)	35.	(D)
16.	(A)	36.	(B)
17.	(D)	37.	(E)
18.	(B)	38.	(A)
19.	(C)	39.	(D)
20.	(B)	40.	(C)

1.	(C)	climbing	banking left	north
2.	(D)	level flight	no bank	west
3.	(C)	climbing	banking left	west
4.	(B)	level flight	no bank	north
5.	(A)	climbing	no bank	north
6.	(A)	climbing	banking left	east
7.	(D)	level flight	banking right	north
8.	(C)	descending	banking left	southeast
9.	(D)	level flight	banking left	south
10.	(C)	level flight	banking left	west
11.	(B)	descending	no bank	east
12.	(B)	level flight	banking right	west
13.	(C)	level flight	no bank	south
14.	(A)	level flight	no bank	east
15.	(A)	descending	banking right	southwest
16.	(B)	level flight	banking left	north
17.	(D)	descending	banking left	west
18.	(C)	descending	no bank	southeast
19.	(D)	climbing	banking left	east
20.	(A)	climbing	no bank	west
21.	(A)	climbing	banking right	west
22.	(C)	level flight	banking right	south
23.	(D)	climbing	banking right	north
24.	(D)	climbing	no bank	east
25.	(B)	descending	no bank	west

Block Counting

1.	(D)	16.	(A)
2.	(C)	17.	(C)
3.	(A)	18.	(E)
4.	(C)	19.	(B)
5.	(B)	20.	(D)
6.	(C)	21.	(B)
7.	(B)	22.	(A)
8.	(B)	23.	(C)
9.	(A)	24.	(E)
10.	(E)	25.	(D)
11.	(B)	26.	(D)
12.	(D)	27.	(B)
13.	(A)	28.	(E)
14.	(C)	29.	(B)
15.	(B)	30.	(A)

AVIATION INFORMATION

1. **(C)**

(A) is incorrect. Ailerons require pilot input.

(B) is incorrect. The nose of the aircraft rises when the tail is pushed down.

(C) is correct. When the elevators are raised, the tail of the aircraft is pushed down, which increases the pitch and raises the nose of the aircraft.

(D) is incorrect. The elevators do not control left turns.

(E) is incorrect. The elevators do not control right turns.

2. **(C)**

(A) is incorrect. The ailerons affect the longitudinal axis of the aircraft during turns.

(B) is incorrect. The elevators affect pitch.

(C) is correct. The rudder affects yaw; it controls the vertical axis of the aircraft.

(D) is incorrect. The spoilers reduce lift, increase drag, and control speed.

(E) is incorrect. The position of the wings adjusts the airflow pressure, controlling lift and drag.

3. **(B)**

(A) is incorrect. The teeter hinge allows the blades to flap.

(B) is correct. The swashplate allows for directional movement of the aircraft.

(C) is incorrect. The ducted fan is a component of the NOTAR aircraft design.

(D) is incorrect. The tail boom is a structural component that supports the tail rotor assembly.

(E) is incorrect. The skids are used as landing gear for rotary-wing aircraft.

4. **(A)**

(A) is correct. This climb is used to clear obstacles that may be in the flight path.

(B) is incorrect. This climb is used to cover the most distance, not the most altitude.

(C) is incorrect. This climb will not produce the greatest altitude.

(D) is incorrect. This is not a type of climb.

(E) is incorrect. This is not a type of climb.

5. **(B)**

(A) is incorrect. A coaxial rotor system cancels torque effect by using counter rotating rotor heads.

(B) is correct. Translating tendency causes a rotary-wing aircraft to drift laterally due to tail rotor thrust.

(C) is incorrect. Gyroscopic precession is when a force input is applied yet the force output is felt 90 degrees later in the plane of rotation.

(D) is incorrect. The tail rotor cancels out the torque effect.

(E) is incorrect. An effective translational lift results from increased efficiency of the main rotor system as directional flight is established.

6. **(D)**

(A) is incorrect. The aircraft pitch would indeed change; however, this is not the best complete answer.

(B) is incorrect. The airspeed would increase and the nose of the aircraft would pitch downward.

(C) is incorrect. The airspeed would indeed increase due to the change of airflow around the wings caused by the cyclic or control wheel; however, this is not the best answer.

(D) is correct. This is the best answer because it describes the combination of changes to the aircraft.

(E) is incorrect. Changes in the foot pedals control the rudder, which affects any yawing of an aircraft.

7. **(C)**

(A) is incorrect. A change of heading would not reduce airspeed.

(B) is incorrect. Decreasing altitude will result in an initial higher airspeed.

(C) is correct. Approaching the red line means the aircraft is reaching the maximum airspeed for the aircraft.

(D) is incorrect. Increasing airspeed will exceed the maximum airspeed of the aircraft.

(E) is incorrect. Increasing thrust will increase airspeed to an excess level if all other forces remain the same.

8. (C)

(A) is incorrect. Above ground level (AGL) is an altitude measurement.

(B is incorrect. Degrees are used in directional headings.

(C) is correct. Feet per minute (fpm) describes a rate of climb.

(D) is incorrect. Airspeed is measured in knots.

(E) is incorrect. Mean sea level (MSL) is an altitude measurement.

9. (D)

(A) is incorrect. Lag has a delay of 6 to 9 seconds; trend information is in real time.

(B) is incorrect. Lag has a delay of 6 to 9 seconds.

(C) is incorrect. Although trend information is in real time, lag is not.

(D) is correct. Trend information displays in real time in relation to the movement of the cyclic.

(E) is incorrect. Trend information does display in real time.

10. (C)

(A) is incorrect. The rudder controls adverse yaw.

(B) is incorrect. The wings and ailerons control bank.

(C) is correct. The lateral axis controls pitch when the nose moves up and down.

(D) is incorrect. The longitudinal axis controls roll.

(E) is incorrect. The vertical axis controls yaw.

11. (C)

(A) is incorrect. The teeter hinge allows the blades to flap.

(B) is incorrect. The rotor hub is the center attachment point for the rotor head components.

(C) is correct. The blade grips allow the main rotor blades to feather.

(D) is incorrect. The skids are used as landing gear for rotary-wing aircraft.

(E) is incorrect. The pitch horn couples the blade cuff to the pitch links.

12. (A)

(A) is correct. The angle of attack (AOA) is the angle between the chord (pitch) of the aircraft wing and the direction of relative wind.

(B) is incorrect. The artificial horizon is the line that represents the horizon of the earth and the aircraft attitude on the attitude indicator.

(C) is incorrect. The minimum limits of aircraft performance are shown on the vertical speed indicator.

(D) is incorrect. The pressure altitude is displayed on the altimeter when the setting window is adjusted to 29.92 Hg.

(E) is incorrect. A stall is when aircraft airspeed experiences decreased lift and lower airspeed, causing the AOA to be exceeded.

13. (A)

(A) is correct. The pilot must be acknowledged with the aircraft call sign to establish communications.

(B) is incorrect. This is true for Class C and D controlled airspaces but not true for Class B airspace.

(C) is incorrect. Approval for clearance is required for Class A through D controlled airspaces.

(D) is incorrect. When aircraft clearances are required, it applies to all types of aircraft.

(E) is incorrect. If clearance is required for entering an airspace, clearance is also required for exiting it.

14. (D)

(A) is incorrect. This would increase airspeed.

(B) is incorrect. This would increase airspeed.

(C) is incorrect. Extending the ailerons and flaps would decrease thrust, but this is done during landing to slow the aircraft.

(D) is correct. When increasing pitch, thrust must be increased to provide lift and maintain vertical speed or a stall will result.

(E) is incorrect. The rudder has no effect on thrust.

15. (A)

(A) is correct. This is the acronym for aircraft gross weight, also known as all-up weight (AUW). This weight changes during the flight due to consumables (i.e., oil and fuel).

(B) is incorrect. This is the acronym for maximum landing weight.

(C) is incorrect. This is maximum ramp weight.

(D) is incorrect. This is maximum takeoff weight.

(E) is incorrect. This is operating empty weight.

16. (D)

(A) is incorrect. A shallow turn is less than 20 degrees and does not need aileron pressure to return the aircraft to level flight, unlike medium and steep turns.

(B) is incorrect. While medium turns do require aileron pressure to return the aircraft to level flight, a shallow turn is less than 20 degrees and does not need aileron pressure to return the aircraft to level flight.

(C) is incorrect. A shallow turn is less than 20 degrees and does not need aileron pressure to return the aircraft to level flight.

(D) is correct. These turns are between 20 and 45 degrees and greater than a 45-degree bank. The pilot inputs aileron pressure to return the aircraft to level flight for both of these types of turns.

(E) is incorrect. There is no such turn.

17. (C)

(A) is incorrect. Weight, lift, thrust, and drag must be in balance in order to hover.

(B) is incorrect. An effective translational lift results from increased efficiency of the main rotor system as directional flight is established.

(C) is correct. Advancing and retreating blades of the rotor system generate unequal lifting forces: a dissymmetry of lift.

(D) is incorrect. Gyroscopic precession is when a force input is applied yet the force output is felt 90 degrees later in the plane of rotation.

(E) is incorrect. Autorotation is when the rotor blades are driven by relative wind rather than by the aircraft's powerplant.

18. (E)

(A) is incorrect. The cyclic controls the pitch and roll axis of the aircraft.

(B) is incorrect. The collective changes the pitch of the blades simultaneously.

(C) is incorrect. The tail rotor pedals control the yaw axis of the aircraft.

(D) is incorrect. Translating tendency causes a rotary-wing aircraft to drift laterally due to tail rotor thrust.

(E) is correct. The throttle maintains the engine within optimal flight parameters.

19. (E)

(A) is incorrect. This describes indicated altitude.

(B) is incorrect. This describes pressure altitude.

(C) is incorrect. This describes density altitude.

(D) is incorrect. This describes true altitude.

(E) is correct. Absolute altitude is indeed the height above ground level (AGL).

20. (C)

(A) is incorrect. AOA is the angle between the direction of the airflow and the chord on a wing—the imaginary reference line that extends from the leading edge to the trailing edge.

(B) is incorrect. A degree is the directional measurement for an aircraft.

(C) is correct. Airspeed is measured in knots.

(D) is incorrect. Mean sea level (MSL) is an altitude measurement.

(E) is incorrect. Rate of climb is a type of climb performed to navigate above obstacles during takeoff.

Follow the link below to take your second AFOQT practice test and to access other online study resources:

www.triviumtestprep.com/afoqt-online-resources

Made in the USA
Las Vegas, NV
16 January 2025

16524934R00149